Dear Rabbi Cohen –

I hope you find
these stories as inspirational
as I did –

[illegible]

משנה

ArtScroll Series®

Rabbi Nosson Scherman / Rabbi Meir Zlotowitz
General Editors

Reflections

of the

by

Rabbi Paysach J. Krohn

author of

The Maggid Speaks, Around the Maggid's Table, In the Footsteps of the Maggid, Along the Maggid's Journey, Echoes of the Maggid *and* ***Bris Milah***

Published by

Mesorah Publications, ltd

Maggid

Inspirational Stories
from around the globe
and around the corner

FIRST EDITION
First Impression ... October 2002
SECOND EDITION
First Impression ... November 2002
Second Impression ... June 2003

Published and Distributed by
MESORAH PUBLICATIONS, LTD.
4401 Second Avenue / Brooklyn, N.Y 11232

Distributed in Europe by
LEHMANNS
Unit E, Viking Industrial Park
Rolling Mill Road
Jarrow, Tyne & Wear, NE32 3DP
England

Distributed in Australia and New Zealand by
GOLDS WORLD OF JUDAICA
3-13 William Street
Balaclava, Melbourne 3183
Victoria, Australia

Distributed in Israel by
SIFRIATI / A. GITLER
6 Hayarkon Street
Bnei Brak 51127

Distributed in South Africa by
KOLLEL BOOKSHOP
Shop 8A Norwood Hypermarket
Norwood 2196, Johannesburg, South Africa

ISBN:
1-57819-751-1 (hard cover)
1-57819-752-X (paperback)

Typography by CompuScribe at ArtScroll Studios, Ltd.

Printed in the United States of America by Noble Book Press Corp.
Bound by Sefercraft, Quality Bookbinders, Ltd., Brooklyn N.Y. 11232

RABBI
ISRAEL GROSMAN
BATEI WARSAW
JERUSALEM, ISRAEL

ישראל גרוסמן
רב ור"מ ודומ"ץ
פיעה"ק ירושלים תובב"א
מחבר ספרי שעורי כתובות שעורי גיטין
שעורי קדושין שעורי ב"ק שו"ת הליכות ישראל
שו"ת משכנות ישראל שו"ת נצח ישראל

בתי ורשא ירושלים

Tel: 5371056 :טל

בעז"ה י"ג תשרי תשס"ט

[illegible]

הרב ישראל גרוסמן
דומ"ץ רב ור"מ
בעיה"ק ירושלים ת"ו
JERUSALEM ISRAEL
RABBI ISRAEL GROSSMAN

דוד קאהן

ביהמ"ד גבול יעבץ
ברוקלין, נוא יארק

בס"ד

רחימאי דנפשאי הרב פסח יוסף נר"ו

שמח לבי מהבשורה שהנך ממשיך בדרכך הקודש להוציא לאור ספר שני של סיפורי מעשיות שנקרא על שם הגה"צ רב שלום שוודרון זצ"ל המגיד מירושלים.

הלא בהדפסת הספר הלזה תתקיים החזקה של אתמחי גברא ואתמחי קמיע פעמיים. החל מערב חנוכה תשמ"ג שהתחלת בהדפסת ספרי המגיד הצלחת ללמד השקפת התורה ברוח ישראל סבא והרכבת תורה שבכתב עם תורה שבעל פה לפרש [illegible] לאלו ששותים דברך בצמא. ואמינא לך בכחך זה והושעת את ישראל.

אוהבך ודורש שלומך
דוד קאהן
ב' דר"ח מרחשון תשס"ג

Rabbi Shlomo Teitelbaum
85-30 124th Street
Kew Gardens, NY 11415
(718) 847-9828

שמחה שלמה טייטלבוים
קהל עדת יראים
קיו גרדענס, נ.י.
(718) 846-1571

בס"ד

מכתב ברכה

יום א' לסדר ושנת "ואת הנפש אשר עשו בחרן"

פסח דבריך יאיר, ויוסף הוא המשביר לכל עם
הארץ בדרשותיו הנפלאים אשר דרש דרש כמין חומר
לקרב לבות בני ישראל לאבינו שבשמים בתורה
ואמונה טהורה הה"ה גברא רבה ויקירא רודף צדקה
פה מפיק מרגליות ידיד נפשי כבר יובל שנים מוה"ר
פסח יוסף הכהן שליט"א ונהלה דקהלתינו עדת יראים
עלה במדריגות נעלות בזיכוי הרבים אשר הוצג חן
בשפתותיו דורש טוב לעמו דובר צדק ומגיד מישרים
וכבר זכה לדלות מים מבארי וצדיקי עולם ובפרט מהגאון
הרב שלום שבדרון המגיד המפורסם מירושלים עיה"ק זצ"ל
ועכשיו הוא נוהג בו טובת עין להביאם בדפוס לחלקם
ביעקב ולהפיצם בישראל להשקות בהם עדרי צאן הצמאים
לדבר ה' והנני מברכו שיזכהו השי"ת שתקבלו דבריו בלב
בדם ודברים היוצאים מן הלב נכנסים אל הלב ויפוצו
מעינותיו החוצה ורבים יהנו לאורו וזכות הרבים תעמוד
לכם להגדיל בכל מילי דמיטב מתוך רב אושר עונג
ושמחה ורב נחת דקדושה מכל יוצ"ח ודקרו"ר ויזכה לראות
ישועת ה' בקרוב עין בעין בביאת גוא"צ בב"א

הכותב וחותם לכבוד התורה
שמחה שלמה טייטלבוים

Table of Contents

Part F: Perceptions and Perspectives 251

Indices 279

Author's Preface

אֶפְתְּחָה פִּי בְּשִׁיר וּרְנָנִים לְהוֹדוֹת וּלְהַלֵּל פְּנֵי שׁוֹכֵן מְעוֹנִים

It is with deep feelings of appreciation and gratitude to Hashem that I present this book to the reading public. *Chazal* explain that at times Hashem bestows on individuals a חוּט שֶׁל חֶסֶד, *a touch* (lit. a thread) *of kindness* (see *Megillah* 13a and *Chagigah* 12b). Rabbi Mendel Kaplan (1913-1985), a *Rosh Yeshivah* and legendary *moreh derech* (spiritual guide) to hundreds of *talmidim* in Chicago and Philadelphia, explained that though a thread is thin and barely noticeable, an entire garment is woven from many of these unnoticeable threads. Hence, though each thread is significant, it truly becomes noteworthy when it is interwoven with many other threads.

I feel the same way regarding the writing of this book. No single story or parable, regardless of how inspiring or moving it might be, comprises a book. One needs many strands and fibers to craft a book. In combination, they can become a substantial tapestry, warming the reader and enveloping him with inspiration. In that sense I feel as though the *Ribono Shel Olam* has granted me countless threads of kindness.

The Torah tells us that the *Mishkan* was surrounded by curtains that were made of שֵׁשׁ מָשְׁזָר, *interwoven linen* (*Shemos* 27:9). The word שֵׁשׁ also means six, hence homiletically one could say that this book, the sixth in the Maggid Series, is a שֵׁשׁ מָשְׁזָר, a sixth tapestry of stories woven together from threads that were collected from around the globe and around the corner. That the *Ribono Shel Olam* should have granted me these threads of kindness is something for which I will be eternally grateful.

We are different.

Since the publication of the previous Maggid book in this series, *ECHOES OF THE MAGGID*, in March 1999, we as Jews and the world at large have changed. In the last two years, our people have suffered agony and anguish not known since the horrifying days of the Holocaust. The almost constant wave of death, destruction and injury to our brethren in *Eretz Yisrael*, and the shattering, cataclysmic events of September 11, 2001, have caused us to become more keenly aware of the enemies of *Klal Yisrael* throughout the world. We are concerned and insecure about the future.

The pain of our nation was crystallized in a speech given recently by a *bar mitzvah* boy in the settlement community of P'sagot in Israel. As he came to the end of the *drashah* that his father had taught him, he said that he would like to say something to Hashem. Obviously, he had something to say that no one had taught him. What was it? Surprised and curious, his parents and the guests sat with bated breath, waiting to hear his message.

"Ribono Shel Olam," he began, "I have now joined Your exclusive club, the club that allows me to be counted as a member of *Klal Yisrael*. I can be counted in a *minyan* — I can be included in a *zimun*. It is customary that when one joins a club or an organization he is given a bonus or a gift as a welcoming gesture. For example if someone joins an airline's 'frequent flyer club' he is given a certain amount of free miles. If someone signs a contract with a particular cell phone company, he might be granted a few hundred free minutes or a reduced rate for two months.

"Perhaps then I too am entitled to a bonus or gift. I ask You, Hashem, please don't give it to me. I have a friend in my class whose father was killed a few weeks ago by the Palestinians. He, too, is having a *bar mitzvah* soon, but he has no father to teach him his *drashah.* Please find someone who will teach it to him with the love and patience his father would have had. *Ribono Shel Olam,* I have another friend in this settlement who lost his mother in a drive-by shooting by Arabs. He too is having a *bar mitzvah* soon. Please find him someone who will go with him to buy his new suit with the same love and concern his mother would have had. *Ribono Shel Olam,* give my friends and others like them any bonus You may have wanted to give me."

With tears in his eyes — and in the eyes of everyone listening — that special *bar mitzvah* boy sat down and wept.

When in *Klal Yisrael* did we ever have *bar mitzvahs* like that?

When I heard this story from Rabbi Meir Goldwicht, who was at that *bar mitzvah,* it brought to mind an insight by the *Baal HaTurim* regarding the daughter of Pharaoh, who saw an infant (whom she would later name Moshe) in a basket in the reeds by the river. The Torah says: וַתִּפְתַּח וַתִּרְאֵהוּ אֶת הַיֶּלֶד וְהִנֵּה נַעַר בֹּכֶה, וַתַּחְמֹל עָלָיו וַתֹּאמֶר מִיַּלְדֵי הָעִבְרִים זֶה, *She opened it [the basket] and saw the child, and behold a youth was crying. She took pity on him and said, "This is one of the Hebrew boys" (Shemos 2:6).*

It is generally understood that the words יֶלֶד, *child,* and נַעַר, *youth,* are both referring to Moshe. The intent of the verse is, therefore, that she saw the child in the basket and he was crying. The *Baal HaTurim* however suggests that the word נַעַר, *youth,* refers not to Moshe, but to his brother Aharon. She saw the *child* in the basket, but then she also saw a *youth* — Aharon — standing by the basket and crying. At that sight she said, "This is one of the Hebrew boys." If one boy is crying because of the travail of another boy — that's a sure sign he is Jewish — for the trait of compassion is the essence of a Jew.

Just like that *bar mitzvah* boy in Israel.

These are days when people are seeking solace, inspiration, direction and encouragement. So many individuals feel the emptiness expressed by Yirmiyahu *HaNavi*: יְתוֹמִים הָיִינוּ וְאֵין אָב, *We have become orphans, without a father (Eichah* 5:3*).* More people attend lectures in Israel, America, Canada, Europe, Mexico or any other place in the world than ever before. We pray today as we haven't prayed in years as we try to come closer to the *Ribono Shel Olam* and understand His ways.

Chazal teach: אֵין פּוּרְעָנוּת בָּאָה לָעוֹלָם אֶלָּא בִּשְׁבִיל יִשְׂרָאֵל, *Punishment comes to the world only for the sake of [improving] Klal Yisrael (Yevamos* 63a; *see Rashi, Shemos* 7:2*).* Remarkably the verse brought as a proof to this concept is one that makes us think of recent history: הִכְרַתִּי גוֹיִם נָשַׁמּוּ פִּנּוֹתָם, *I have eliminated nations, their towers have become desolate (Zephaniah* 3:6*).* On the word פִּנּוֹתָם, *Metzudas Zion* comments: הֵם הַמִּגְדָּלִים הַגְּבוֹהִים, *they are the tall towers!* In the next verse, Hashem says: אָמַרְתִּי אַךְ תִּירְאִי אוֹתִי תִּקְחִי מוּסָר, *I said, just fear Me, accept chastisement* (ibid. v. 7).

Surely, in times like the present we must see Hashem's message, take heed and change.

The Gemara (*Berachos* 33a) tells of a poisonous snake that was biting people in the town of Rabbi Chanina ben Dosa. Frightened, the people ran to Rabbi Chanina for advice and protection. He went and put his heel over the snake's lair. The snake bit his heel — and died! Rabbi Chanina then slung the dead snake over his shoulder, walked into the *beis midrash* (study hall) and proclaimed, "See, my children, it is not the snake that kills, it is sin that kills."

But whose sin today is causing havoc and catastrophe? Perhaps the answer lies in the Talmudic explanation of the verse: וְכָשְׁלוּ אִישׁ בְּאָחִיו, *Man will stumble because of his brother (Vayikra* 26:37*),* which the Sages understand to mean that one man in the Jewish community will stumble (i.e. be punished) *because of the sins* of another member of the community. Why? שֶׁכּוּלָּן עֲרֵבִים זֶה בָּזֶה, *because all [Jews] are responsible for one another (Sanhedrin* 27b*).*

It is not enough to refrain from sin. One must try as much as he can to be sure that others do not sin, as well. For if one does nothing to deter others from sinning, in a sense he is also guilty. We are responsible for one another. The *Arizal* was once asked why he recited the confessional prayers on *Yom Kippur* when he knew very well that he hadn't transgressed most of that long list of sins mentioned. He replied, "It's true I may not have committed some of them, but I know people who did transgress and perhaps I could have stopped them or prevented them from doing so again. I did not do that and so I too am guilty."

As Rabbi Yehudah Zev Segal, the Manchester *Rosh Yeshivah,* wrote, "In essence all Jews are one. Our souls are all united and in each soul there is a portion of all the others." We all share what is known as the נְשָׁמָה, *soul,* of *Klal Yisrael.* This concept is the basis of the principle: כָּל יִשְׂרָאֵל עֲרֵבִים זֶה בָּזֶה, *All Jews are responsible for one another (Shevous* 39a*).* Since each Jewish soul possesses a portion of all the others, when a Jew sins his wrong affects not only his own soul, but also the collective soul of Israel. [Conversely when one does good, the collective soul of all Jews is enhanced.] (See *Inspiration and Insight* Vol. II, p. 91.)

We are all responsible for much that is going on in *Klal Yisrael;* so it is the entire Jewish nation collectively that must improve.

How do we change? How can we improve and become elevated? Perhaps one method is to read and study about inspirational people who have led lives of Torah and *yiras Shamayim,* absorbing in our consciousness their examples of *chessed* and concern, and learning from those who display faith and love of Hashem even in the most trying circumstances.

Perhaps, then, this book with its stories of such people can in small measure inspire us. I have been moved by each of these stories and I hope you will be inspired as well. Some of the people I have written about are well known, others are ordinary people whose attitudes and actions are remarkable and noteworthy. The bond that unites the subjects of these stories is that they are worthy of emulation. I believe we can glean from their accomplishments, incorporate them in our lives and become exalted and elevated.

I had the *zechus* to know a man who had the capacity to lift the spirits of Jews in trying times. He was the revered and beloved Maggid of Jerusalem, Rabbi Sholom Schwadron (1912-1997).

Overflow crowds flocked to his *drashos,* as he guided, chided and inspired young and old throughout Israel and the Jewish world. In the same speech he could be warm, loving and encouraging, yet stern, strict and demanding; he made people laugh and cry. Mostly, he made them think. Through an incredible chain of events, my family became very close with Reb Sholom and it is primarily because of him that I came to write these Maggid books. (See introduction to *THE MAGGID SPEAKS* and *ECHOES OF THE MAGGID.)* I am eternally grateful to him, and know that my family and I can never adequately express our gratitude to him.

Reb Sholom will always be my role model as the ideal speaker. He gave people hope, he put a smile on their faces, yet he guided them to spiritual improvement with his inspirational thoughts. His stories were fascinating and elevating. People would leave his *drashos* and say, "He was talking to me." And that is the ultimate bond between speaker and listener.

He cannot be replicated. We have his writings, pictures, and recordings, but they can only help us reflect on what he was in real life. And even though Reb Sholom himself is intangible today — like a reflection in the water that can be seen but not touched — his messages are still real and palpable. It is my fervent prayer that my words, be they written or spoken, be a *Reflection of the Maggid.*

אָבִינוּ מַלְכֵּנוּ תְּהֵא הַשָּׁעָה הַזֹּאת שְׁעַת רַחֲמִים וְעֵת רָצוֹן מִלְּפָנֶיךָ.

Dedication

David *HaMelech* writes: אָנָּה ה׳ כִּי אֲנִי עַבְדֶּךָ אֲנִי עַבְדְּךָ בֶּן אֲמָתֶךָ, *Please Hashem — for I am Your servant, I am Your servant, the son of Your maidservant (Tehillim* 116:16*).* Rabbi Avigdor Miller (1908-2001) explains that David's intent in the second part of the verse was not merely to state his family lineage; rather, he says that he became the devoted servant of Hashem because he had a mother who was the exemplary maidservant of Hashem. Interestingly, David's mother's name is not mentioned anywhere in *Tanach.* She seems to have been "behind the scenes," yet she exerted such a strong influence on her son that he became who he was because of her. [Her name was actually נִצֶּבֶת בַּת עֲדָאֵל, Nitzevess the daughter of Ada'eil (*Bava Basra* 91a).]

With these thoughts in mind I dedicate this book to my mother, Mrs. Hindy Krohn, who has always been a woman "behind the scenes." She is a woman of few publicly spoken words, yet a woman of insight, character, unbending faith in the *Ribono Shel Olam,* and the influential Matriarch of her family, which *baruch Hashem* includes children, grandchildren, and great-grandchildren.

More than anyone, she gave me my love for writing. In grade school, in Torah Vodaath in Brooklyn, "English Composition" became the subject I loved because she would compose the essays with me (and sometimes for me). We would often sit at night and read editorials and newspaper articles and underline poetic and lilting expressions and discuss the nuances of phrases. We would analyze the inflection of a sentence and the rhythm of a paragraph. We watched for the clever combination of clarity and conciseness. One of the best parts of being in summer camp was receiving her letters, which were always upbeat, descriptive, and laced with just enough understated humor to make me anxious to get home the day after Color War.

She has always been and still is a very private person. She talks freely only to her nearest and dearest. If there were a thousand women at a lecture of mine (It would have to be mine. I doubt she has ever left the house to attend anyone else's lecture.), she would be the last person you would pick out as my mother. I am tall and she is short; I am verbal and she is quiet; I love crowds and she tolerates them; I move quickly and she moves deliberately; I know I haven't reached my potential and she thinks I have exceeded it.

She believed in me long before anyone else did. When I wrote the *Bris Milah* book for Artscroll in March 1985, a project she and I worked on for two-and-a-half years, another *mohel* called to tell me that though he liked the book, he could have written it, and he should have written it and would have written it, had he only thought of the idea. When I repeated his words to my mother, she said, "Only you *could* have written it, only you *should* have written it, and only you *actually* wrote it."

I became a *mohel* at age 21, even before I was married, taking over for my father, Rabbi Avrohom Zelig Krohn, when he passed away at the untimely age of 47. Understandably some people were reluctant to use a very young *mohel*, and calls for my services were not frequent. When I would ask my mother if anyone had called, she always said the same two words, which showed her confidence, concern and sensitivity. Those words were "Not yet." Honest but hopeful, factual but encouraging. To me those words meant, "Calls will come. They just haven't come yet. People will find out that you are good. Hang in there and it will happen."

My parents' home was open to anyone who needed a meal or a kind word. My father was an accomplished *talmid chacham*, thoroughly knowledgeable in a vast array of Torah topics, be they *halachah, aggadah, safrus, shechitah,* or *milah.* He owned and was familiar with thousands of *sefarim.* He was innovative, sagacious, practical, handy, a melodious *baal tefillah* and a delightful speaker. Couple that with my mother's talents as a pianist, writer, mentor, guidance counselor and advisor, and you have a home where his office and her kitchen became comfortable places for a broad spectrum of people. Some were brilliant, others were talented, still others were lonely, broken people who craved to be listened to. The conversations in our home were fascinating and entertaining. Tommy, the eclectic artist; Yosef (with his French berét), the *Shas* and Shakespeare genius; Baruch, the (legally) blind chiropractor; Libby, the sophisticated intellectual; Yitzchok, the dashing doctor from Ireland; "Rebbi" (Rav Label Chait), who made learning a thrilling experience; the hapless and hopeless soothsayer of gloom and doom; the untamed teenager from Argentina; the tender but sometimes misguided orphan; the three different Dovids, each with his own distinctive situation; and, of course, Rav Sholom and Rav Yisroel [Grossman, who came with Rav Sholom] — all had a broad effect on our upbringing. My parents' attentiveness to them and others was an example to my siblings and myself until this very day. We saw the microcosm of *Klal Yisrael* in our dining room and learned from our parents how every type of *Yid* is special and significant. We pray that our homes can be like theirs.

My mother has edited almost every word of every article and book that I have written — except the words of this dedication. So I close with this personal note. Please forgive me for not telling you about this in advance. You would have tried to dissuade me — but I wanted people to know what you are and what you mean to me. You have been our family's strength, our guiding light, our role model. The love and reverence that all your children and grandchildren have for you is living proof of what you mean to all of us.

With deepest love, affection and gratitude,

Your oldest child,
Paysach.

Acknowledgments

One of the most rewarding aspects of writing a book like this is getting to know extraordinary people throughout the Jewish world. I thank the *Ribono Shel Olam* for allowing me to know these people and I thank each of them for the time they spent with me and the opportunities they have afforded me. They opened their hearts and their homes and without their help this work could not have been accomplished.

Mr. Ezra Abrahams (Melbourne), R' Asher Arielei (Jerusalem), Mr. and Mrs. David Aronovitz (Johannesburg), R' Berel Belsky (Brooklyn), R' Yaakov Ben-Haim (Brooklyn), R' and Mrs. Ezra Berkowitz (Zurich), Dr. and Mrs. Eli Bio (Amsterdam), my *rebbi*, R' Dovid Cohen (Brooklyn), R' Boruch Mordechai Ezrachi (Jerusalem), R' Yitzchok Ezrachi (Jerusalem), R' Yehoshua Fishman (Brooklyn), R' and Mrs. Shmuel Dovid Friedman (Brooklyn), Mr. Aaron Gestetner (Montreal), R' Shimon Gifter (Brooklyn), R' Ezreal Goldfine (Johannesburg), R' Yisroel Grossman (Jerusalem), R' Avrohom Gurwicz (Gateshead), Mr. and Mrs. Sammy Homburger (Golders Green), Mr. and Mrs. Shmuel Zvi Heimann (Stamford Hill), R' Avrohom Katz (Gateshead), R' Chaim Boruch Katz (Gateshead), R' Chaim Kaufman (Gateshead), Mr. and Mrs. Mordechai Levin (Arosa), R' Daniel Levy (Zurich), R' and Mrs. Yehuda Leib Lewis (Amsterdam), R' and Mrs. Nesanel Lieberman (Gateshead), R' and Mrs. Eliezer Liff (Jerusalem), R' Yosef Mendelowitz (Jerusalem),

R' Raphael Mendlowitz (Silver Spring), R' Brachya Perlow (Johannesburg), R' and Mrs. Michael Orelowitz (Cleveland), R' Shmuel Orenstein (Manhattan), Mr. Yossi Ortner (Vienna), R' Avrohom Yonah Schwartz (Vienna), R' Yosef Pardes (Vienna), R' Jonathan Rietti (Monsey), R' Yaakov Salomon (Brooklyn), R' Sholom Schechter (Jerusalem), R' Raphael Shmulevitz (Jerusalem), Dr. Reuvain Silverman (Teaneck), R' and Mrs. Ziska Slominanski (Mexico), R' Shlomo Teitelbaum (Kew Gardens), Mr. Nechemia Roosen (Amsterdam), R' Avrohom Tenenbaum (Monsey), R' Yehuda Treger (Antwerp), R' and Mrs. Boruch Wasyng (Antwerp), R' Usher Weiss (Jerusalem), Mr. and Mrs. Yermiah Witriol (Brooklyn), and R' Shlomo Wolbe (Jerusalem).

I thank Miss Shoshana Lewin (Stamford Hill) for suggesting the title of the book; Mr. Michael Ibragimov for providing transportation when I needed it; my nephew Chaim Meir Bryks for cataloguing the source material; and Mr. Michael Rothschild from the Chofetz Chaim Heritage Foundation (Monsey) and his team of videographers — Shmuel Borger (Brooklyn) and Chaim Snow (Brooklyn) — for the opportunities they have afforded me with their worldwide *Shmiras HaLashon* programs every *Tishah B'Av*.

Over the nearly two decades that I have been fortunate to be associated with Rabbi Nosson Scherman and Rabbi Meir Zlotowitz, my admiration and reverence for them has grown with each year. Reb Nosson's deft pen has enhanced my words, his wise counsel has guided my thoughts, and his stately demeanor has set my standards. Reb Meir's global scope of Torah dissemination is breathtaking, his dedication and determination in seeing a project to fruition is inspiring, his artistic taste is ingenious and his genuine encouragement is motivating. Our generation's Torah study, *mitzvah* observance and entreaties to Hashem have been enhanced by them and the team they have put together. How fortunate are they … and we.

I thank Eli Kroen for his majestic work on the cover; Avrohom Biderman and Leah Seeve for steering the book through all its stages; Mrs. Ruchy Reifer, Miss Tzini Hanover, Miss Menucha Mitnick and Mrs. Leah Weiner for their meticulous typesetting; Mrs.

Charlotte Friedland and Mrs. Mindy Stern for their crafty and stylish editing and proofreading; and the rest of the splendid group that brings us closer to the *Ribono Shel Olam* with all their publications.

My wife Miriam often says that I have three full-time jobs — *mohel,* writer and speaker. That is an exaggeration of course; one may not perform a *bris* at night, writing is forbidden on Shabbos and I usually don't accept daytime speaking engagements. But be it as it may, in order to balance these three careers one needs an extraordinarily organized administrative secretary, a capable managerial business agent, a precision-oriented time consultant, a gifted sounding board, and a practical advisor. She is all that plus a dedicated housewife, mother and grandmother, inspiring teacher, and *Limudei Kodesh* Studies Coordinator at Shevach High School. Thus if I have three jobs she has ten! Thanking her is like a right arm thanking a left arm. It's one unit working hand in hand.

May we and our children and grandchildren be inspired by the thoughts and actions of the wondrous people mentioned in this book. May we all live to see the day when Eliyahu, the מַלְאַךְ הַבְּרִית, *the Angel of the Covenant,* heralds the coming of *Mashiach,* so that we can return to Jerusalem and witness the building of the third *Beis HaMikdash.* May it happen in our time.

זֶה הַיּוֹם עָשָׂה ה׳ נָגִילָה וְנִשְׂמְחָה בוֹ

Paysach J. Krohn	פסח יוסף קראהן
Rosh Chodesh Cheshvan 5763	ראש חודש חשון תשס"ג
Kew Gardens, New York	
October, 2002	

Part A:
Courage and Character

A Jet Fighter's Radar

It was the end of the first day *Succos* in 5760/1999 and I had just finished giving a *drashah* (lecture) in the Ezras Torah *Shul* in the Sanhedria HaMurchevet section of Jerusalem. A Yerushalmi *avreich,* a *kollel* fellow in his early 30's, accompanied by his 7-year-old son, approached me and said, "I have a story for you."

Those words are delightful to me, for I am always searching for stories or parables with messages of inspiration. "I would love to listen to you," I said, "but my family is waiting for me to make *Kiddush* in the *succah*. As *galus* (Diaspora) Jews we still have another day of *Yom Tov* to celebrate." I invited him to come by a little later and tell his story to our family.

His first words to all of us later that evening in the *succah* were astounding and riveting. "I used to be a jet fighter pilot for the Israeli air force." With his beard and *payos* (sidelocks) he looked anything but that. And then R' Yaakov Sherman, formerly known as Koby, told this incredible story.

It was 21:30 (9:30 p.m.) as five Israeli jet fighter planes stood on the tarmac in formation ready to roar up into the sky. They were to streak across the black sky and practice bombing maneuvers at hundreds of miles an hour as they prepared for war. In his cockpit, the lead pilot, Koby, checked the dials on the various gauges and meters on the display, secured his helmet and got set for takeoff. His plane would be flanked in the air by four other jet fighters, two on his right and two on his left.

There was no reason to suspect that tonight's maneuvers would be out of the ordinary. This team of pilots, Koby, Arik, Nati, Ofir, and Gadi had worked in tandem for weeks. Their nightly routine was methodical and familiar as they performed their drills with pinpoint precision in total darkness.

Each night Koby would take off first in a thunderous streak heading out and up. Moments later the four jets would follow in a roar that rattled the tarmac. Once in the sky they assumed a position that resembled five fingers stretching forward. Koby was in the lead, Arik and Nati were slightly behind on his right, and Ofir and Gadi were slightly behind on his left. Koby would scan a potential bomb site, determine a precise target, and shoot a flare illuminating the site. The bombers escorting him would come forward and release their missiles. After releasing his flare, Koby would thrust his jet upward and begin flying in a huge arc up and then around and back over the bombing area to assess the accuracy and the damage the bombers had wrought.

On this clear night, Koby, tense and taut, roared off the runway into the darkness and began searching for an appropriate site. When he settled on a target he radioed his team to be in position and ready. With an explosion of fire he released his flare, which lit up the area like five bolts of lightning.

Koby banked his jet to the right as he prepared to climb. He had done this maneuver dozens of time before, but tonight his head began to spin, as vertigo — a condition of confusion and disorientation — overtook him. Pilots are trained to recognize this potentially disastrous situation, but tonight Koby's condition was too intense for him to recognize. Vertigo causes confusion and dizziness so that one cannot determine direction or altitude. Without realizing it, Koby had turned his plane upside down, yet was still flying at the same high speed. Bewildered, Koby was sure he was flying right side up.

Instinctively he thrust his jet in the position that he thought was upward. However because he was flying upside down, his jet was hurtling downward at a frightening speed, heading for an imminent explosive crash on the ground. He checked his altimeter to determine his position. To his shock and utter disbelief the altimeter indicated that he was losing altitude and hurtling toward earth.

As a safety precaution, Israeli jet fighters are equipped with two altimeters to protect pilots struck by vertigo. In a confused state a pilot might rationalize that an altimeter is defective, however with two altimeters displaying the same information, even the disoriented pilot would presumably acknowledge the danger confronting him. The readings on the twin gauges jolted Koby into stark reality.

Koby radioed the four pilots behind him and screamed in a panic, "Tell me my position. Am I going up or down?"

In a microsecond their radar indicated his descent. "You're going down," yelled Nati, "reverse your position!"

Koby took hold of the yoke, the stick that controls the direction and position of the plane, and held it tight. He would have to yank it back toward himself to cause the plane to turn back over so that it was right side up. However in his state of mind he was convinced that this maneuver would turn the plane upside down as it sped toward earth, killing him on impact. With his body demanding that he do one thing and his mind insisting that he do another, he did "what was the hardest thing I ever did in my life." Terror stricken, he pulled the yoke toward himself. Slowly the plane turned over and, having been redirected, it headed skyward.

A minute later Koby's head cleared. He realized what had happened and flew over the bombed-out area to assess his team's latest bombing maneuvers. A while later he was able to land on his airbase back home.

Now sitting in the *succah,* R' Yaakov (Koby) said, "Years later, after I became a *baal teshuvah,* I realized that the flight that night was a fight between man and his *yetzer hara* (evil inclination). At times we lead our lives certain ways and not only are we positive that we are traveling on a straight path but we are sure that we are growing, traveling spiritually upward, making progress and even striving higher. We act, eat, and speak without hesitation, not aware that in reality we are afflicted with spiritual vertigo! We think we are going up, but in reality we are going down!

"Who then can correct us if we have spiritual vertigo? It is the *rebbi*, the teacher, the friend who can look at our ways 'from the outside' with objectivity. They can guide us as my copilots did for me, for they see the deficiencies that we fail to recognize because of our own subjectivity. If we seek their advice, we can be redirected so we indeed achieve great heights and spiritual altitude."

A Shield of Distinction

In October 1938, the hatred that the German populace had for Jews boiled like a hot cauldron on a raging fire. Nazi SS men indiscriminately dragged Jews off the streets or from their homes, humiliated them and carted them off to slave labor camps, where torture and cruel death often awaited them. It was only a matter of time until a volcanic explosion of violence by civilians would erupt. Every day there were tremors indicating the shocks to come. Tension was high and fear was constant.

R' David Tzvi Cohen and his wife Sarah Zisel lived with their four children on Linien Strasse in the Jewish district of Berlin. Shops and stores owned by Jews lined the streets of the district, and dozens of *shuls* and temples — many of them architecturally beautiful — were spread throughout the area. The Cohens, who lived on the second floor of an apartment building, had good relations with their German gentile neighbors, particularly the Reinmann family, who lived on the third floor.

On Thursday morning, November 10, 1938, *Frau* (Mrs.) Reinmann came downstairs and said to the Cohens with urgency, "I hear there is going to be a pogrom and it may even be today. You would be safer if you left this neighborhood for now."

The Cohens had also heard rumors to that effect, but who could know which threat was real and which was not? *Frau* Reinmann assured them that she had her information from reliable sources. Unbeknownst to the Cohens and most Jews, the night before at 11:55 p.m., Gestapo Chief Heinrich Mueller had sent a telegram to all police units ordering them not to interfere with actions that would be taking place against all Jews, especially their synagogues. Fire companies were instructed not to protect the synagogues but to make sure that the flames did not spread to Aryan property.

Trusting *Frau* Reinmann, the Cohens decided to act at once and flee with their children to the other side of town, to the home of Mrs. Cohen's parents, David Shaye and Braindel Shankal on Elsasser Strasse where few Jewish families resided. Surely it would be safer there to weather a possible storm of violence.

The Cohen's 12-year-old daughter Esther asked her parents if she could come to her grandparents an hour later. She wanted to finish her homework and she had all her books at home. Esther was a feisty child and her parents trusted her instincts. She knew the route to her grandparents' home and assured her parents she would be there as soon as possible. The Cohens left with their three other children as Esther remained home alone.

Within an hour, Esther heard wild screaming and rioting. She ran to a window facing the street and saw a mob of what seemed like a thousand people rampaging down Linien Strasse, roaring in piercing maniacal voices at the top of their lungs, "Get the Jews! Kill the Jews!" She watched in terror as pandemonium reigned. The mob smashed windows, looted stores, threw rocks, hurled insults, and threatened the lives of Jews anywhere and everywhere throughout the Reich. Esther put her hands on her open mouth as she watched in frightened disbelief.

Frau Reinmann was right. This was a pogrom of the worst order. Esther knew she could not remain in the building for if she were found her life would be in danger. She was trapped. Trembling and isolated, she tried to devise a plan to save herself. If only she could get to her parents on the other side of town she would be safe.

Esther began reciting any *Tehillim* she knew by heart, all the while thinking desperately of a plan of escape. She was often told that she didn't look Jewish because of her fair skin and blonde hair. Perhaps now she could use that to her advantage. She tousled her hair and combed it the way the German girls in the Hitler Youth Association did. She looked into a mirror and was revolted at what she saw.

She was afraid, though, that it still wasn't enough of a decoy. She adjusted her jacket and clothes in a provocative way, so that no one could imagine she was an Orthodox Jewish girl. She hated dressing that way. She felt cheapened and degraded, but there was no choice. Her life hung in the balance. She decided she would go outside and walk nonchalantly, hoping no one would suspect she was Jewish, for logically no Jewish girl in her right mind would brazenly walk among such an anti-Semitic mob.

With the words of *Tehillim* on her lips, she reached up to kiss the *mezuzah* as she left her apartment. "*Ribono Shel Olam,* please save me," she whispered softly.

As she walked down the stairs in the hallway she suddenly remembered an expression she often heard from her mother, "*Ahfilu fahr dee feer vent, darf mehn zich shemmen.*" ("Even for the four walls [in a home] one should feel shame.") Her mother meant to convey the message that *tznius* (modesty of dress) was a code of behavior that was required even in the privacy of one's home. She was startled that those words would come to her just now. She rationalized that she had to look like "them" to spare her life. Surely her mother would understand and even encourage her behavior. But now, in the empty darkened hallway, she was having doubts. Perhaps this *was* a message from Above.

Esther decided that come what may, she would not go out the way she was dressed. She rebuttoned her blouse to her neck, tucked it into her skirt and straightened the collar of her jacket, but kept her hair tousled. As she walked out into the street the noise burst at her with a crescendo. She mumbled more words of *Tehillim,* making sure, however, that no one realized she was praying.

The yelling and screaming of the mob was deafening. She walked hesitantly, checking to see if the horde had reached her grandmother's fabric store on the first floor of their apartment building. (They hadn't reached it yet, but later the shop was looted and ransacked.)

She walked as quickly as she could, avoiding eye contact with anyone. She tried to keep to the middle of the street, away from the flying glass and swinging clubs that smashed into every Jewish window in sight. She dodged wild-eyed men whose faces were contorted in animalistic rage and sidestepped men who looked liked brutal murderers. The bloodcurdling catcalls rolled over her like ferocious tidal waves. She tried not to panic as her mouth went dry from fear.

In 10 minutes, that seemed like ten days, she was past the mob. As soon as she was sure she wasn't being observed, she began to run as fast as she could. When she came to her grandparents' home, she knocked on the door rapidly. Her heart was beating wildly as she waited for a response. Did her parents make it? Had the Nazis come here earlier? Was anyone home?

The door opened and she ran right past her sister into her mother's arms and wept uncontrollably. The emotion and tension of the last hour burst forth in a torrent of tears. At first she could not speak, but kept looking back at the door, hoping she had not been followed. Then slowly, between sighs and sobs, she told her anxious parents and grandparents about her frightful experience.

When she finished, Mrs. Cohen took Esther's face in her hands and said softly, "Don't you realize, my child, you saved your own life?"

Esther was bewildered. "Esther," her mother said again, "look, you are wearing your gold necklace with a *Magen Dovid* on it. Had you left your buttons open, the *Magen Dovid* would have identified you as a Jew. Your *mitzvah* protected you without your even knowing it."

Shlomo *HaMelech* writes in *Mishlei (1:8)*: שְׁמַע בְּנִי מוּסַר אָבִיךָ וְאַל תִּטֹּשׁ תּוֹרַת אִמֶּךָ, *Hear my child the discipline of your father, and do not forsake the teaching of your mother.* In the context of this story the next *pasuk* is remarkable: כִּי לִוְיַת חֵן הֵם לְרֹאשֶׁךָ וַעֲנָקִים לְגַרְגְּרֹתֶיךָ , *For they are an adornment of grace for your head and a chain for your neck* (ibid. 1:9).

The horrific events later that night will always be remembered in Jewish history as *Kristallnacht* (Crystal Night or the Night of Broken Glass). Within a period of 48 hours, 1,300 synagogues were burned, 30,000 Jews were arrested and sent to concentration camps and 7,000 businesses were smashed and looted.

Esther Cohen, today Mrs. Esther Biller of Monsey, New York, survived the war and has lived to raise a precious family. Her son, Reb Aryeh, a loving *rebbi* of little children for more than a decade, was kind enough to share his mother's story with me.

Marked for Eternity

Titanic.

The word itself is a paragraph if not a book. The word evokes images of the colossal, the massive, that which is larger than life, something of enormous proportions. Indeed the builders of the great ocean liner, the Titanic, had just such prodigious thoughts in mind. The Titanic was the most enormous ship ever built, a staggering 46,329 tons. It accommodated over 2,000 passengers. Its publicists advertised its durability with haughtiness befitting the size of the ship, as they bragged that it was "the ship that even G-d couldn't sink."

The world would soon know differently. A hundred thousand people came to Belfast, Ireland, on April 3, 1912, to see the Titanic embark on its maiden voyage, and within days, millions the world over knew of the calamity that would become a legend in world history. Stories abound about the heroism, sacrifice and misfortune that occurred that night, as the Titanic sank after crashing into a twin peaked iceberg on the open seas of the North Atlantic. I had never heard of a "Jewish story" regarding the Titanic, thus when Mrs. Alyssa Hershkop in Beit Shemesh, Israel, insisted that she had a "great Jewish story" about the Titanic, I was skeptical.

However, research and interviews with descendants of the passengers on that voyage proved she was right. A remarkable episode with Jewish overtones did indeed transpire on that fateful trip. The emotion roused by this story is truly — yes — of titanic proportions.

I am grateful to Mr. and Mrs. Gilbert and Roberta Binder and Mrs. Marie Aks of Virginia Beach, Virginia, for providing recordings and personal information about this story.

In 1910, Mr. Sam Aks of Turek, Poland, immigrated to England where he married the former Leah Rosen. They lived in London for a while after their wedding, and then they decided to move to America where there were better business opportunities. They settled on moving to Norfolk, Virginia.

By this time Leah was expecting their first child and her parents felt strongly that in her condition she should not make such an arduous trip across the ocean. They felt it would be too exhausting for her and dangerous for the unborn child. It was decided that Sam would travel alone, set up a home in Norfolk and a few months after the child was born, Leah would come with the infant.

The newspapers and media at the time were ablaze with the news of the opulent, gigantic ocean liner, the Titanic, that was to make its historic maiden voyage from Southampton, England to New York City, in April of 1912. The White Star Line, the Flagship Company of the Titanic, confidently claimed that their luxury liner was safe, sturdy and even majestic.

On April 10, Mrs. Leah Aks and her baby, with 912 other passengers, boarded the ship in Southampton, England, accompanied by hoopla, fanfare and ceremony. Leah and her infant were in steerage, the third-class cabin, with many other immigrants to America. The high society, wealthy people were in the luxurious first-class cabins. More passengers boarded at other ports before the Titanic crossed the ocean.

Four days later, shortly before midnight on April 14, as the ship was ninety-five miles south of the Grand Banks in Newfoundland, it sideswiped and crashed into an iceberg that towered 100 feet over the deck. [Ninety percent of an iceberg is hidden beneath the water.[1] Thus the iceberg was literally a mountain of ice close to 1,000 feet from top to bottom. Its massive knife-like edges beneath the water surface punctured and gashed the ship along 250 feet of its hull.] Twenty minutes later, after consulting with the ship's designer, Thomas Andrews, Captain Edward Smith realized that the ship would sink within two hours. Everyone on board would lose their lives unless they could get on lifeboats and be rescued by passing ships.

Incredibly there were not enough spaces in the lifeboats for everyone. Though there were 2,200 passengers and crew on board, there was room for only 1,178 on the lifeboats. More than a thousand people would surely die! One is astounded at the negligence of not being prepared for disaster. As the boat began tilting there was panic and pandemonium. The captain and crew ordered that women and children would be saved first.

In the third-class cabin, women were ordered to the front and men to the rear. Leah Aks held her son Frank Philip (Ephraim Fishel) in her arms and tried to get out onto the deck, but the gate in front of the cabin jammed and no one could get out. She stood pressed against the gate, screaming for help. A sailor saw her with her baby in her arms and he reached over the gate and lifted her and the child out, so that she could run to the deck where women and children were being put into lifeboats. (Most of the people in the third-class cabin could not get out and 75 percent of them drowned. The first-class cabin fared better, as only 40 percent died.)

Leah ran up to the deck with her child and waited by the railing, trying to get on line to be rescued. It was frighteningly cold. People were shoving and pushing frantically trying to get onto lifeboats. Meanwhile, down below water poured thunderously through the gaping holes, flooding the bottom of the ship.

As Leah stood on the deck, one of the wealthiest women on board, Lady Madeleine Astor, saw her and the baby huddled against the cold. Lady Astor, who was expecting a child, removed her beautiful eight-foot shawl and gave it to Leah saying, "Here

1. This peculiarity gave rise to the popular saying, "That's the tip of the iceberg," meaning a situation that contains hidden dangers or problems under the surface.

wrap your baby, it's so cold out here." Her teeth chattering, Leah thanked her profusely.

During this time, a man had pushed onto a lifeboat that was about to be lowered into the water. When cabin stewards saw him, they forced him out of the boat and pulled him back on deck, yelling that women and children were being rescued first. Somehow this man managed to get onto another lifeboat and once again the stewards saw him and forced him off the lifeboat, fighting with him, as they insisted that women and children were being given priority.

Back on the deck, the man saw Leah standing there with her baby now wrapped in the shawl. He was enraged. His eyes were wild as he stalked back and forth consumed by anger and frustration. In a demented moment of madness he ran toward Leah and screamed, "You think women are first! You think children are first! I'll show you," and he grabbed the infant from Leah's arms and threw him overboard!

Leah shrieked in horror and cried out for her child. Men on board lunged at this maniac but the deed had been done. People were yelling and screaming — but now it was Leah's turn to get on a lifeboat. "I won't go without my baby," she cried. But the officers told her she had to save her own life. There was no point in staying on the sinking ship. The women around her tried to console her, but Leah cried hysterically as she was placed on the lifeboat and lowered into the water.

The lifeboats drifted for three hours until the Cunard liner, the Carpathia, came and rescued those who were fortunate enough to get off the Titanic. Only 705 were saved, 1,523 people died.

Two days later, the grief-stricken Leah Aks was walking on the deck of the Carpathia when she saw a woman holding a child. The child lunged toward Leah. She recognized him. Leah screamed, "That's my baby! That's my child!"

The woman holding the child, Mrs. Elizabeth Ramell Nye, was dressed in a long black dress embroidered with a huge cross. "No it's not," she insisted. "This child was entrusted to me!" (Others contend that the woman was possibly Argene del Carlo from Italy.)

A wild argument ensued and Mrs. Nye claimed that while she was in the lifeboat, a child came flying into her waiting arms. To her that was a sign from Heaven that she had to care for the child the rest of her life.

People took sides in the argument. Soon the captain of the Carpathia, Arthur H. Rostron, was called to decide the issue. Leah was crying hysterically while Mrs. Nye was insisting on her position. She would not be denied this child.

When Captain Rostron arrived and heard the points of the argument, he told both women to come with the child to his quarters where he could reflect and decide the matter.

In the captain's quarters, Leah suddenly called out, "I can prove this is my child." The 18-year-old Leah spoke firmly and with certainty, "I am Jewish and my son was circumcised!" In Europe at that time, only Jewish children were circumcised.

When Captain Rostron saw that indeed the child had had a *bris,* 10-month-old Ephraim Fishel was reunited with his mother. Eventually the Carpathia brought all the survivors to New York.

Frank Philip Aks was raised in his rightful Jewish home. Eventually he married and had children and grandchildren. Frank passed away in 1991 at the age of 80. His wife, Marie, recently told me that as a youngster he would walk for miles on Shabbos to *daven* in the Orthodox *shul* in Norfolk, known as the Cumberland Street *Shul.*

After the traumatic events of the ill-fated journey, Leah was so grateful to Captain Rostron and his crew that years later when she had a daughter she named her Sarah Carpathia Aks. Incredibly there was some confusion among the hospital secretaries and they recorded her name on her birth certificate as Sarah Titanic Aks!

When I told this story to Rabbi Dovid Cohen of Brooklyn, he showed me the following *Midrash.*

When Hashem told Avraham *Avinu* to circumcise himself, Avraham consulted with three of his friends and confidants, Aner, Eshkol and Mamrei. Aner said, "You are [nearly] 100 years old, will you now risk your life by inflicting such pain to yourself?" Eshkol said, "Would you dare [put such an indelible] mark on yourself [and thereby look obviously different] from all your enemies? [That alone could be life threatening.]" Mamrei was the only one who encouraged Avraham to have faith in Hashem and follow His direction (*Bereishis Rabbah* 42:8 *and* 44:7).

Said Reb Dovid, "Isn't it noteworthy, that the mark that Eshkol thought would bring scorn on Avraham *Avinu* and even endanger his life was just the mark that reunited this child with his mother and saved him, so that he would be raised with his family as a Jewish child?

Healing a Trampled Sole

A number of years ago in Flatbush, New York, a very private, soft spoken gentleman, who always sat near the back of the *shul*, told his rav that he wanted to donate a *Sefer Torah*. The gentleman, Mr. Shimshon Blau,* told the rav that he had commissioned a *sofer* (a scribe) to write a *Sefer Torah* for him and now the job was nearly complete. The rav was incredulous. Mr. Blau was not known to have substantial funds and the cost of a new *Sefer Torah* was more than $30,000.

The rav spoke to the *sofer* and learned that Mr. Blau had indeed been paying small sums of money over the years and recently had made the last payment. The *Sefer Torah* would be finished in a few days.

On Shabbos the rav announced the good news to his congregants and everyone went over to Mr. Blau to wish him *mazel tov* and thank him for his generous gift to the *shul*. Plans were made for the *Hachnasas Sefer Torah*.

A few weeks later on a bright Sunday afternoon, the community gathered at Mr. Blau's home and escorted him as he carried the *Sefer Torah* from his home to the street where he walked under a

*The name has been changed.

chupah to bring the Torah to the *shul.* Dancing and singing accompanied those who took turns carrying the Torah, and a special meal was tendered in the *shul* in honor of the occasion.

A few days later, a neighbor asked Mr. Blau if there was a particular reason he decided to have the *Sefer Torah* written. At first he was hesitant to talk about it, but eventually he relented and told his heartbreaking story.

When I called Mr. Blau to hear the story directly from him, he said, "Rabbi, please don't make me tell the story again. I haven't slept a full night in the last fifty-five years." I wasn't going to press the issue, but then, of his own volition, he began reliving the episode. It is one of the most moving stories I have ever heard. People literally gasp when they first hear it. It is hard not to be moved to tears.

Shimshon Blau was only 16 years old when the Nazis took him, his parents and his sisters from Lodz, their hometown in Poland, to one of the notorious concentration camps. Shortly after their arrival the parents were separated from the children and Shimshon never heard from them again. He was placed in a slave labor barracks and suffered humiliation and heartache every day.

One night as he was lying in bed, a Nazi soldier came in to check on the prisoners. He walked from bed to bed — and then he saw Shimshon. Suddenly he lunged at Shimshon's feet, grabbed his leather boots and yelled, "Those boots are now mine."

Shimshon was shocked. The leather boots had been given to him by his parents shortly before the family had been captured by the Nazis. Shimshon treasured them because they were his last connection to his beloved parents. He had no pictures, no letters, no memento that he could hold onto in a private moment for strength and rejuvenation. The gift of the boots had become a precious memory.

Shimshon cried uncontrollably. This cruel act by the Nazi was the axe that severed the last tangible bond with his parents. It was devastating. Shimshon cried for hours. Eventually he fell asleep.

The next morning he went out of his barracks barefoot and found the soldier who had taken his boots. In desperation he ran over to him and begged, "Please give me a pair of shoes. I have nothing to wear on my feet. I'll freeze to death." He did not dare to antagonize the soldier by asking for his own boots back.

Much to Shimshon's surprise, the soldier told him. "Wait here, I'll be back in five minutes with some shoes for you."

Shimshon shuddered in the cold as he waited for the soldier to return. In a few minutes the Nazi came back with a pair of shoes and gave them to the startled but grateful teenager.

Shimshon went back to his barracks and sat on his bed to put on his new shoes. He looked them over carefully. They were made of wood, but he knew he would have to wear them regardless of what they were made of or how uncomfortable they would be. As he was about to put his foot into the shoe, he looked into its instep and gasped. The instep was a piece of parchment from a *Sefer Torah*!

Shimshon froze in terror. How could the Nazis be so heartless? How could he step down on the words that Hashem Himself had told Moshe *Rabbeinu* to write for all generations? But he knew he had no choice. There was nothing else to wear on his feet and it was either these shoes or frostbite and death. Hesitant with guilt, he put them on uneasily.

Now, years later, Shimshon said, "With every step I took, I felt I was trampling on Hashem's *Sefer Torah.* I swore to myself then that if I ever got out of the camps alive, no matter how rich or poor I was, someday I would have a *Sefer Torah* written and give back to Hashem the honor that I took from Him by trampling on His Torah. That's why I gave the *shul* a *Sefer Torah.*"

In his sincerity, Shimshon felt he was trampling on Hashem's Torah. Who could blame him? But what about us? We must ask ourselves, "Are we in any way trampling on G-d's Torah? Do we, unwillingly and sometimes even willingly, violate basic precepts of His Torah, which is in essence trampling on His words?

Shimshon Blau surely rectified his "misdeed." We as observant Jews should do no less.

Code Blue in Boston

For fourteen years, Dr. Chona Chaim (Howie) Lebowitz divided his time between providing medical services in his hometown of Boston and in the holy city of Jerusalem. A graduate of Harvard Medical School, where he later taught, Dr. Lebowitz is an internist with an impeccable reputation.

More than a decade ago, Dr. Lebowitz began his religious studies in Yeshiva Aish Hatorah in Jerusalem, where he became enamored by the brilliance and guidance of the *Rosh Yeshivah,* Rav Noach Weinberg, and became one of the teachers in Aish Hatorah's Discovery program. These days Dr. Lebowitz spends his time learning in the Mirrer Yeshiva in Jerusalem and is often consulted on medical matters by the most renowned *rabbanim* in *Eretz Yisrael.* He sees patients after *seder* and at night. [Since the writing of this story he and his family have moved to Lakewood, N.J.]

On *Simchas Torah* Dr. Lebowitz told me a riveting story that happened years ago in Boston. The episode gave him a new perspective and does the same for all who hear it.

As Senior Resident in Brigham and Women's Hospital in Boston, Dr. Lebowitz was in charge of its often-frenzied emergency room. The ER at Brigham, like other emergency rooms throughout the world, is a flurry of activity as doctors and nurses attend patients according to the severity of the situation. A stroke patient can't be kept waiting, every moment counts; a patient with a possible broken ankle — as painful as it is — must wait until the car crash victim bleeding profusely is attended to. In many hospitals, the emergency room comprises a row of cubicles, separated by thin curtains, where immediate and not so immediate attention is given to the myriad cases that arrive unannounced throughout the day and night. All this activity takes place to the steady din of staccato beeps of monitors and cardiographs and constant clacking on computer keyboards as information is entered on forms, registrations and medical records.

One afternoon, as Dr. Lebowitz was making his rounds in the emergency room, the loudspeaker blared a "Code Blue" alert, the words that indicate an emergency life-threatening situation. A woman had suffered a severe heart attack in the cafeteria upstairs and was in cardiac arrest. Dr. Lebowitz grabbed his equipment and raced upstairs, where he found doctors already working on the woman.

All patrons had been cleared from the cafeteria, as a hospital security officer stood guard at the door, not allowing anyone in except medical personnel. Dr. Lebowitz rushed toward the huddle of people in the middle of the room. "How is she doing?" he asked one of the doctors who was kneeling on the floor attending the stricken woman.

"I'm afraid it's too late," the doctor replied. "We've been working on her for a while already."

"Let me try," Dr. Lebowitz said, quickly moving toward the patient. He inserted an intravenous catheter directly into her heart to get her started on epinephrine, which would prevent further progression of the blood clot to her coronary arteries. He applied two large paddles known as defibrillators to her body, so that he could send an electric shock to the heart to jumpstart it back into a normal rhythm.

Dr. Lebowitz tried numerous times to get a heartbeat, but he was unsuccessful. The other doctors began to leave the cafeteria, shaking their heads in disappointment that a patient had died right before their eyes.

However, Dr. Lebowitz would not give up ... not yet. He tried a fifth and a sixth time to stimulate a heartbeat, but it wasn't happening. He realized the end was near, if it had not already come. He would try one more time.

He pressed the control button on the defibrillator with added emphasis. He glanced at the cardiac monitor. The razor-thin line that had been flat darted upwards! There was life! A doctor called out in disbelief, "You've got a heartbeat!"

Infused with hope and determination, Dr. Lebowitz worked frantically to continue the heart's revival and with concerted effort managed to stimulate a feeble pulse. He ordered medics to transfer the patient to the third floor intensive care unit, where she would be treated and observed every moment. Once in the ICU, her progress was slow but steady.

Dr. Lebowitz returned to the emergency room to continue his full-time duties. Periodically he would call up to the ICU unit to get the latest update on the woman's condition. Six hours later he was told the good news that she was being allowed to sit up in bed. Dr. Lebowitz wondered if he should go up and visit the woman. She wasn't his patient. She would surely not recognize him and he did not need her thanks. He was in medicine to help people, not for gratitude and recognition.

The more he thought about it the more he wanted to see her. Her family name was Kelly,* obviously she was not Jewish. His name, Lebowitz, was unmistakably Jewish. "If I do visit her," he thought, "it would be a *kiddush Hashem* (santification of Hashem's Name), for she will surely realize that a Jew saved her life. That's important in the long run. Let her know that Jewish people are compassionate to everyone."

As Dr. Lebowitz walked to her room he wondered how he should introduce himself. When he entered the room he didn't have to say a word. A man sitting next to her called out, "He's the one! He's the one who saved your life! That's the one I've been telling you about."

"And who are you?" Dr. Lebowitz said, extending his hand to the gentleman.

"I'm her husband and I saw how you worked to save my wife's life."

"Where were you?" Dr. Lebowitz asked.

"I was with her when it happened, but then they whisked me out of the room and I stood watching from behind the glass wall."

The woman began crying uncontrollably. Dr. Lebowitz stood there somewhat embarrassed, waiting for her to compose herself. When she did, she spoke softly and said words Dr. Lebowitz will never forget.

"What do I say? Thank you? That's what you say to someone who holds a door open for you, not to someone who has just given you back your life. But I will tell you this. When I go home and see my children I will remember you and say, 'Thank you Dr. Lebowitz.' In a week from now when I take a walk with my husband I will think of you and say, 'Thank you Dr. Lebowitz.' The next time I go out with my friends, I will think of you and say, 'Thank you Dr. Lebowitz. 'And the next time I have a birthday, I will remember you and say, 'Thank you Dr. Lebowitz.'"

*The name has been changed.

Her words were simple but heartfelt — gentle but powerful.

When Dr. Lebowitz left the room he walked out into the hospital corridor and said to no one and to anyone, "When I come home and see my wife and family, I'm going to say, 'Thank you — Hashem,' and the next time I *daven* and feel connected to Hashem I will remember and say, 'Thank you Rav Noach Weinberg,' and the next time I learn *Chumash* I will say, 'Thank you Rav Noach Weinberg.' The next time I walk up the stairs and don't get out of breath I will say, 'Thank you Hashem.'"

Dr. Lebowitz returned to the emergency room a humbled and grateful person.

Bound to His Father

The following is one of the most moving stories I have ever heard. I am grateful to Rabbi Zvi Teitelbaum, principal of the Yeshiva of Greater Washington in Maryland for sharing it with me. The young man in this story is a prize student in his yeshivah.

In the summer of 2000, 16-year-old Mordechai Kaler volunteered to help in the Hebrew Home for the Aged in Greater Washington. One of his responsibilities was to invite the residents to attend the daily services in the synagogue on the first floor. Some agreed and others refused, but even those who declined were pleasant about it.

There was one man on the second floor, however, who had been quite nasty and had even cursed another volunteer when he was asked to join the *minyan*. The volunteer was taken aback by the man's tirade, so Mordechai undertook the challenge of speaking to the angry gentleman.

Mordechai found the man sitting in a wheelchair in a lounge filled with residents of the home. After introducing himself, Mordechai said softly but firmly, "If you don't wish to join the services we can respect that, but why should you curse the volunteer? He is here to help and he was just doing his job."

"Young man," the elderly gentleman said sternly, "wheel me to my room. I want to tell you a story."

When they were in the room alone, the old man told his story of horror, pain and sadness. He came from a prominent religious family in Poland and when he was 12 years old, he and his family were taken to a Nazi concentration camp. They were all killed except for him and his father.

In their barracks there was a man who had smuggled in the *tefillin shel rosh,* the *tefillin* worn on the head. Every day the men in the barracks would try to seize an opportunity to put on that *tefillah,* even for a moment, when there were no Nazi S.S. guards nearby. The men knew that they hadn't fulfilled the *mitzvah* of donning *tefillin shel yad,* but their love for *mitzvos* compelled them to do whatever they could.

The man continued, "But for my father that wasn't enough. My *bar mitzvah* was coming up and he wanted that at least on the day of my *bar mitzvah* I wear a complete set of *tefillin*. He had heard that in a barracks down the road, a man who had been killed had had a complete pair of *tefillin*.

"On the morning of my *bar mitzvah,* my father, at great risk, went out early to the other barracks to get the *tefillin.* I was waiting by the window with trepidation. In the distance I could see him rushing to get back. As he came closer I could see that he was carrying something cupped in his hands.

"As he got to the barracks, a Nazi stepped out from behind a tree and shot and killed him right before my eyes! When the Nazi left I ran out and took the pouch of *tefillin* that lay on the ground next to my father. I managed to hide it."

The old man peered angrily at Mordechai and said vehemently, "How can anyone pray to a G-d Who would kill a boy's father right in front of him? I can't!"

The man pointed to the dresser against the wall and said, "Open the top drawer."

In the drawer Mordechai saw an old black *tefillin* pouch, crusted from many years of not being used. "Bring me the pouch," the man ordered. Mordechai complied.

The man opened it and took out an old pair of *tefillin*. "This is what my father was carrying on that fateful day. I keep it to show people what my father died for, these dirty black boxes and straps. These were the last things I got from my father."

Mordechai was stunned. He had no words — no comfort to give. He could only pity the poor man who had lived his life in anger, bitterness and sadness. "I'm sorry," he finally stammered softly. "I didn't realize." Mordechai left the room resolved never to come back to the man again. When he came home that evening, he couldn't eat or sleep.

He returned to the home the next day, but avoided the old man's room. A few days later, as Mordechai was helping the men who had come to the *shul*, one of them said, "I have *yahrzeit* today and I need to say *Kaddish*. We only have nine men here today. You think you could get a tenth man?" Mordechai had already made his rounds that morning and had been refused by many of the residents. They were too tired, not interested or half asleep. The only one he hadn't approached was the old man on the second floor.

Reluctantly and hesitantly he went upstairs. He knew the old man would scold him, but he still had to make an effort. He knocked on the door gently and announced himself.

"It's you again?" the old man asked

"I'm so sorry to trouble you," Mordechai said softly, "but there's a man in *shul* who needs to say *Kaddish* today. We need you for a *minyan*. Would you mind coming just this one time?"

The old man looked up at Mordechai and said, "If I come this time, then you'll leave me alone?" Mordechai wasn't expecting that response. "Yes," he said in a whisper, "I won't bother you again."

To this day, Mordechai doesn't know why he then said what he did. It could have infuriated the old man, but for some reason Mordechai blurted out, "Would you like to bring your *tefillin*?"

Mordechai braced himself for a bitter retort — but instead the man said again, "If I bring them, will you leave me alone?"

"Yes," Mordechai said, "I will leave you alone."

"All right," the man replied, "then wheel me downstairs and make sure that I'm in the back of the *shul*, so I can get out first."

Mordechai wheeled the old man to the *shul* and brought him to the back. "May I help you?" Mordechai asked as he took the *tefillin* out of the pouch. The gentleman put out his left hand. Mordechai helped him put on his *tefillin* and left the synagogue to do other work.

After the services, Mordechai returned and the *shul* was empty — except for the old man. He was still wearing his *tefillin* and tears were running down his cheeks. "Shall I get a doctor or a nurse?" Mordechai asked.

The man didn't answer. Instead he was staring down at the straps of *tefillin* wrapped on his left arm, caressing them with his right hand and repeating over and over, "*Tatte, Tatte* (Father, Father), it feels so right." The old man looked up at Mordechai and said, "For the last half hour I've felt so connected to my *Tatte*. I feel as though he has come back to me."

Mordechai took the man back to his room and as he was about to leave, the old man said, "Please come back for me tomorrow."

And so every morning Mordechai would go to the second floor and the old man would be waiting for him at the elevator holding his *tefillin*. Mordechai would wheel him into the *shul* where he would sit in the back wearing his *tefillin*, holding a *siddur*, absorbed in his thoughts.

One morning Mordechai got off the elevator on the second floor but the man wasn't there. He hurried to his room, but his bed was empty. Instinctively he became afraid. He ran to the nurses' station and asked where the gentleman was — and they told him. He had been rushed to the hospital the previous afternoon and late in the day he had had a stroke and died.

A few days later, Mordechai was given an award by the Jewish home for his work as a volunteer. After the ceremonies a woman approached him and thanked him for all he had done for her. Mordechai had no recollection of the woman. "Excuse me," Mordechai said, "do I know you?"

"I am the daughter of that man you helped," she said softly. "He was my father and you did so much for him. You made his last days so comfortable. When he was in the hospital he called me frantically and asked me to bring him his *tefillin*. He wanted to *daven* one more time with them. I helped him with his *tefillin* in the hospital and then he had his stroke."

He died wearing them.

Bound to his Father — in Heaven.

Towers of Strength and Loyalty

September 11, 2001 — the day will be a frame of reference as long as Americans breathe on the planet earth. On the bloodiest day on American soil since the Civil War, when planes filled to capacity with fuel for cross-country trips were hijacked by Muslim terrorists and flown into the Twin Towers of the World Trade Center in New York, the Pentagon in Washington, D.C., and a farm in Shanksville, Pennsylvania, murdering nearly 3,000 people, a stunned nation was numbed and plunged into mourning, as the world reacted with fright and sympathy.

The close coordination and nearly flawless execution of these attacks brought a sudden awareness to Americans that even we, the strongest nation in the world, are vulnerable to mass violence and destruction.

As the upper portion of the North Tower became obscured in black smoke after the first plane struck it, and a 300 foot fireball cascaded along the façade of the South Tower after the second plane crashed into it, thousands of stories of death and rescue unfolded simultaneously. Police, firefighters and rescue workers evacuated 25,000 people in half an hour, the largest rescue effort in American history. Throughout the weeks and months after 9/11, stories emerged about those who were saved and those who were lost, stories of unimaginable commitment and indescribable grief, of those blessed with fortuitous timing and those victimized by ill-fated timing, of those who were reunited with loved ones and those whose lingering hope for the survival of their relatives and family members slowly dissipated into agonized sorrow.

I went to be *menachem avel* Reb Yankel Zelmanowitz, whose brother Avremel perished in the collapse of the North Tower. As his eyes filled with tears, Reb Yankel shook his head in disbelief and said, "I saw Avremel in *shul* that morning as I did many mornings. For some reason, before he left we embraced intensely for a long moment and wished each other a good day. We never did that after *davening*. That morning we did it. It was almost like a special good-bye."

> His poignant description brought to mind a Talmudic teaching *(Megillah* 3a*)* regarding a prophetic vision Daniel saw. Three other prophets who were with him — Chaggai, Zechariah and Malachi — did not see it, but it frightened them. The *Gemara* asks, "Since they did not see the vision, why were they frightened?" The Gemara replies, אִינְהוּ לָא חָזוּ מַזָּלַיְהוּ חָזוּ, *Even though they did not see, their representative angels did see [the vision]. Rashi* (ibid.) explains that every person has an angel that represents him in heaven. This is what is meant by a person's *"mazel."* Hence, if a person fears something and doesn't know why he fears it, it may be because his *"mazel"* saw something that he could not see with his physical eyes.
>
> Did Avremel's *"mazel"* see something that morning after *davening?*

Three days after the cataclysmic events, on Friday, September 14, the President of the United States, Mr. George W. Bush, spoke at a prayer service held at the Washington National Cathedral. He spoke of the grief and sorrow of the nation, of offering prayers for the dead and missing, and of the recognition in tragedy that G-d's purposes are not always our own. Then he spoke of Americans "who are generous, and kind, resourceful and brave." Millions of people throughout the world heard him say, "We have seen our national character in eloquent acts of sacrifice. Inside the World Trade Center, one man who could have saved himself stayed until the end at the side of his quadriplegic friend ..." The President was referring to the "eloquent act of sacrifice" performed by Avremel Zelmanowitz.

Avremel, who was a computer programmer for Blue Cross/Blue Shield, worked on the 27th floor of One World Trade Center, the North Tower. When the first plane hit it, killing many on the upper floors and trapping others by fire and falling debris on lower floors, people began evacuating the building.

In Avremel's office there was a quadriplegic man, an Irish fellow named Ed Beyea, who had been paralyzed from the neck down in an accident when he was 22. He needed a constant health care attendant and was confined to a wheelchair. Ed's attendant, a devoted 68-year-old woman named Erma had been in a cafeteria on an upper floor getting some breakfast. As smoke barreled through the hallways and stairwells she ran downstairs coughing, trying to catch her breath and get fresh air. Erma ran into the Blue Cross/Blue Shield office but knew she could not help Mr. Beyea. He weighed close to 300 pounds and it would take a few strong men to carry him downstairs. Firefighters had been summoned to come and get him. Avremel told Erma that she should leave the building, and he would stay with Ed until the firefighters came.

Ed broke into a profuse sweat as he heard people running and screaming through the halls. He was helpless and understood that he could be abandoned and left to die at any moment. But to his amazement, Abe, the one he had always called "The Mentsch" was staying with him when no one else would.

An extraordinary *kiddush Hashem.*

It was at that point that Avremel called his sister-in-law, Mrs. Chavie Zelmanowitz, on the phone. She pleaded with him to leave the building but he insisted that he had to wait with Ed until rescue workers arrived to carry him down the stairs. No one will ever know if Avremel, Ed and the firefighter, Captain William Burke of Engine 21 in Manhattan, who came to assist, lost their lives in that office waiting for help (as the President indicated) or if it happened when they were already making their way down the stairwell.

Eventually though, Ground Zero yielded remains, so that Avremel could be buried in *Eretz Yisrael,* on *Har Hazeisim* in Jerusalem, alongside his parents.

What compelled Avremel to act as he did? What possessed him to act in such noble fashion to the point of risking his life for the sake of another human being in trouble? Where does a man, standing at death's door, get the strength to defy the basic instinct of survival and think of someone other than himself?

As Reb Yankel spoke about his brother, he revealed a fascinating episode that happened in *shul* on Shabbos, three days before September 11.

Avremel *davened* in Rabbi Chaim Halberstam's *shul,* Shaarei Tzion, in Flatbush. One of the congregants, Avraham Mintz, a Lubavitcher *chassid,* had become seriously ill a few months earlier. Rabbi Meshulem Halberstam, son of the rabbi and a *dayan* (rabbinical judge) in the community, suggested that it would be appropriate to learn something from the writings of the *Baal HaTanya,* Rabbi Schneur Zalman of Liadi (1745-1812), the first Lubavitcher Rebbe, as a *zechus* (benefit) for Mr. Mintz, so that he would merit a *refuah sheleimah* (complete recovery).

The members agreed and so every Shabbos Rabbi Meshulem Halberstam led a study group in the classic work *Tanya* for the benefit of Mr. Mintz. Avremel, himself a *talmid chacham,* was part of the group. He listened attentively, but hardly ever spoke up or interrupted with questions. He had a sharp inquisitive mind but reserved his comments until the class was over. On the Shabbos of September 8th the group was studying the end of the eighteenth chapter.

The Baal HaTanya writes: וְלָכֵן אֲפִילוּ קַל שֶׁבְּקַלִים וּפוֹשְׁעֵי יִשְׂרָאֵל מוֹסְרִים נַפְשָׁם עַל קִדּוּשׁ ה׳ עַל הָרֹב, וְסוֹבְלִים עִנּוּיִם קָשִׁים שֶׁלֹּא לִכְפּוֹר בַּה׳ אֶחָד, *Therefore, as a rule, even the simplest of the simple and [even] Jewish sinners sacrifice their lives for the sanctity of G-d's Name and suffer harsh torture rather than deny G-d's unity.*

At this point Avremel spoke up. "I thought," he said, "that only great people like the *Asarah Harugei Malchus* (Ten Martyrs — ten Sages of the Mishnaic period who were brutally killed by the Romans), could make a *kiddush Hashem* of such magnitude. A simpleton who has no understanding of Hashem would not understand the significance of what he is doing and thus it would not be a *kiddush Hashem* in the true sense of the words."

Rabbi Halberstam replied, "Every Jew, regardless of his level, can sanctify Hashem's Name by his noble deeds." To prove his point he continued with the words of the *Baal HaTanya:* וְאַף אִם בּוּרִים וְעַמֵּי הָאָרֶץ וְאֵין יוֹדְעִים גְּדֻלּוֹת ה׳, וְגַם בַּמְעַט שֶׁיּוֹדְעִים אֵין מִתְבּוֹנְנִים כְּלָל, וְאֵין מוֹסְרִים נַפְשָׁם מֵחֲמַת דַּעַת וְהִתְבּוֹנְנוּת בַּה׳ כְּלָל אֶלָּא בְּלִי שׁוּם דַּעַת וְהִתְבּוֹנְנוּת, *Even if they are unlearned and illiterates, who are ignorant of G-d's greatness, and do not delve into the little knowledge they possess, so that by no means does their self-sacrifice result from any knowledge or contemplation of G-d, rather [they are prepared to sacrifice their lives] without any knowledge or reflection …*

Again, Avremel spoke up. The members of the group turned in surprise to listen to him. This was so unusual; he never said anything during the *shiur,* but on the matter of self-sacrifice and *kiddush Hashem* he had his opinions.

Less than 72 hours later, Avremel would make the ultimate sacrifice. Certainly he was intelligent, and undoubtedly he knew what the gentile Ed was thinking as he displayed a loyalty that was noble and heroic. Maybe as fear and panic surrounded them, Avremel was at peace with himself because he believed there was enough time for them to be rescued and he believed that he was fulfilling the commandment of *kiddush Hashem* with his heroic loyalty. For had Ed lived he would surely say of Avremel afterwards, "Fortunate is that person who learned Torah, fortunate is his father who taught him Torah, fortunate is his teacher who taught him Torah." [These are the words that describe people's reaction to one who performs a *kiddush Hashem* (see *Yoma* 86a *and Bach).*]

Ed can't say those words about Avremel. We can.

יְהִי זִכְרוֹ בָּרוּךְ, *May his memory be blessed.*

Priority Baggage

In the summer of 2001, I had the opportunity to spend a week with a large group of English families who came together in a family camp setting in Sestriere, a small vacation town in the Italian Alps. I was fortunate to meet many extraordinary people from various walks of life, some of whom told me incredible stories. One such individual was Mrs. Yocheved Kahn, a Torah educator from London (see *Echoes of the Maggid*, p. 204).

In the 1980's, when travel behind the Iron Curtain was rigorously restricted, Mrs. Yocheved Kahn traveled to the Soviet Union with a group of men and women to teach Torah clandestinely in basements and attics. The group, directed by Mr. Ernie Hirsch of England, brought *sefarim, mezuzos, tefillin* and *matzos* to Jews who desperately longed for them. More than most others, Mrs. Kahn could relate to the perils and fears of her Russian students, for as a child she, too, had been confronted with fright, persecution and separation.

Mrs. Kahn was born in 1939, in Apeldoorn, Holland, as Nazis were spreading their ghastly terror throughout Europe. Dutch Jews were terrified that the Nazis would soon invade their country. When Yocheved was 2½ years old, her parents reluctantly gave her to a gentile woman, who promised to care for her and protect her from the Nazis. Two weeks later, Yocheved's parents along with hundreds of others were taken to the transit camp in Westerbork, a tiny town in northeastern Holland. Tragically, she would never see her parents again, as they were transferred to extermination camps in Poland where they perished.

After the war, when she was 6 years old, Yocheved was reunited with an uncle and aunt in Utrecht, and they raised her until she married. Throughout her youth, Yocheved searched for people who could tell her about her parents. One evening in 1958 when she was 19 years old, she met Mrs. Gerda Hirsch who told her a story that has given Yocheved strength, pride and purpose until this very day.

"So you are the daughter of Reb Shlomo and Rosa Leuvenberg?" Mrs. Hirsch said. "I must tell you a story about your parents that only I know. No one else could possibly tell it to you because only I, among all the people who witnessed it, lived to tell about it."

Yocheved listened with bated breath.

It was Friday morning, *Parashas Balak,* in the early summer of 1941 when the Nazi S.S. troops began their roundup of Jews in Amsterdam. Jews were snatched from their basements, attics, walk-in closets and any other place they sought to hide. The captives had to leave most of their belongings behind but many took a rucksack — what we in America call a backpack — that contained some necessities, a few precious possessions and money. The Jews were herded into trains that would go north, toward Westerbork.

As people on the train found places among the stifling crowd, there was a surprising release of tension. Everyone realized that all who were present were Jewish and the fate of one would be the fate of all, thus there was no need to hide their identities anymore. Though worried and frightened, they were calm because they were among their own.

The loaded train tarried in the station for hours. When it finally began to move, it traveled but a few miles and then stopped for no apparent reason, waiting endlessly. People made easy conversation throughout the afternoon. As the sun began to set, someone announced that it was time to *daven Minchah.* Many of the men stood up to begin *Ashrei.* When the *Kaddish* after *Ashrei* had been recited, the men and women who knew *Shemoneh Esrei* by heart began praying silently.

As night began to spread over the horizon, the discussion began about *davening Kabbalas Shabbos* (the Friday evening service).

Mrs. Hirsch continued her narrative, "Very few people had *siddurim* so your father announced that he would recite aloud the words of the first chapters of *Kabbalas Shabbos* and everyone could follow along." Reb Leuvenberg recited the words of *Le'chu Ne'rananah* loudly, slowly and carefully. He went through the six chapters of *Tehillim* that are recited Friday night, leading up to *Lechah Dodi,* the beautiful and inspiring hymn to welcome the Shabbos, written by the 16th-century Kabbalist, Rabbi Shlomo Alkabetz. Remarkably, even on this night of confusion, fear and uncertainty people joined Mr. Leuvenberg in greeting the Shabbos with song.

For some it would be the last time they sang these words.

The men finished *Kabbalas Shabbos* and *Maariv* with special intensity. Their spirits had been renewed, their pride in their

Jewishness aroused. And now it would be time to eat, but no one thought of eating anything without first hearing *Kiddush*. There was no wine on the train for *Kiddush*, so the people sat wondering what to do next.

"And then," exclaimed Mrs. Hirsch to Yocheved in a hushed intense voice, "your mother took out of her rucksack two *challos* that she had baked that morning! Of all the things to take in her rucksack, your mother chose what was to her most important — Shabbos *challos*! Others may have taken jewelry, pictures or money, but your mother took *challos*!

"Your father made *Kiddush* for everyone over the *challos*, and afterwards people shared with each other the small parcels of food they had taken along."

It is Mrs. Rosa Leuvenberg's priorities that inspire her daughter, Mrs. Yocheved Kahn, to this very day.

There is an interesting sidebar to this story.

When Yocheved was brought back to her uncle and aunt after the war, she was reluctant to stay there. After having been with a kind gentile family, the Sandstras, for five years in the small fishing town, Enkhuizen, in northern Holland, she felt like a daughter to them. Mrs. Kahn recalls that when she first saw her uncle, Rabbi Aaron De Haas, he was sitting at his desk reading from a large book that had strange letters. It seemed so foreign. She cried and begged to go back with the Sandstras, but they refused her pleas, telling her she was related to the De Haases and not them.

On the first Friday night, as she sat at the Shabbos table, when the De Hasses began singing *zemiros*, she was suddenly brought back to a memory of years before. She recognized those tunes! Unexpectedly she felt a connection that she instinctively knew was true and powerful. Tears welled in her eyes. She wanted to sing along even softly, but she couldn't utter a sound. The lump in her throat choked off any possibility of making a sound.

It was then that the six-year-old child knew that she had returned to where she belonged. One day she would figure out where the painful pieces of the puzzle had gone.

The Warmth of a Chill in the Evening

Rabbi Mordechai Neustadt is the founder of the *Vaad L'Hatzolas Nidchei Yisrael,* an American organization that clandestinely helped Russian Jews under Communist rule learn about their Jewish heritage.

The *Vaad* would send rabbis and teachers to Moscow for two-week stints, in order to teach and guide the growing number of Soviet Jews who were thirsting for knowledge of their heritage. The teaching had to be done in secret; otherwise Russian authorities would confiscate their *Chumashim* and *siddurim.* At times the loss of a job and even jail sentences would be the lot of someone pursuing religious studies. Many of those who traveled to Russia brought with them *talleisim, tzitzis* and pairs of *tefillin* to be dispensed behind closed doors to whoever had the courage and fortitude to use them.

The primary leader of observant Russian Jews at the time was Rabbi Eliyahu Essas, who had covertly been a courageous and daring teacher and mentor of hundreds of newly observant Russian Jews. In the spring of 1989, Rabbi Essas was leaving the USSR to settle in Israel. A rotation of substitute rabbis was needed until a permanent one could be found. Rabbi Neustadt asked Rabbi Yechiel Michel Chill of Monsey, New York, to go to Moscow and serve as a temporary rabbi for a few weeks.

Shortly after his arrival, Rabbi Chill met a brilliant young student, Moshe, who had a sharp inquisitive mind and a great thirst for Torah knowledge. Rabbi Chill spent a long time discussing religion with him, as Moshe longed to learn all he could about authentic Judaism. The two men developed a mutual admiration, as each revered what the other stood for.

The day before Rabbi Chill left the Soviet Union he said to Moshe, "If you are ever able to come to America, make sure you call me. I will help you in any way I can." The two did not know if they would ever see each other again

One afternoon six months later Rabbi Chill received a call, "It's me, Moshe," came the voice on the other end of the line.

"Where are you calling from?" asked an excited Rabbi Chill.

"I am here in Cornell University in Ithaca, New York," replied Moshe, sounding concerned and troubled. "I was able to get an exit visa and I am now enrolled here as an exchange student, but I have no kosher food and no Torah books. The border police in Russia took away my *tefillin*. Is there any way you can help me?"

Rabbi Chill first tried to explain to Moshe the system of kosher food in America with the various *hashgachos* (kosher certifications), but it was too foreign a concept for Moshe to understand. In the Soviet Union, one knew certain foods were either kosher or non-kosher but there were no symbols on food packages to indicate whether or not one was permitted to eat them.

"Stay where you are," said Rabbi Chill. "I'll be up there in a few hours."

Rabbi Chill and a friend, Rabbi Tzvi Goodman, went immediately and purchased a new pair of *tefillin*. They procured a *siddur* with Russian translation and other Torah literature that Moshe could understand. They bought enough kosher food, bread, and drinks to last a month, and then made the four-hour trip from Monsey to Ithaca, which is in the northwestern part of New York State.

The atmosphere on the Cornell campus was festive as final examinations had just been completed and the spring term had officially ended. The celebratory mood only accentuated Moshe's loneliness. He stared out his window observing the joy and frolic of the students below. His English was labored, so his communication skills were awkward. He could not feel the sense of accomplishment that everyone around him seemed to share.

He waited for his visitors with heightened anticipation. How wonderful it would be to see a friendly, familiar face.

The sky was dark and the streetlights were all lit when Rabbis Chill and Goodman walked into Moshe's dormitory room. Rabbi

Chill and his scholarly friend embraced warmly and immediately began reminiscing about their religious discussions in Russia.

Moshe was amazed at everything the rabbis brought him. He became alive and animated. The rabbis had lifted his spirits and given him hope. He would never forget this evening and the generosity of these men. After two hours, Rabbi Chill explained that he would have to head back to Monsey. Aside from being the rabbi of his synagogue, Rabbi Chill was the eleventh grade *rebbi* at the Rabbi Samson Raphael Hirsch High School for boys in Washington Heights. He had to get home and get some rest in order to get to school on time the next morning.

The next morning when Rabbi Chill stood before his class he said to his students, "Boys, if I appear a bit tired this morning, I would like you to understand that I had a very long night last night." Then he added half in jest, "So please be easy on me."

He went on to detail his meeting with Moshe in Moscow a few months earlier, culminating in the eight hours of driving he and a friend did the night before, to bring kosher food, *tefillin* and *sefarim* and lift the spirits of a special Jew who was trying to be observant under all circumstances. Rabbi Chill had a twofold purpose in telling his *talmidim* of the previous night's episode. Aside from his explaining his obvious exhaustion, he felt it was a good lesson in caring for a fellow Jew. Perhaps the event would leave an impression and someday in the future one of his students would perform a similar gesture to a Jew in need.

A year later, on a Sunday morning, a twelfth grader, Jeremy Strauss, who had been in Rabbi Chill's class the previous year, came running in to Rabbi Chill's classroom and exclaimed, "*Rebbi*, you won't believe what happened in our neighborhood, (Englewood, New Jersey) this past Shabbos."

Jeremy told the following story. "My father and I came to *shul* on Shabbos and we noticed someone who looked like he might need a place to eat. My father invited him to be with us and he accepted.

At the *seudah* (Shabbos meal) he told us that he was a recent *baal teshuvah.* My father asked him if there was a story behind his wanting to be religious and he replied that there certainly was.

"He said that he had been a student in Cornell University in Ithaca and at the end of the semester he got a new roommate, a fellow from Russia. He told us that the Russian fellow seemed lost and out of place. On the second evening that the Russian was there, two rabbis came and brought him food and books, and showed him a love and respect that the roomate had never seen before. The *baal teshuvah* said, 'I kept thinking all night that I had never seen anything like this. I must find out about the religion that creates such love for a fellow Jew. I began looking into what Judaism was all about and that's where the road to being observant began.' So *Rebbi,*" Jeremy continued, "you may not have realized it but your kindness not only helped Moshe, but was the reason why his roommate became a *baal teshuvah!*"

And then Jeremy added something that was astounding, "You know what else he told us? The Russian fellow was his roommate for only two nights! After that he moved to a different dormitory."

> The *Hashgacha Pratis* (Divine synchronization) of the timing is so obviously impeccable.

A Blessing in Disguise

On a trip to Minneapolis, Minnesota, I had the opportunity to meet Dr. Nesanel Breningstall, a world-renowned pediatric neurologist. As we sat talking in his home, he began telling a story that was vaguely familiar to me. "Wait a moment," I said. "I heard that beautiful story a number of years ago but I never knew to whom it happened nor precisely when it happened and so I never told it or wrote about it."

"Well, I'm the person in that story," Dr. Breningstall said with pride, "and I'll be happy to tell you the details."

I sat fascinated, for indeed the story is remarkable.

As a highly regarded expert in his field, Dr. Breningstall attends neurology conferences and seminars throughout the world. In the fall of 1987, he came to Jerusalem to participate in the 17th Epileptic International Congress. (Epilepsy is a chronic nerve disease characterized by brief convulsive seizures and loss of consciousness.) A few hundred doctors were in attendance, listening to the distinguished speakers present their latest findings in the field.

During one of the sessions, Dr. Breningstall noticed a Yerushalmi Jew with beard and *payos* (sidelocks) listening attentively. His dress was glaringly incongruous to the other attendees, but this was Jerusalem; thousands of such Jews lived in the city. After the session, Dr. Breningstall approached the Yerushalmi gentleman and asked him, "Are you a doctor?"

"Oh, no," came the reply.

"So what brings you here?" asked Dr. Breningstall.

"My daughter suffers from epileptic seizures," the Yerushalmi said, "so whenever I hear about such conferences in Israel, I attend them, so that I can be up to date on the latest developments in the field. This way I can help my daughter get the best help available."

Dr. Breningstall was impressed with this father's dedication and commitment. The two men became friendly and they spoke for the duration of the conference. The three-day conference ended Friday afternoon. After the last session, the Yerushalmi approached Dr. Breningstall and asked, "Where are you planning to be for Shabbos?"

"To tell you the truth," replied the doctor, "I was going to be alone in my hotel."

"Why don't you spend Shabbos with us?" said the Yerushalmi. "You'll have a memorable Shabbos."

Dr. Breningstall readily agreed and the two made up to meet at a particular *shul* for *davening* that evening.

After *Kabbalas Shabbos,* as the two of them made their way home from *shul*, the Yerushalmi said, "I have five daughters but you'll see, you won't be able to tell which is the daughter who suffers from the seizures. She has them only once in a while and she integrates so well with the other children that our home seems perfectly normal."

"Perhaps you are right," said Dr. Breningstall. "We shall see."

The Yerushalmi came home, introduced his guest to the family and then made *Kiddush.* The meal proceeded and the children indeed laughed and interacted beautifully with each other. They all took turns helping their mother serve and each recited *divrei Torah* (Torah thoughts) they had heard in class throughout the week.

During the meal, the father turned to Dr. Breningstall and said, "*Nu,* what do you say? Which daughter is it?"

Dr. Breningstall looked around the table carefully and then nodded unobtrusively to one of the girls and said softly, "That one."

The Yerushalmi was flabbergasted. His mouth fell open in disbelief. "You are exactly right, but how could you have known that?"

Dr. Breningstall paused for a moment and then said delicately, "When you *bentsched* (blessed) each one of your children (after the singing of *Shalom Aleichem),* you spent the most time with her."

Redeeming Features

The Gurwicz family has played a vital role in developing Gateshead, England as Europe's primary Torah center. In 1947, Rabbi Leib Gurwicz (1906-1982) joined his brother-in-law, Rabbi Leib Lopian (1909-1979), to give the highest *shiur* in the Gateshead Yeshivah. The two *Reb Leibs* (lit. lions) served as *Roshei Yeshivah,* with Rabbi Gurwicz serving in that capacity for three decades. His eldest son, Rabbi Avraham Gurwicz, serves today as *Rosh Yeshivah.*

In the summer of 2000, I met one of Reb Leib's sons, Reb Yitzchak David, a consulting engineer who lives in Gateshead. As Reb Yitzchak David and I spoke about his family, Gateshead, and Torah learning in Europe, he asked me, "Do you know the story of my father's *shidduch?*"

When I had to admit that I didn't, he smiled broadly and said, "This one is for you." How right he was! The following fascinating story is a blend of history, heroics, pathos, prophecy and redemption.

In the early 1930's, the revered Rabbi Elyah Lopian (1872-1970), who was then head of Yeshivah Eitz Chaim in London, was looking for a suitable match for his daughter Liba. He went to the various yeshivos in Poland, then the Torah center of the world — and spoke with *Roshei Yeshivah* — seeking the finest young man for his daughter. (The *Rosh Yeshivah,* Rabbi Zelik Epstein told me he remembers seeing Rav Elyah at the time, speaking with various *Roshei Yeshivah.*)

When Rav Elyah came to Baranovitch, the *Gaon* Rabbi Elchonon Wasserman told him that the most exemplary young scholar at that time was "Leibel Malater," Leib Gurwicz, who was born in Malat, Lithuania, where his father Rabbi Moshe Aaron Kushelevsky was the rav. (R' Leib had to change his family name from Kushelevsky to Gurwicz because of Polish passport problems and the tense political situation between Russia and Poland. He took his mother's maiden name of Gurwicz, by which he was known for the rest of his life.)

Rav Elyah met R' Leib, and was impressed with his brilliance and refined character. The sage and the student spoke of the possibility of marriage to Liba. Soon afterwards the young couple became engaged and *t'nnaim* (agreement to marry) were written. In the *t'nnaim* it was agreed that Liba Lopian would leave London and go to Baranovitch, because R' Leib's potential was widely known and all who knew him felt that he was destined to be a great *Rosh Yeshivah*. At that time, the pinnacle of learning was in the yeshivos of Eastern Europe, so it was logical that he should live there.

R' Leib continued his intensive learning in Baranovitch. During the period of the engagement, however, Reb Elyah's rebbetzin, Sarah Leah, passed away at the young age of 49. There were thirteen Lopian children at home, and the *kallah,* Liba, was the oldest girl. She thought at great length about her family situation and conflicting obligations to her future husband versus those to her widowed father and siblings, and she wrote her *chassan* a letter. She explained that in good conscience she could not leave her father with the burden of caring for all the children at home. "If you want to break the *shidduch,* I fully understand and accept that. I know that your learning is an imperative and I therefore had agreed to come to Baranovitch. But the situation being what it is now, I cannot leave my father alone. I will bear no anger or resentment and I will respect your decision whatever it may be."

Understandably R' Leib was startled and troubled upon reading the letter. What was he to do? He was convinced that she was his destined wife but how could he leave the Torah atmosphere of Eastern Europe?

He decided he needed the guidance of the *tzaddik* of the generation. As soon as he could, he traveled to Radin to seek the counsel of the Chofetz Chaim. It was 1932 and the Chofetz Chaim was 94 years old. He was very frail and few were allowed in to talk with him.

When R' Leib arrived he was told that no one could disturb the great *tzaddik.* He pleaded with the attendant to allow him in, but the most the attendant would do was take the question from R' Leib and relay it to the Chofetz Chaim. R' Leib could see that the Chofetz Chaim was sitting in his *tallis* and *tefillin.*

Before the attendant reached him, the holy sage looked at R' Leib and said, "בָּרוּךְ פּוֹדֶה וּמַצִּיל, *Blessed is He Who redeems and rescues."* (The phrase is from the daily *Baruch She'amar* prayer.) R' Leib was perplexed; what did that have to do with his situation?

Was the Chofetz Chaim responding to his question? Or was he in the middle of *davening Shacharis* and reciting *Baruch She'amar*?

Reb Leib said to the attendant, "Please tell the rav that this is a matter of a *shidduch."* The attendant walked toward the Chofetz Chaim and again the *tzaddik* waved his hand toward R' Leib and repeated, "בָּרוּךְ פּוֹדֶה וּמַצִּיל, *Blessed is He Who redeems and rescues."*

R' Leib was exasperated. He felt that the opportunity to speak to the Chofetz Chaim was slipping away. He begged the attendant, "Please explain the problem to him. I have to decide about a certain *shidduch."*

The Chofetz Chaim looked again in the direction of R' Leib and repeated what he had said before, "בָּרוּךְ פּוֹדֶה וּמַצִּיל, *Blessed is He Who redeems and rescues."* R' Leib realized that the Chofetz Chaim was clearly giving him a message — but what was it? He would have to interpret the message himself and after much thought he decided that the Chofetz Chaim was telling him, "Go ahead. There will be blessing. Don't give up the *shidduch.*"

R' Leib and Liba were married in 1932 and they moved into Reb Elyah's home with all the children. Rebbetzin Gurwicz somehow managed to be a devoted wife, mother and daughter all at once, in a yeoman effort to maintain the stability and serenity in the home.

Years later in 1940, when World War II was raging and people were trying to escape Eastern Europe, they needed sponsors in foreign countries in order to get immigration visas. Because R' Leib lived in London, he was able to sponsor his sister, brothers-in-law and numerous friends, including Rabbi Nosson Ordman, father of Rabbi David Ordman of *Arachim,* who otherwise would have been trapped like the millions of others who perished in the Holocaust. They all came to England where they built new lives for themselves and their families.

It was only then that the Gurwicz family understood the saintly words of the Chofetz Chaim. He had repeated the words, בָּרוּךְ פּוֹדֶה וּמַצִּיל, *Blessed is He Who redeems and rescues.* Indeed there was blessing in the marriage. There was redemption thanks to the visas that R' Leib made possible. There was rescue to England where his relatives survived and rebuilt their lives.

The Mother of All Prayers

The prophet Yeshayahu assures us of a future time in Jerusalem when people will appeal to Hashem for their needs and all their pleas will be answered. He adds וְהָיוּ עֵינֶיךָ רֹאוֹת אֶת מוֹרֶיךָ, [At that time] (*your eyes shall behold your Teacher* (*Yeshayahu* 30:20), a reference to the wondrous situation when the Jewish people will be able to learn Torah directly from Hashem (see *Rashi, Bamidbar* 23:23).

This expression is used homiletically to exhort us to establish a close visual contact with our teachers and mentors. In *Eruvin* 13b, Rebbi (Rabbi Yehudah HaNasi) states that he was sharper than his colleagues because he was able to learn

Torah directly from the great Rabbi Meir, even though he was seated behind him and unable to see his face. Rebbi said, "If I had seen him from the front, I would be even sharper, for it is written: וְהָיוּ עֵינֶיךָ רֹאוֹת אֶת מוֹרֶיךָ, *And your eyes shall behold your teacher.*

Maintaining a close relationship with a Torah mentor is an imperative for our daily growth in Torah learning, *mitzvah* observance and *yiras Shamayim* (fear of Hashem). The Talmud teaches: גְּדוֹלָה שִׁמּוּשָׁהּ שֶׁל תּוֹרָה יוֹתֵר מִלִּמּוּדָהּ, *Serving Torah giants is greater than studying Torah [under them]* (*Berachos* 7b). Observing a Torah scholar's actions and demeanor provides us with the practical way to apply the Torah's teachings and commandments.

How fortunate are those who maintain a close connection to the *talmidei chachamim* of their generation.

R' Yehoshua Ozer Halperin of Manchester is one such person. For years he was a *talmid* and then an attendant of the Manchester *Rosh Yeshivah*, Rabbi Yehudah Zev Segal (1910-1993). In the yeshivah in Manchester, there were only eighty boys, and it was easy for him to be close to his *Rosh Yeshivah*. But when Yehoshua Ozer went to study in the Mirrer Yeshiva in Jerusalem, he was overwhelmed. There were over 800 *talmidim* — how could he, a foreigner, even think of getting close to one of the *Roshei Yeshivah*? There were so many others who probably wanted to do the same thing. One day he heard that the *Rosh Yeshivah*, Rabbi Chaim Shmulevitz (1902-1978), had been told by his doctors that he had to take daily walks for his health. Yehoshua Ozer immediately went into the *Rosh Yeshivah's* apartment and offered to accompany Rav Chaim on his required daily stroll.

"The *Rosh Yeshivah* will take his walks at 5:30 in the morning," explained the rebbetzin. "He doesn't want a *bachur* to have to get up so early just for him."

"I am up then anyway," Yehoshua Ozer said. "I am an early riser and I have a *chavrusa* (study partner) at that time. We can rearrange our learning schedule."

"But the *Rosh Yeshivah* can't walk near the yeshivah," the rebbetzin said. "The streets here in Beis Yisrael are too hilly and it would be too strenuous for the *Rosh Yeshivah*."

"That too is no problem," said Yehoshua Ozer, thinking fast. "My uncle in Bayit Vegan has an old car that he is not using. He will give it to me so I can drive the *Rosh Yeshivah* to any area where he wishes to walk."

Within the next week the rebbetzin and Yehoshua Ozer scouted various parks in Jerusalem checking the available walking paths, the hills, the surroundings, and the benches where the *Rosh Yeshivah* could rest. They finally settled on *Gan Haaztmaut* (Independence Park) behind the Plaza Hotel. Each morning, Yehoshua Ozer would get up at 5 o'clock and prepare to meet the *Rosh Yeshivah* for the drive to the place where they would walk for half an hour. On those walks the young *talmid* from England established a strong bond with the venerable *Rosh Yeshivah*. Yehoshua Ozer soon recognized the brilliance, compassion and sensitivity of Reb Chaim, and became part of the Shmulevitz family, accompanying the *Rosh Yeshivah* on many public and private occasions.

One day, Reb Chaim asked Yehoshua Ozer if he could take him to *Kever Rachel* (Rachel's tomb) in Beis Lechem. Yehoshua Ozer said he would be honored to do so. What transpired on that trip has left an impression on him until this very day.

On the way out of Jerusalem on the highway to Beis Lechem, Rav Chaim began thinking of all the people he wanted to pray for: the sick, the grieving, the childless and the financially troubled. He began crying. At first it was a soft cry but soon his body heaved with uncontrollable sobbing.

As he entered the hallway of *Kever Rachel* he tried to muffle his cry. When he approached the tomb itself he called out in bitter wailing, *"Mamme! Chaim'keh is duh."* ("Mother, Chaim'keh is here.")

As his eyes welled with tears he recited numerous chapters of *Tehillim* and then began mentioning the many names of people he had in mind. His eyes were tightly shut as he mentally visualized the various people he had prayed for and their misfortunes. Then he called out in Yiddish, *"Der Ribono Shel Olam hut dir gezught Mamme, as du zultzt nit vainin, uhber ich, Chaim'keh, zug, 'Vain, Mamme vain!'"* ("Hashem said to you, Mother, 'Don't cry,' but I, Chaim'keh, say to you, 'Cry, Mother, cry!'")

[This was a reference to the verse in *Yirmiyahu* 31:15 where Hashem says to Rachel, מִנְעִי קוֹלֵךְ מִבֶּכִי וְעֵינַיִךְ מִדִּמְעָה כִּי יֵשׁ שָׂכָר לִפְעֻלָּתֵךְ נְאֻם ה׳ וְשָׁבוּ מֵאֶרֶץ אוֹיֵב, *Restrain your voice from weeping and your eyes from tears; for there is reward for your accomplishment — the word of Hashem — and they will return from the enemy's land.]*

On the way back to Jerusalem, someone asked Reb Chaim, "If Hashem told Rachel not to cry, how can the *Rosh Yeshivah* implore Rachel to cry?"

Rav Chaim's answer was classic.

"A father can tell a daughter not to cry, but a son can appeal to his mother that she should cry!"

No Chariots in Oak Park

Chesky Shoenig of Oak Park, Michigan, was a sweet, beloved 13-year-old boy adored by his parents, admired by his friends and revered by his teachers in Yeshiva Bais Yehudah. In the winter of 1996, he came down with a lingering illness. As the doctors tried to contain his malady, they came to the reluctant conclusion that he was more seriously ill than they originally thought.

One afternoon, in January 1997, they arrived at their grim diagnosis — Chesky had leukemia. He had had it as a 19-month-old infant, and it had been in remission for more than ten years. Its reappearance was devastating. The news came as a crushing blow to the close-knit Jewish community of Detroit. *Tehillim* was recited for Chesky in every *shul* and school. The Shoenigs went to all lengths to research the disease and tried every treatment available, but Chesky's condition worsened. His parents were beside themselves with grief and agony.

One morning, in *shul*, a man approached Chesky's father, and said, "Don't worry, Elya, your son will be okay. He'll be cured."

"And what's makes you so sure?" asked Mr. Shoenig, wondering why the man was so confident.

"It's a *pasuk* we say every day in *davening,*" the man replied. אֵלֶּה בָרֶכֶב וְאֵלֶּה בַסּוּסִים וַאֲנַחְנוּ בְּשֵׁם ד׳ אֱלֹקֵינוּ נַזְכִּיר, *Some with chariots and some with horses, but we — in the Name of Hashem, our G-d, we call out* (*Tehillim* 20:8).

"We Jews live by a different set of rules," the man said. "Perhaps it would be hopeless for a child from the other nations, but not your Chesky. As bleak as things seem now, Hashem cares for His children. Chesky will make it."

For the rest of the day, Mr. Shoenig thought about that verse. By nightfall he had become convinced that the man was right. Indeed that was the intent of David *HaMelech* when he wrote those words. Jews did have different standards and values than the nations of the world. Ours was a spiritual life, an exalted way of living prescribed by Hashem and revealed to us in the Torah and through the words of *Chazal.* Yes, now Elya Shoenig knew — his cherished Chesky would have a complete recovery.

Thus, a few months later, when Chesky had his bone marrow transplant done at the Harper Hospital in Detroit, it came as no surprise to Mr. Shoenig that his son was doing better than anyone else on the floor. He repeated that *pasuk* numerous times a day, convincing himself that this was only a temporary nightmare. Chesky would surely improve and eventually grow to adulthood like all his friends in Oak Park.

Sadly, it was not to be. When Chesky returned from the hospital, new complications developed. Doctors, frustrated parents and friends could only plead with their *Tehillims* that Hashem spare this precious child. Then, on a Friday afternoon in November 1997, little Chesky Shoenig returned his soul to heaven.

Thousands attended his funeral. The community wept as one. His life seemed too short. And the eulogies, searing as they were, could not assuage the pain of Chesky's nearest and dearest.

A few days after the *shivah* (the seven-day period of mourning), Elya Shoenig remembered that verse in *Tehillim* and it bothered him. Hadn't the *pasuk* assured him that his son would be well? What happened to the encouragement it had given him? Had he missed something?

For months he was haunted by the now enigmatic *pasuk*. At times he was angry that his hopes had been built up, but regardless of what had happened, he had to understand the verse. What had he misunderstood?

And then one day, while he was reciting the verse during *Shacharis*, an idea struck him. David *HaMelech* was not describing battles *during* the war, but rather an appraisal *after* the war.

When a nation loses an armed conflict, it second-guesses itself as it re-evaluates its strategies and tactics. "If only we had done this ... If only we had implemented different maneuvers ... If only ... if only ... we would have been successful." That is the meaning of אֵלֶּה בָרֶכֶב וְאֵלֶּה בַסּוּסִים, *Some with chariots and some with horses ...*

But Jews don't look back. They understand that if a battle was lost, it was because Hashem intended it to be so, וַאֲנַחְנוּ בְּשֵׁם ד׳ אֱלֹקֵינוּ נַזְכִּיר, *but we — in the Name of Hashem, our G-d, we call out.*

Now, thought Mr. Shoenig, the next verse in the chapter fits perfectly. הֵמָּה כָּרְעוּ וְנָפָלוּ, *They slumped and fell* — because of their frustration and false perception that things could have been different, וַאֲנַחְנוּ קַמְנוּ וַנִּתְעוֹדָד, *but we arose and were invigorated* (*Tehillim* 20:9), because we Jews understand that this is the way it was meant to be, and with our faith in Hashem's mercy and righteousness, we have the strength to continue with life.

It is this insight that carries the Shoenig family to this day — an extraordinary concept that should help countless others in time of grief and tragedy.

Part B:
Dedication and Devotion

Soaring Greatness

The *Midrash* (*Vayikra Rabbah* 11:8) teaches: נִמְשְׁלוּ יִשְׂרָאֵל לְעוֹף. מַה הָעוֹף הַזֶּה אֵינוֹ פּוֹרֵחַ בְּלֹא כְּנָפַיִם כַּךְ יִשְׂרָאֵל אֵין יְכוֹלִים לַעֲשׂוֹת דָּבָר חוּץ מִזְקֵנֵיהֶם, *The Jewish nation is compared to a bird. Just as a bird cannot fly without wings, so too the Jewish people are immobilized and incapable of action without the counsel of their elders.*

The message of the *Midrash* seems clear: We are dependent on our זְקֵנִים, (lit. elders) for their guidance and direction. Their life experience and Torah wisdom are precious and priceless. Indeed, *Chazal* teach that the word זָקֵן is an acronym for זֶה שֶׁקָּנָה חָכְמָה, *he who has acquired wisdom* (*Kiddushin* 32b, see *Rashi*).

In a moving eulogy for Rav Elazar Menachem Man Shach (1898-2001), delivered at an Agudath Israel convention, Rabbi Mattisyahu Salomon, the *Mashgiach* of Beth Medrash Govoha in Lakewood, New Jersey, provided an illuminating insight into the words of this teaching. "It doesn't say that a bird cannot live without wings," the *Mashgiach* said. "Surely a bird can walk and putter around even if it has no wings. Without wings, however, a bird cannot soar, it cannot reach great heights. The *Midrash* is telling us that Jews need the wisdom and the guidance of their elders so they can soar and reach lofty levels."

In this touching episode recounted by R' Shaya Goldberg of Brooklyn, we see the respect and thoughtfulness two elderly Torah sages had for each other. By emulating their example of humility and dignity we can soar to live elevated lives.

Shaya studied in Yeshivas Ner Yisroel in Baltimore, Maryland, for eleven years, and during that time established a close relationship with the *Rosh Yeshivah*, Rabbi Yaakov Yitzchak Ruderman (1900-1987). The *Rosh Yeshivah* had taken a personal interest in Shaya almost immediately after his arrival to Ner Yisroel.

In 1970, after he became engaged, Shaya asked Rav Ruderman if he would be able to come to New York for the wedding and be the *mesader kiddushin* (performer of the marriage ceremony). The *Rosh Yeshivah* apologized and explained that unfortunately he would not be able to attend. He had made a commitment to be in another city that night. Shaya was crestfallen, but he understood that his elderly *Rosh Yeshivah* had many other responsibilities.

Shaya had been raised on the Lower East Side of Manhattan and lived with his family on FDR Drive, in the same apartment building as Rabbi Moshe Feinstein (1895-1986). Shaya and his father, Avraham Shlomo (Sammy), often davened with Reb Moshe and were friendly with the Feinstein family. When Mr. Goldberg heard that Rabbi Ruderman could not attend his son's wedding, he felt that the right thing was to have Reb Moshe be the *mesader kiddushin.*

Mr. Goldberg revered Reb Moshe and was thrilled at the possibility of having the great Torah sage perform his son's wedding. He thus approached Reb Moshe and explained, "Yeshivah *bachurim* today like to ask their *Roshei Yeshivah* to be *mesader kiddushin,* so my son asked Rav Ruderman. Rabbi Ruderman can't come and you were the one I wanted all along. We would be honored if you could come."

Smiling warmly, Reb Moshe shook Mr. Goldberg's hand and said, "I understand and I thank you for the honor. I will be happy to come with the rebbetzin."

A few days before the wedding, Rabbi Ruderman told Shaya that his schedule had changed and he was able to attend the wedding. Shaya was overjoyed.

When Shaya came home for Shabbos and told his father the great news, Mr. Goldberg's mouth fell open. "I've already asked Reb Moshe to be *mesader kiddushin.* I can't go now and tell him that he is not needed."

"Well, I surely can't go to Reb Moshe," replied Shaya. "First of all, I didn't ask him and secondly I asked my *Rosh Yeshivah* weeks ago."

"Then let's go to Reb Moshe together," Mr. Goldberg said.

As they walked to Reb Moshe's apartment, they were apprehensive about their predicament. What could they possibly say to Reb Moshe, the *gadol hador* (the Torah giant of the generation), that would not be uncomfortable for all of them? They knocked on the door softly.

Reb Moshe himself appeared at the door. He took one look at them, and before the Goldbergs said a word, he smiled and said, "Do you think I'm coming to the wedding to get an honor? I'm coming because we are friends and neighbors for years. I'm happy to attend as a guest."

The Goldbergs were stunned! How could he have figured out the situation so quickly and with one sentence put them at ease? They hadn't uttered a word, but with his sagacious intuition Reb Moshe saw the whole picture. He wished the Goldbergs well and changed the subject.

At the *kabbalas panim* (reception before the *chupah*), Rabbi Ruderman sat next to the *chassan*. When Reb Moshe arrived, he, too, was ushered to the head table. Rabbi Ruderman said to him, "Obviously you will be the *mesader kiddushin*."

A discussion ensued between the two elderly sages. "You are the *bachur's Rosh Yeshivah*. It is proper that you should be the *mesader kiddushin*," insisted Reb Moshe.

"But you are the *mara d'asra* (the leader of the community), so you should be the *mesader kiddushin*," Rabbi Ruderman countered.

Rabbi Ruderman and Reb Moshe each offered reasons why the other should be given the highest honor at the wedding. Finally Rav Ruderman exclaimed with exuberance the answer he was sure would settle the matter, "But you are older, so it's proper that you should be the *mesader kiddushin*!"

"You are right," said Reb Moshe with joyous finality, "I am older, so you have to listen to me, and I insist that you be the *mesader kiddushin*."

Rabbi Ruderman smiled at Reb Moshe's retort. Now he had no choice.

When it came to filling out the *kesubah* (the marriage contract) which is usually done by the *mesader kiddushin*, Rabbi Ruderman asked Reb Moshe to do it. Before Reb Moshe could protest, Rav Ruderman said, "I am the *mesader kiddushin* and this is how I am *mesader* (lit. arranging) the *kiddushin*."

Indeed, Rabbi Ruderman performed the wedding as *mesader kiddushin* and Reb Moshe was given the honor of reading the *kesubah* he had written. And those who were aware of how things finally fell into place still talk about it to this day with awe at the humility and sensitivity of the two great men.

Good Neighbor Policy

In 1997 Rabbi Mattisyahu Salomon assumed the prestigious position of *Mashgiach* (spiritual dean) at Beth Medrash Govoha in Lakewood, New Jersey. Ever since Rav Mattisyahu arrived from the renowned Torah community of Gateshead, England, he has become a beloved and cherished figure throughout Torah circles in America. His *shmuessen* in Lakewood, his lectures at conventions and seminars, and his heartfelt advice to countless people who seek his counsel have made him one of the most revered Torah educators in our generation. May Hashem give him the strength and health to continue.

This story reveals his remarkable sensitivity. His actions are worthy of emulation.

Shortly after the Salomons came to Lakewood, they moved into a home on Sixth Street, a block from the yeshivah. Their neighbors were the Epsteins, with whom they soon developed a strong mutual friendship. The families had children the same age and a *simchah* for one was a *simchah* for the other. In autumn of 1999 one of the Salomon girls became engaged. There was great joy in the Salomon home and delight and excitement in the Epstein home as the girls looked forward to dancing at their close friend's wedding.

Tragically this was not to be. A few weeks later, just days before *Rosh Hashanah,* the Salomon's beloved neighbor, Rabbi Shimon Epstein, suddenly passed away. Rabbi Epstein was a *talmid chacham*, a *mohel* and *shochet,* and was known in Lakewood for the inordinate amount of *chessed* and charity that he performed, often done in secretive, sensitive ways. Having lived in Lakewood for more than thirty-five years, his funeral was attended by thousands, including many who had long ago moved to other communities.

The Epstein family was plunged into mourning, and as mourners the children would not be permitted to attend festive gatherings such as weddings for the next twelve months. Hence attending the Salomon wedding was out of the question. This only added anguish to their unexpected suffering.

During the following weeks the Salomons made a conscious effort not to talk about the wedding plans within earshot of the Epsteins, but the wedding day moved inexorably forward. It would be a day of great celebration in Lakewood befitting a *simchah* in the *Mashgiach's* family.

On the day of the wedding the Epstein daughters went to work and came home as they usually did, around 6 o'clock. When they arrived there was a note on the table, "To our dear friends the Epsteins: Please do not prepare dinner this evening. Your dinner will be served to all of you shortly. We will miss you at the wedding but we wanted you to share in our *simchah* and so the caterers will be at your home with the wedding dinner. May we share future *simchas*. The Salomons."

Within an hour a truck came from the wedding hall in Lakewood with the full course meal, including dessert, for every member of the Epstein family.

And if that was not enough, as the Epsteins were enjoying this unexpected meal someone came and brought them pictures that had just been taken at the wedding. Rav Mattisyahu had arranged that someone take pictures of the *badekken* and *chupah,* run with the finished film to a local photography store that developed pictures within an hour and then deliver the processed pictures to the

Epsteins. Thus, as they were enjoying the wedding meal they could enjoy wedding photos!

> In the last of the *Sheva Berachos* we thank Hashem for creating the traits of אַהֲבָה אַחֲוָה שָׁלוֹם וְרֵעוּת, *love, brotherhood, peace and companionship.* The events of the evening totally exemplified those words.

Blackboard Whitewash

In the fall of 1999, the *Jewish Image Magazine* of Chicago asked eminent Jewish personalities to recall a memorable incident or comment from one of their *rebbeim* that left a lasting impression. Among those interviewed were Rabbi Yisroel Reisman, rav of the Agudas Yisroel of Madison in Brooklyn, Rabbi Nosson Scherman, general editor of Artscroll/Mesorah Publications and author of the commentary on the *Artscroll Siddur* and *Stone Edition Chumash,* Rabbi Dr. Aaron Twerski of the Brooklyn Law School, and Rabbi Nisson Wolpin, editor of the *Jewish Observer*.

Rabbi Wolpin and Rabbi Reisman recounted impressions from Rabbi Avraham Pam (1913-2001) of Yeshiva Torah Vodaath. Rabbi Wolpin recalled a time in the 1950's when Rabbi Pam was his *rebbi.* The rabbi started teaching a long *Tosafos* right before dismissal. One of the students complained that there would be no time to finish the *Tosafos,* so why bother starting it?

With his inimitable soft demeanor, Rabbi Pam referred to a comment inserted in the middle of *Rashi's* commentary on *Bava Basra* 29a: "*Rashi's* commentary ends at this point. The commentary for the remainder of the tractate is that of [his grandson] R' Shmuel ben Meir [commonly known as the *Rashbam*]." There is an additional note that says, "This is when *Rashi* died."

"*Rashi,* in his holiness, surely had a premonition of when he would die," said Rabbi Pam. "One would expect that *Rashi* would spend his last day on this earth saying good-bye to his relatives and friends. Why would he spend his last moments writing a commentary that he knew he couldn't finish? The answer is that *Rashi* understood that there was no better way to spend his last moments of life. He thereby taught us that in teaching, writing and learning, it isn't a question of finishing. One must start and continue for as long as he can."

Rav Pam smiled and then said, "It is for this reason that we now begin the long *Tosafos* even though we will run out of time before we finish it."

Rabbi Reisman recalled that Rabbi Pam would often say, "There are teachers who teach subjects and teachers who teach students. While those who teach subjects may indeed impart a great deal of information, those who teach students make a great impact on their lives."

Rabbi Dr. Aaron Twerski recalled a comment his *rebbi,* Rabbi Nachum Sacks, made when he taught the ninth grade in Skokie's Bais Medrash L'Torah. When a *talmid* asked a question, Rabbi Sacks would say enthusiastically, "You're 100 percent right, but I'll show you where you're wrong!" (Dr. Twerski said that he uses this line today in his law classes.) It acknowledged the student's logic and insight, yet allowed the *rebbi* to show him where he had gone wrong.

However, it was the incident that Rabbi Nosson Scherman recalled that left me spellbound. I used the incident in a lecture to principals and teachers at a Torah Umesorah convention, for it is a glowing example of the Talmudic credo, יְהִי כְבוֹד תַּלְמִידְךָ חָבִיב עָלֶיךָ כְּשֶׁלָּךְ, *Let the honor of your student be as dear to you as your own* (*Avos* 4:15, see also *Rashi, Shemos* 17:9).

An extraordinarily sensitive *mechanech,* Rabbi Hirsch Kaplan, taught the sixth grade of Yeshiva Torah Vodaath in the Williamsburg section of Brooklyn. If children misbehaved in class he would often put their names on the blackboard as an incentive for the boys to improve their behavior. When a boy behaved better, his name was erased.

One day Rabbi Kaplan had a few names on the "Bad List" when the beloved principal of the school, Rabbi Dr. David Stern, walked into the room unexpectedly. As Dr. Stern spoke to the class, Rabbi Kaplan slowly backed up until he was flush against the blackboard.

As the principal spoke, Rabbi Kaplan shuffled his back from right to left against the chalk-written names on the board. When the principal finished his talk and turned to leave the room, Rabbi Kaplan escorted him to the door. It was only then that all the students clearly saw the back of Rabbi Kaplan's black *kapota* (long jacket), which was completely white from the chalk of the "bad names" he had erased, so that Dr. Stern would not see them.

That act displayed selfless love, as it preserved the dignity of 10- and 11-year-old children. It remains to this day one of the most inspiring sights that Rabbi Nosson Scherman has ever seen.

Final Farewell

When Rabbi Aryeh Zev Ginzberg, Rav of the Chofetz Chaim Torah Center in Cedarhurst, New York, studied in Israel he established a close relationship with numerous Torah sages, particularly with the *gadol hador,* the *Rosh Yeshivah* of the Ponevezher Yeshivah in Bnei Brak, Rav Elazar Menachem Man Shach (1898-2001). Rabbi Ginzberg often came to Rabbi Shach's home to consult with him, and in the course of these visits he became friendly with the *Rosh Yeshivah's* attendants and family members.

One afternoon in December, 1976, Rabbi Ginzberg came to Rabbi Shach's home, but was told that he would not be able to see the great sage. "Not even you can get in today," Rabbi Shach's grandson said softly but firmly.

Rabbi Ginzberg was surprised. "Is everything all right? Is the *Rosh Yeshivah* feeling well?"

"He is recuperating from yesterday," came the reply. "Yesterday was a very hard day for the *zaide* (grandfather) and today he must rest."

The grandson then told the following story.

Yesterday had been cold and nasty, as windswept rain battered Bnei Brak. In the middle of the storm Rav Shach called his grandson and said, "Please arrange a car for me. I have to travel to a town near Haifa."

The grandson protested. "But *zaide*," he said, "the weather is terrible and you could get sick going out on a day like this."

"If you don't arrange a car for me," said Rav Shach, "I'll go myself and take a bus. I must go to a *levayah* (funeral) near Haifa."

"Who died?" the grandson asked. He hadn't heard of any prominent *Rosh Yeshivah* or rabbi whose death would warrant Rav Shach's making such an arduous two-hour trip.

"A certain woman passed away and I must go to her *levayah*," Rav Shach said. "Please arrange the car."

The grandson recognized how serious his grandfather was, and arranged a car and driver immediately. When he inquired about the woman's identity, Rav Shach refused to give any information. The grandson knew better than to press the issue.

The trip to the cemetery in the north took over two hours. The grandson was positive that they would find a large crowd in attendance to pay final respects to this important woman, whoever she was. Surely if Rav Shach himself at his advanced age insisted on making this trip, the woman deserved great honor. Yet to his amazement there was barely a *minyan* there. True the weather was bad, the rain had not let up and the temperature was close to freezing but still — so few people! Why had his grandfather insisted on attending this funeral?

Upon inquiry the grandson found out that the woman had no children, few relatives and that most of her friends had already passed on. Some distant relatives and a few neighbors had gathered to pay final respects.

The funeral was short, sad and simple.

When it was over, Rav Shach recited the Mourner's *Kaddish.* The pelting rain continued as the wind howled in the vast lonely expanse of the cemetery. The driver who brought them was waiting nearby, and the grandson ushered Rav Shach to the waiting car.

Suddenly Rav Shach stopped walking. He let go of his grandson's hand and closed his eyes. His shoulders hunched in the cold as the rain dripped from his hat and coat. The grandson waited a few moments and then tried to get his grandfather to go to the car. Rav Shach shook his head indicating that he wasn't ready to leave.

He stood in the rain, shivering, immersed in his thoughts — and then made his way to the car.

Throughout the long trip back Rav Shach hardly spoke, and his grandson, realizing that the *Rosh Yeshivah* did not want to speak, remained silent. When they finally got home, the grandson could not contain his curiosity. "*Zaide*," he said, "who was that woman and why did you feel that you had to go her *levayah*?"

Rav Shach told his grandson a story that few people, if any, had ever heard from him before.

When he was merely 12 years old, it was announced that a yeshivah for *illuyim* (brilliant boys) was opening. The *Rosh Yeshivah* was extremely selective and every applicant was carefully scrutinized and tested. Each *bachur* was informed that if he could not rent a room, he would have to make do with the meager living conditions in the yeshivah. This meant that the older boys would have the "luxury" of being able to sleep on the benches, while the others would have to sleep on the floor. Food was sparse, but edible.

Most of the successful applicants were already in their teens. Rav Shach, at 12, was one of the youngest boys accepted, but despite his age he was allowed to sleep on a bench. [Undoubtedly it was because he was recognized for his brilliance and piety.]

During the spring, summer and fall, the situation was tolerable, but in the freezing winter, the days were hardly tolerable and the nights were unbearable. There was no place in the building where the boys could keep warm, and the constant pangs of hunger accentuated the poor living conditions. The young boy was exhausted from lack of sleep and it affected his learning.

One Wednesday, he received a letter from his uncle. "Come join me in my business." The uncle, his mother's brother, was a prosperous blacksmith. He had no children and was getting on in years. He assured his young nephew that he would teach him the trade and that eventually the business would be his. "Why stay where you are in poverty and hunger?" the uncle wrote. "If you come join me you will be set for life."

For more than a day, the young *talmid* mulled over the letter. By Thursday night he decided that his uncle was right. Things were too difficult in the yeshivah; he could join his uncle's business and still make time for learning. He decided he would stay in yeshivah for Shabbos and leave right after *Havdalah.*

Friday morning a woman came into the *beis midrash* and spoke to the *Rosh Yeshivah*. She explained that she had just gotten up from sitting *shivah* for her husband. "My husband was a salesman," she told the *Rosh Yeshivah,* "and he traveled far and wide to buy and sell his wares. Last week when he was traveling, the horse and carriage he was in turned over and he was killed. We live far away from here but I came here to sit *shivah* with his family. He sold blankets and I have a few of them with me. I have no interest in bringing them back to my home. I won't be able to sell them and I have no need for them. Take them for your *talmidim*."

She brought in a few heavy Russian blankets filled with goose down, known as *perenehs* and gave them to the *Rosh Yeshivah*. The *Rosh Yeshivah* gave one of them to Rav Shach. "That Friday night I was warmer than I had been all winter," said Rav Shach, "and when I woke up in the morning I decided that with the heavy blanket I could survive the cold winter, so I stayed in the yeshivah. I had been very close to abandoning learning, but because that woman brought the blankets when she did, I stayed where I was. From then on there was never a question of how I would direct my life.

"The woman had a sad life. She went back to her hometown and unfortunately never remarried. Later she moved to *Eretz Yisrael* and I heard that she lived near Haifa. When I found out that she passed away, I felt that I had to be at the *levayah*."

The grandson had never heard this story before and it answered every question but one. "But *zaide,* why after the *levayah* did you not go into the car right away? Why were you standing out there in the cold and rain?"

Rav Shach's answer was classic and instructive. "It has been so many years since that incident with the blankets," he said. "Over the years one tends to forget the way things were and so I wanted to stay out in the cold to remind myself how freezing I was in those days, so that I could have the proper *hakaras hatov* (gratitude) to the woman for all that she did."

The first words Jews say every morning upon awakening are מוֹדֶה אֲנִי לְפָנֶיךָ, *I gratefully thank You,* an expression of our thanks to Hashem for letting us live to see a new day. The last words David *HaMelech* wrote in *Tehillim (150:6)* are: כֹּל הַנְּשָׁמָה תְּהַלֵּל יָ-הּ, *Let every neshamah* (soul) *praise Hashem.* The *Midrash* expounds on the similarity between the words *neshamah,* soul, and *neshimah,* breath. Thus, the verse can be understood as, *For every breath of life that man breathes he must praise his Creator* (*Bereishis Rabbah* 14:9). *Hakaras hatov,* gratitude and appreciation, are basic Jewish concepts (see *Sforno, Bereishis* 29:35). In his quiet and dignified manner, Rav Shach showed the intensity and sincerity that should accompany such feelings.

One can only imagine the Heavenly reward awaiting the woman who, in a sense, preserved this Torah giant and leader for *Klal Yisrael* — a man who was a paragon of *hasmadah* (diligence in Torah study), holiness and piety that spanned a full century. As Rabbi Aryeh Zev Ginzberg says, "It wasn't merely a blanket to warm a young *talmid* the woman donated, it was a *mantel* (cover) to shelter a *Sefer Torah.*"

May Eye Bless You

Nowadays, when a *gadol hador* (leading Torah sage of a generation) passes away, a plethora of articles are immediately written about his life's history and accomplishments. An erupting volcano of stories pours forth in eulogies, magazines, and newspaper columns. Within weeks of his passing, books in Hebrew and English are being written. Hence it is rare to find a new story involving a *gadol* about whom so much has already been written.

Yet at a recent wedding in Montreal, Reb Yankel Abramczyk told me a touching new story concerning a revered *gadol* about whom much is known. The splendor of the story was enhanced by a wondrous discovery by Reb Yankel himself.

I thank Rabbi Moshe Yaakov Kanner of Toronto and my son-in-law, Rabbi Ephraim Perlstein of Far Rockaway, for additional details and insights on this episode.

One afternoon, Rabbi Alexander Dinkel, a *maggid shiur* (Talmudic lecturer) in Yeshiva Kol Torah in Bayit Vegan, Israel, told the *Rosh Yeshivah,* the great sage, Rabbi Shlomo Zalman Auerbach (1910-1995), that he would have to leave a bit earlier than usual. He explained that he had to check out an apartment one more time, as he and his family were considering moving there.

"Can I come along with you?" asked Reb Shlomo Zalman.

Rabbi Dinkel was surprised. Why would a man whose every moment was precious, whose every word of Torah study was sacred, want to be involved in the mundane chore of checking the suitability of an apartment for a young couple and their family?

"I hate to bother the *Rosh Yeshivah,*" Rabbi Dinkel stammered. "I can tend to the matter myself."

"It's fine," replied Reb Shlomo Zalman. "Just let me know when you are ready to go and we'll go together."

A little later Rabbi Dinkel called a taxi and he and the great sage went directly to the apartment. Reb Shlomo Zalman seemed inquisitive as he walked around. "Is this where the dining area will be? Is this where the children will play?" He inquired about each room and wanted to know for what it would be used.

Rabbi Dinkel was astounded that Reb Shlomo Zalman was paying such attention to detail. Finally he asked, "Why did the *Rosh Yeshivah* insist on coming here with me?"

The answer was as radiant as Reb Shlomo Zalman's smile.

"I wanted to place [the blessing of] an *ayin tovah* (benevolent eye) on your home."

Obviously Reb Shlomo Zalman's intent was affectionate — but what exactly is an *ayin tovah?*

A month after Reb Yankel Abramczyk heard this story, he was studying the Torah portion of that particular week, *Va'eschanan.* In it Moshe *Rabbeinu* describes his pleading to Hashem that he be allowed to enter the Land of Israel. Moshe begged Hashem: אֶעְבְּרָה נָּא וְאֶרְאֶה אֶת הָאָרֶץ הַטּוֹבָה אֲשֶׁר בְּעֵבֶר הַיַּרְדֵּן, *Let me now cross and see the good land that is on the other side of the Jordan (Devarim* 3:25). *Sforno* comments that Moshe's intent was וְאֶרְאֶה, *[By] my gazing upon the land,* הָאָרֶץ הַטּוֹבָה, *there would be everlasting benefit for Israel.*

According to *Sforno's* interpretation, the expression וְאֶרְאֶה, *and see,* is not simply a request to see in the usual sense, but to effectuate a major influence upon Israel's permanent residence and success in *Eretz Yisrael.*

Apparently one can effectuate goodness for others by viewing their possessions with kind and good-hearted eyes. Undoubtedly this was Reb Shlomo Zalman's intent.

Interestingly, *Ramban (Bamidbar* 1:45*)* writes that when the census of Jews was taken in the wilderness, every Jew was to appear before Moshe *Rabbeinu* and Aaron — כִּי יָשִׂימוּ עֲלֵיהֶם עֵינָם לְטוֹבָה, *so that they [Moshe and Aaron] will set their eyes upon them for good* (see also *Yirmiyahu* 24:6*)*. Here, too, eyeing someone favorably brought about blessing.

In this light, the *Yismach Yisrael,* Rabbi Yisrael Yitzchak Danziger of Aleksander (1853-1910), offered a novel interpretation of a Talmudic teaching in *Kesubos* 17a. Hillel teaches that if someone made a bad purchase, יְשַׁבְּחֶנּוּ בְּעֵינָיו, *one should still praise it in the purchaser's eyes.* (The principle of harmony and peaceful relations overrides the problem of speaking a falsehood.)

Based on the aforementioned *Sforno* and *Ramban,* the *Yismach Yisrael* translates the words יְשַׁבְּחֶנּוּ בְּעֵינָיו as, *you shall enhance it with your [own] eyes!* By viewing it favorably, you will bring blessing to the item, so that it becomes worthwhile and advantageous to its owner.

Too often people afflict others with an *ayin raah* (detrimental eye). Their jealousy and selfishness do not allow them to be glad for another's success. Hence they view another person's possessions or accomplishments with envy and an unspoken prayer for that person's failure (see *Avos* 5:22).

Reb Shlomo Zalman's attitude was the antithesis of *ayin hara* — he possessed the trait of Avraham *Avinu* — *ayin tovah* (see *Avos* ibid.) and that's why he was so beloved.

What a Difference a Date Makes

Yosi Heber of Detroit is a corporate executive who is also a unique *talmid chacham.* To help those who learn *Daf Yomi,* Yosi produced a series of 122 cassettes, which contain a summary of every *mesechta* in *Shas.* Each tape contains a synopsis of twenty *blatt,* enabling the listener to quickly review what he has learned. This enables people to review their learning as they proceed through the seven-and-a-half year *Daf Yomi* cycle. To teach *Shas* one must know *Shas* — quite an achievement for a young man.

One of the major problems facing many young Jewish men and women today is the problem of *shidduchim,* i.e. finding the appropriate marriage partner. These people are capable, bright and articulate, but they unfortunately have not yet met the partner with whom to build their future. Yosi was in that category for many years until, finally, while working in England in 1994, he became engaged.

Yosi called one of his friends in London and said excitedly, "I'm a *chassan!*"

"*Mazel tov* — when are you getting married?"

"August 22nd," said Yosi.

"August 22nd?" the man asked derisively. "Who cares about August? What's the Hebrew date?"

Yosi was taken aback. Yes, *yamim tovim,* bar mitzvah days, and *yahrzeits* are reckoned by the Hebrew date, but in the common vernacular just about everyone uses the English date. And besides, is that the way to talk to a new *chassan*? The gentleman had taken a bit of "the wind out of Yosi's sails." Meekly he gave his "friend" the Hebrew date, the fifteenth of *Elul,* and the conversation ended shortly afterwards.

Yosi could not wait to share the good news with his beloved *rebbi* and *Rosh Yeshivah,* Rabbi Avraham Pam (1913-2001) in New York. Considering the time difference between England and America, he waited until it was appropriate to make the call. When he heard the soft silken voice of Rav Pam, he exclaimed, "*Rebbi,* this is Yosi Heber. I wanted to share good news. I just became a *chassan!*

"Mazel tov, mazel tov," said Rav Pam. "I am so happy to hear this *besurah tovah* (good news). When are you getting married?"

Yosi hesitated for a moment and then said, "August 22nd."

"That's wonderful," exclaimed Rav Pam. "Do you know something? That's my anniversary. Yosi, now every year we'll be able to share our anniversaries together. That's so nice."

Yosi was amazed at the coincidence, touched that Rav Pam would disclose something so personal, and thrilled to share a meaningful day with his *rebbi.* Every year, without fail, he made sure to send Rav Pam and his rebbetzin an anniversary card with a nice note and an updated picture of his growing family. Eventually Yosi and his family moved back to the United States where he renewed his personal connection with his revered *rebbi.*

In the summer of 2001, Rav Pam, who had been ailing for more than a year, was so seriously ill that doctors feared for his life. Throughout the Torah world people were reciting *Tehillim* for the cherished, gentle man who had served *Klal Yisrael* for sixty years as a *rebbi, Rosh Yeshivah* and member of the *Moetzes Gedolei HaTorah.* Sadly the situation became increasingly worse.

As Yosi kept hearing of Rav Pam's declining health, he wondered if his *rebbi* would survive till the anniversary date of August 22. He sent his anniversary card a few days early, on August 10, even though he wondered if Rav Pam or the rebbetzin would even have the patience to read it.

Rav Pam passed away on August 17th. Tragically the rebbetzin was sitting *shivah* on what would have been their fifty-eighth anniversary.

During the *shivah,* Yosi came to the modest Pam home on East Seventh Street in Kensington, Brooklyn. Hundreds of people from all walks of life came to console the family: *talmidim,* former *talmidim, rabbanim, askanim, balabatim,* friends and relatives. There was a constant flow of humanity in and out of the home. With the same graciousness that had exemplified their great father, Rav Pam's three sons, R' Aaron of Flatbush, R' David of Toronto and R' Asher of Lakewood tried to acknowledge each of the visitors. One of them asked Yosi, "What is your name?"

"Yosi Heber," was the soft reply.

"You're the one with the anniversary cards?" asked one of the sons.

Yosi smiled, embarrassed and surprised that Rav Pam's children would even know about the annual cards. "My parents appreciated the cards every year," another of the sons said. Yosi thanked them for telling him that and went on to tell the sons how much their father meant to him as a *rebbi* and *moreh derech* (guide in life).

After a while Yosi asked if he could be *menachem avel* the rebbetzin. He was pointed toward the kitchen. Rebbetzin Sarah Pam was sitting on a low chair near a table, having something to eat. The door was behind her and she did not see Yosi.

Someone bent over the rebbetzin and whispered, "Yosi Heber is here."

She stood up and faced Yosi. Her eyes filled with tears as she said, "Yosi, thank you for the card this year. It came last Tuesday and as soon as I got it, I took it to the *Rosh Yeshivah* in the hospital. He was unconscious but I read it to him anyway and he responded to it." Then she paused and said soflty, "In fact it was the last thing in his life that he responded to." Two days later, on Thursday night, he passed away.

Yosi was speechless. He was glad that he thought to send the card when he did and astounded that she would take it to the hospital and read it to her husband. Then the rebbetzin added a few words that Yosi will never forget. "Yosi," she said, "I heard that you had a baby this year. The picture that you sent with the card didn't have the new baby. Would you mind sending a new picture? We'd like to have an updated picture."

Yosi recalled the warm feeling he had years ago when he first mentioned his engagement to Rav Pam. Both Rav Pam and the rebbetzin had the capacity to focus on the joy and concern of others even during times of their own personal duress. Rav Pam had made him feel special then, his wife made him feel special now. Throughout their lives together, Rav Pam and his wife personified the teaching of Shlomo *HaMelech*, דְּרָכֶיהָ דַרְכֵי נֹעַם וְכָל נְתִיבוֹתֶיהָ שָׁלוֹם, *[The Torah's] ways are ways of pleasantness and all its paths are peace (Mishlei* 3:17*).*

A Living Will

In an incisive essay on *chessed* (benevolence) Rabbi Eliyahu Dessler (1892-1954) emphasizes that a person must strive to be a *nosein* (a giver) not a *noteil* (a taker). He writes that those who continually *take* are absorbed by self-interest and self-love, which can ultimately lead to denial of Hashem's existence, whereas those who are benevolent experience an upsurge in spirituality for "all [spiritual] growth is dependent on [one's development of] the power of giving." (See *Michtav MeEliyahu,* Vol. 1, p. 140 ff*).*

Rabbi Chaim Shmulevitz (1902-1978), too, condemns *takers.* He comments that the severity of the sin of taking interest from a borrower lies in the character of the lender. Hypocritically, he is convinced that he is a *giver* (for he has lent money), but in essence he is a *taker* (as he insists on getting back more than he lent). (See *Sichos Mussar, Maamar* No. 8, 5731.)

In this touching story we appreciate a different type of *giver.* I had the privilege to know the people involved, Rabbi Simcha Wasserman (1899-1992) and his rebbetzin, Feige Rachel, when they lived with a wonderful family, the Rowes, in our neighborhood of Kew Gardens, New York, when Reb Simcha was recuperating from a serious illness. The Wassermans were both soft-spoken, kind, considerate and sensitive people, who devoted their lives to inspiring *talmidim* and *talmidos* in Europe, America and Israel.

Reb Simcha and his wife had a very special relationship. They were married more than sixty years but sadly they were childless. They revered each other and were a constant source of strength to one another during numerous frustrations and unrealized aspirations in the various communities in which they lived. (See *Along the Maggid's Journey*, p. 61.)

The rebbetzin often said that she could not live a day without Reb Simcha. She expressed the hope that she would die before he did so that she would be spared the pain and anguish of living even a day without him.

As she got older, however, it occurred to her that if she died before her husband, there would be no immediate relative to mourn him. Thus, she relinquished her original idea and said, "It would be better if Reb Simcha would pass away first, for at least he would have someone to sit *shivah* for him."

(For his part, he said in his will that he wanted no eulogies at his *levayah* (funeral), but if the rebbetzin were still living there could be one brief eulogy, for her sake.)

On the second day of Marcheshvan 5753, Rav Simcha Wasserman passed away. Thousands mourned him at his funeral in Jerusalem and hundreds came to be *menachem avel* the rebbetzin during the *shivah.*

Incredibly, on the twelfth day of Marcheshvan, a few days after the *shivah* ended, the rebbetzin passed away.

Perhaps the rebbetzin understood that by wishing she would die first she was acting as a *noteil* (taker), focusing only on the kindness and benevolence she always received from her husband. When she realized that only she was eligible to pay her great husband the ultimate respect of sitting *shivah*, she sought to elevate her life by becoming a *nosein* (giver). In deference to her piety, her wish was granted.

At a *Sheva Berachos* tendered in Bnei Brak for his newlywed daughter, Rav Mordechai Broide, *Rosh Yeshivah* of Yeshivas Beis Eliyahu in Elad, Israel (near Petach Tikvah), told two stories that occurred years apart, in different parts of Europe. Seemingly they had no connection. However, as Rav Broide wove the tapestry of the stories together, a magnificent quilt of information began to evolve. When he finished, a beautiful pattern had emerged which was especially designed to make the stories relevant to the event that was being celebrated. (Additional details of the story were culled from the newly published *Meir Einay Yisrael,* Vol. 4, p. 503.)

When the yeshivah of the Chofetz Chaim (1838-1933) was first founded in Radin, Poland, numerous people subsidized the meals for the *talmidim* (students) of the yeshivah. Each person agreed to underwrite the cost of the meals for a particular day of the week. Thus, the financial burden of the yeshivah was lightened.

When this process was no longer possible, the yeshivah sought to institute a system called *teg* (lit. days) where every boy would be assigned to eat in a particular home on a particular day / days of the week. Based on this schedule, the *talmidim* would be sustained by the families near and around the yeshivah.

In Radin, there was an extremely pious, kind, caring Jew, known as R' Gedalye (Kaplan) the water carrier. Aside from his daily chores, R' Gedalye was always available to help people carry their heavy loads. His recognizable trademark was the thick ropes that were always slung over his shoulder. When necessary the ropes could be tied around anything that had to be carried from place to place.

When R' Gedalye heard about the proposal to have the *bachurim* leave the yeshivah to have their meals in people's homes he went to the Chofetz Chaim and respectfully protested. "It is *bitul Torah* (waste of time from Torah study)," he said. "I volunteer to pick up the meals for the *bachurim* so that they can remain in the yeshivah and not have to spend their time going back and forth to their hosts of the day."

The Chofetz Chaim was impressed with R' Gedalye's gesture and took him up on his offer. Thus, every day R' Gedalye would make the rounds in the community picking up the meals for the *bachurim,* so they could remain in the yeshivah and spend that extra time learning. This went on for years.

On those rare occasions when R' Gedalye did not pick up the meals because there was no food to be had, the yeshiva *bachurim* would quip, "Today we are having our own T*zom* (fast of) *Gedalye"* (a reference to the fast day, immediately after *Rosh Hashanah).* R' Gedalye was beloved by the *bachurim* and revered by the Chofetz Chaim.

One summer day, R' Gedalye contracted a terrible illness and was bedridden. As the weeks wore on he became more ill and soon began getting frail. As R' Gedalye's dutiful and dedicated wife, Tamara, tended to her sick husband, the Chofetz Chaim would send his daughter Sara'leh to R' Gedalye's home every Friday with wine, *challos* and sufficient food for Shabbos. She would then set the table for Tamara and her two young daughters, Sima Yehudis and Sarah Musha, as she delivered her sainted father's blessing that R' Gedalye have a *refuah sheleimah* (complete healing).

By *Rosh Hashanah* R' Gedalye was extremely ill. The morning of *Yom Kippur* the Chofetz Chaim went with a *bachur* from the yeshivah, R' Moshe Meir Alexsondov, to bring food to R' Gedalye. As they walked in the wet and muddied streets, Moshe Meir said to the Chofetz Chaim, "I will go myself, the streets are so muddy, the *rebbi* need not go."

However, the Chofetz Chaim feared that R' Gedalye would not believe the *psak* (religious ruling) that he had to eat unless he heard it personally from the Chofetz Chaim. Thus the great sage went along to be sure that R' Gedalye would indeed eat.

When R' Gedalye passed away two months later on the tenth of *Kislev,* the Chofetz Chaim delivered a stirring *hesped* (eulogy). Among the things he said was: "R' Gedalye was known as the water carrier. But he carried much more than that. With his kindness he carried our burdens and with his faith he carried his life's travails with patience and tolerance."

R' Gedalye had only two young daughters at the time of his passing. The eldest, Sima Yehudis, was all of 11 years old. The Chofetz Chaim made it his personal agenda to see to it that Tamara and her daughters were taken care of. The two children always seemed to be in the Chofetz Chaim's home, as they were treated like relatives. The Chofetz Chaim and his wife were so grateful to R' Gedalye for what he had done for the yeshivah *bachurim* that they felt this was a way to show their endless gratitude.

> Thus ended the first story told by Rav Broide. It was interesting, moving and informative. All who were present thought Rav Broide was about to end his talk, but then he began another story, one that dealt with a well-known *Rosh Yeshivah* in Europe, Rav Chaim Moshe Yehudah Schneider (1885-1955). (Supplementary details of this story were put together from *Sefer Hazikaron* on Rav Scheneider and from conversations with his son, Rav Gedalye of Bnei Brak, and his daughter, Rebbetzin Nechama Gitel Siemiatycki, who lives in Clapton, outside Stamford Hill in England.)

Rav Moshe Schneider, a descendant (from his mother's side) of the *gaon,* Rav Isaac Slonimer (1800-1873), was raised by his parents to be a Torah personality. When he was yet a child, his father would lift him up and show him the rav of the city and exclaim with awe and reverence, "Do you see how prominent and beautiful he is?" It made an everlasting impression.

From his early years he was an exceptional *masmid* (diligent in learning). When he was in his teens he escaped from persecutions in his hometown outside of Vilna, Lithuania, by fleeing to the German border town of Memel. R' Moshe wanted to continue his Torah studies but there was no yeshivah in Memel. So instead, he gathered a number of the sons of Russian businessmen who had also escaped with their fathers from their hometowns and began learning with them. His personal goal at the time was not to stay in Memel but rather to study *Yoreh Deah* and become a rav in America.

This was not to be. Instead, against all odds, he eventually started a small yeshivah in Memel and imbued his *talmidim* with a love for learning and *mussar* (ethical teachings), specifically teaching his favorite work, *Chovos HaLevavos* (the classic work by R' Bachya Ibn Pakudah, the early 11th century *dayan* and *paytan*). As the yeshivah began to grow, Rav Moshe realized it was time to find his partner in life. He wrote letters to *rabbanim* and acquaintances throughout Europe asking if they knew a woman who would be suitable in marriage. In the letter he wrote, "I need someone who would be willing to cook for the *bachurim* of my yeshivah."

People asked him, "What about the system of *teg* where yeshivah boys routinely eat by families near and around the yeshiva? Why not institute that system in Memel? And besides," they added, "is cooking for the *bachurim* a job for a *Rosh Yeshivah's* wife?"

Rav Moshe replied firmly and bluntly, "The yeshivah experience for a *bachur* must be total. He should not have to leave the premises every day for anything. The yeshivah must provide his daily food. And as to the second question — I feel that the less hired help the better! Whatever we can do ourselves for the *bachurim* would lighten the yeshivah's financial burden."

For weeks there was not even one response to his letters. Finally, a letter came from the Chofetz Chaim's son-in-law, Rav Tzvi Hirsch (Halevi) Levinson (1863-1921), saying that his father-in-law had suggested a young woman, Sima Yehudis Kaplan, from Radin, who he thought would be a perfect match. Rav Levinson explained that Sima Yehudis had been raised as a child by her father, R' Gedalye, who shared the exact values Rav Moshe did regarding *bachurim* and their total yeshivah experience. Thus the *shidduch* seemed right.

Rav Moshe Schneider took the suggestion seriously and indeed in 1911, Sima Yehudis became Rebbetzin Schneider. The Chofetz Chaim himself was the *mesader kiddushin* (performer of the marriage ceremony). Sima Yehudis became her husband's distinguished helpmate as he fashioned a life dedicated to teaching and spreading Torah, at times under severely adverse conditions.

After their marriage, the Schneiders returned to the yeshivah in Memel where the rebbetzin ran the kitchen. As the First World War beckoned, with Germany and Russia battling each other, the Schneiders were expelled from Memel since Rav Moshe was considered an enemy of the Germans because of his birth in Lithuania. They settled first in the small island Rugen in the north of Germany and then were expelled to Holzminden, where with the help of Rav Ezra Munk (1867-1940), the noted rav in Berlin, the Schneiders were able to start a thriving community.

They remained in Holzminden until 1917 and after the War, they moved to Frankfurt, where Rav Schneider built and sustained a renowned yeshivah for twenty years. Torah giants such as Rav Chaim Ozer Grodzinsky (1863-1940), the Chortkover Rebbe, Rav Yisrael Friedman (1842-1933), the Slabodka Rosh Yeshiva, Rav Moshe Mordechai Epstein (1866-1933), the Ponevezher Rav, Rav Yosef Kahaneman (1886-1969) and Rav Yechiel Yaakov Weinberg (1885-1966), author of responsa *Seridei Aish,* all visited the yeshiva and declared it to be on par with the *Litvisher* yeshivos in Poland.

With the onslaught of the Nazi regime in the late 1930's, the yeshivah suffered discrimination and arrests at the hands of government officials. Eventually, by orders of the Gestapo it was forced to close. Anyone who could, tried to escape to any country which would issue a visa. In 1939, with the help of the head of London's Rabbinical Court, Rav Yecheskel Abramsky (1886-1976), Chief Rabbi Dr. Joseph H. Hertz (1872-1946), and his son-in-law, Rabbi Shlomo Schonfeld (1912-1982), Rav Moshe Schneider and his wife were able to immigrate to England.

England became enmeshed in World War II, and it was nearly impossible to raise funds for a yeshivah. Yet, Rav Schneider and his Rebbetzin with their fierce determination established the Toras Emes Yeshivah in London, which began in their own home. The yeshivah, known as Rav Schneider's yeshivah, produced *talmidei chachamim* and *mechanchim* for the next generation.

Rav Schneider was very demanding of his *talmidim's* punctiliousness in their *mitzvah* observance. Those who came late for *davening* were subject to fines. A *talmid* once came late and when questioned by Rav Schneider about missing the *z'man* (time) for *krias Shema,* the boy said, "There is still time according to the Gra's *z'man* (the Vilna Gaon's time limit for the recitation of *krias Shema* is later than that of the *Magen Avraham*). Rav Schneider retorted, "Do you also keep the Gaon's hours of (maximum) learning and (minimal) sleeping?" He exhorted the *bachurim* that their *berachos* always be said out loud, be it *Al Netilas Yadaim* or *Hamotzi* or the answering of *Yehei Shemei Rabbah.* He would cite *Sefer Chassidim* (No. 254) which states that those who don't recite their blessings out loud rob others of the opportunity to answer *Amen.*

He encouraged the *bachurim* to talk *divrei Torah* during their meals. If he saw their conversation would veer to mundane topics he would ask a *she'eilah* in *halachah* and have the boys debate it. He always called his *talmidim* by their Hebrew names, the names with which they were called to the Torah, never by their last name, nickname or secular name.

The *Rosh Yeshivah* and the rebbetzin treated each of the beloved *talmidim,* many of whom were refugees, as their own children. When the yeshivah had to escape to Manchester in 1944 because of the German's incessant bombing of London, the Schneiders served as surrogate father and mother to the *bachurim.* As she had done in Memel, Frankfurt and London, the rebbetzin ran the kitchen, and she and her daughters cooked the *bachurim's* meals daily.

Their first son-in-law was Rav Eliezer Lopian, the son of the eminent Rav Elyah Lopian (1872-1970). Years later, when Rav Eliezer was one of the *Roshei Yeshivah* of Toras Emes, his first son-in-law, a *talmid* of the yeshivah, was Rav Mordechai Broide.

Rav Broide told these stories at the *Sheva Berachos* of his daughter — Sima Yehudis, named after her remarkable great-grandmother, Rebbetzin Sima Yehudis Schneider, daughter of R' Gedalye, ward of the Chofetz Chaim. I heard these stories because the *chassan* is my nephew, Shmuel Yaakov Sofer of Far Rockaway, N.Y.

I am honored to be even distantly connected to such illustrious people.

Every morning we bless Hashem for enabling us to walk and reach our destinations. We say: בָּרוּךְ אַתָּה ה' ... הַמֵּכִין מִצְעֲדֵי גָבֶר, *Blessed are You, Hashem ... Who firms (i.e. empowers) man's footsteps.* (Some say אֲשֶׁר הֵכִין ... *Who has firmed.*) The wording of the blessing is based on the verse מֵד' מִצְעֲדֵי גֶבֶר כּוֹנָנוּ, *By Hashem, the footsteps of man are firm (Tehillim 37:23).*

Others understand the blessing differently. Using the *Abarbanel's* understanding of the aforementioned verse (see *Tehillim Mikdash Me'at* ibid.), the word הֵכִין is translated as *prepares.* Thus that daily morning blessing is an acknowledgment that Hashem plans and guides our footsteps so that we appear in particular places at particular times. Being somewhere is never happenstance, it is always an act of Providence. What we do there is up to us. Hashem presents opportunities; we must make the most of them.

The following story is a memorable case in point.

One spring day in 1962, as R' Hershel Weber, a *chassid* in the Williamsburg section of Brooklyn, was leaving the *Poilisher Shtiebel,* a famous *shul* on Ross St., he heard a man who was walking in front of the *shtiebel* cry out that he had a sharp pain in his chest. The man collapsed right in front of R' Hershel.

R' Hershel screamed for help and within seconds people called the police and an ambulance. R' Hershel stood over the man helplessly, assuring him that aid was on the way. R' Hershel saw the man become unconscious and his face turn blue. Tragically, a few minutes later the man was dead on the sidewalk.

A while later two police officers arrived. As they took notes and surveyed the situation, R' Hershel heard one officer say to the other, "If only we had gotten here 10 minutes earlier, we could have saved this guy."

R' Hershel, a *kollel* member, was shaken and traumatized by the event. He convinced two of his friends, R' Hershel Kaff, who owned a bakery, and R' Yoelish Gantz, who owned a cleaning store, to enroll with him in a first aid course at a local Red Cross office so that they could administer emergency medical help in time of need. R' Hershel reasoned that since both Mr. Kaff and Mr. Gantz had people working in their stores, they could get away in case of crisis. All three friends bought small oxygen tanks.

A few months later an elderly gentleman who lived on Morton Street in Williamsburg died in his sleep. When his wife awoke the next morning she realized immediately that something was terribly wrong. She ran to the window facing the street and screamed hysterically for help. At once a crowd gathered inside and outside her home. Someone yelled, "Get Hershel Weber!"

R' Hershel came running with his trustworthy oxygen tank and some very basic medical equipment. As soon as he examined the man he realized at once that there was nothing he could do. The man had been dead for hours.

He left the bedroom dejectedly and said a few comforting words to the newly widowed woman. As he walked down the stone staircase in front of the house and jostled his way through the large crowd of onlookers, someone called out, "*Dee zayst Hershel? Ehr hut im gehargit!*" ("Did you see Hershel? He is the one who killed him!")

R' Hershel was shocked. He had come to help! The one who made the nasty comment must have thought that because Hershel was not a doctor, the old man had died because of inadequate medical care.

R' Hershel began crying uncontrollably. How, he wondered to himself, could one Jew say something like that about another Jew?

For the next two days Hershel was devastated. Every time he thought of that disparaging remark tears came to his eyes. He decided to go to the Satmar Rav, Rabbi Yoel Teitelbaum (1887-1979), the greatest and most influential *chassidic* leader in Williamsburg.

R' Hershel recounted the incident on Morton Street to the Rebbe and then asked, "Wouldn't it be a good idea that there should be a group of Jews that would become well versed in emergency medicine so that they could be available in the community on a volunteer basis whenever the need arises?"

The Satmar Rebbe told Hershel to bring him the *sefer Shaarei Teshuvah,* the classic *mussar* work by *Rabbeinu Yonah* (1180-1263). The Rebbe read from *Shaar* 3:71: וְטוֹב וְנָכוֹן מְאֹד לִהְיוֹת בְּכָל עִיר וָעִיר מִתְנַדְּבִים בָּעָם מִן הַמַּשְׂכִּילִים לִהְיוֹת נְכוֹנִים וּמְזֻמָּנִים לְכָל דְּבַר הַצָּלָה בִּהְיוֹת אִישׁ אוֹ אִשָּׁה מִיִּשְׂרָאֵל שְׁרוּיִים בְּצַעַר, *It is beneficial and most appropriate that there be in every city intelligent volunteers prepared and available for any [hatzalah] assistance — [to help] a Jewish man or woman in anguish.*

The Rebbe looked up at R' Hershel Weber and said, "Start the organization you spoke of and because of that expression in the *Shaarei Teshuvah,* call it Hatzalah!"

And that's how the great Hatzalah organization was created. One man, seemingly in a place by coincidence, recognized an imperative need in the community. Many of us could have been there but Hashem chose to have R' Hershel there because he would make the most of the situation.

We can only marvel at his accomplishment.

Since its inception the volunteers of Hatzalah have saved hundreds, perhaps thousands, of lives and relieved pain and anguish for tens of thousands of Jews. Books could be written about their heroic escapades and heart-rending experiences, but the books will *not* be written because Hatzalah demands absolute confidentiality from its members. Their sacrifice knows no bounds and their commitment no limits. Hatzalah volunteers are heroes who deserve our accolades and community support.

Yet even the most serious of organizations has its lighter moments. The following epsiode which occurred in the Flatbush section of Brooklyn on the holiest day of the year brings a chuckle to all who hear it.

It was *Yom Kippur* and an old man in a Flatbush *shul* was feeling very weak. The *shul* had no air conditioning and the air was thick and stifling. Suddenly, during *Mussaf,* the gentleman collapsed and fell to the floor with a heavy thud. Some people around him thought he had died.

People yelled for Hatzalah and a call was made to the central office. The dispatcher notified the volunteers in neighboring *shuls*, who quickly whipped off their *taleisim* and rushed to the stricken man's *shul*.

Within moments Hatzalah volunteers ran into the sanctuary. One group brought a strecher, and the pale, wan gentleman was gently placed on it and carried out to an ambulance. His skin was colorless and his body was limp, but when he was carried outside into the fresh air, he opened his eyes and to his amazement he saw a group of people around him all dressed in white.

Looking frightenened, he asked in bewilderment, *"Bin ich shoin oiven?"* ("Am I already upstairs [in Heaven]?") The sight of the Hatzalah men around him in their white *kittlach* had him thinking that he was seeing angels.

In reality, he *was* seeing angels. For the volunteers of Hatzalah are truly angels of mercy, healing and compassion.

The Eyes Have It

The *talmidei chachamim* (Torah sages) of a generation are referred to as the עֵינֵי הָעֵדָה (*the eyes of the community*). They are given this appellation because it is through their insights that we attain true Torah perspectives on life. The following is a case in point. It was recounted by Rabbi Avrohom Chaim Feuer, a rav in Monsey and the son-in-law of the Telsher *Rosh Yeshivah*, Rav Mordechai Gifter (1917-2001).

Rabbi Feuer once took Rav Gifter to a noted ophthalmologist in Brooklyn, Dr. Sam Cohen, who is a *talmid chacham*, as well as a renowned doctor. In the course of conversation, Rabbi Feuer mentioned an interesting interpretation by the *Radak* on a verse in *Tehillim*.

David *HaMelech* beseeches Hashem, שָׁמְרֵנִי כְּאִישׁוֹן בַּת עָיִן, *Guard me like the pupil of the eye* (*Tehillim* 17:8). The *Radak* writes that the root of the Hebrew word for pupil, אִישׁוֹן, is אִישׁ, *man*, for when someone looks into the pupil of another person's eye, he sees a man, a reflection of himself. The *Radak* adds that the letters *vav* and *nun* at the end of the word, signify a diminutive. Thus אִישׁוֹן means a *small* man. Indeed, if you look into someone else's eye, you see your reflection appearing like a *small* man.

Upon hearing this *Radak*, Rav Gifter said, "There is a great lesson to be learned here. When one looks at someone else, he tends to view himself as superior, deserving of honor and recognition. However that is not the proper perspective.When one person sees another he should consider the other person as superior to himself, and seek to find the virtues that make the other fellow prominent. As for himself, he should regard himself exactly the way he apears in the pupil of the other fellow's eye, as a diminutive and humble individual."

Small wonder that Rav Gifter had thousands of pupils who saw his greatness.

Moving Mountains

In the summer of 2000, I had the wonderful opportunity to be at the Metropol Hotel in Arosa, Switzerland. The guests included families from London, Zurich, Antwerp, Israel, and America, each with its own background and stories.

Every morning as we walked to the huge balcony behind the hotel for *Shacharis,* the imposing, rugged snow-capped mountains across the way burst into breathtaking view. The raw beauty of the majestic Alps stretching as far as the eye could see was overwhelming and humbling. Struck by the awesome magnificence of Hashem's creations and grateful for the opportunity to pray to Him, I thought of the verse: מָה אֱנוֹשׁ כִּי תִזְכְּרֶנּוּ וּבֶן אָדָם כִּי תִפְקְדֶנּוּ, *What is the frail human that You should remember him? And what is the son of man that You should be mindful of him? (Tehillim* 8:5*).*

One evening after I spoke on that balcony, with the mountains as a backdrop, an elderly, regal gentleman, Reb Chaim

Aryeh Spitz, asked me if I wished to hear a story. "It will take time," he cautioned softly. It was obvious that he was anxious to relate the episode — and I am always eager to hear a good story — and so I acquiesced. We sat down in the back of the makeshift *beis midrash* in the hotel, I called together a few people, we turned on a tape recorder and he began.

When he finished more than half an hour later, I realized once again that Hashem's greatest creation was man — not mountains. Man can move proverbial mountains; and in this remarkable story about the Skulener Rebbe, Rabbi Eliezer Zisya Portugal (1896-1982), we come to appreciate the magnitude of the man and his sense of responsibility for fellow Jews. We witness how the Rebbe jarred granite institutions that eventually tumbled.

Starting with the Bolshevik Revolution in 1917, the Communist government in the Soviet Union was a crushing, oppressive ruler for seventy years. During this era — many millions of people were killed or tortured merely because they were considered "enemies" of the Communist Party. Often the charges against these "criminals" were fabricated, and they were killed for no other reason than that they fell out of favor with the vindictive bloodthirsty rulers.

One of the primary goals of the Communists was to wipe out any form of religion, so millions of Jews suffered persecution, such as job discrimination, rejection from the best schools, lower grades if they were admitted, jailing, torture, expulsion to the frozen tundra of Siberia and even death. This took place not only in the vast expanse of the Soviet Union but in Eastern European countries such as Romania, Hungary, Czechoslovakia and Poland, which were occupied by the Communists. The practice of Judaism virtually disappeared in most Communist areas.

Before, during and after World War II, the Skulener Rebbe and his rebbetzin, Shaina Rachel, protected as many orphaned children as they could. In 1939 there was a pogrom in the Romanian town of Yassi where thousands of Jews were killed. Hundreds of orphans were suddenly desperate and homeless. The Skulener Rebbe convinced numerous religious communities to adopt ten children each and then he opened an orphanage in Cernouti (Chernovitz) that housed and fed close to 400 of the remaining orphans. The most difficult children lived in the Rebbe's home with his family. After the war when the Rebbe moved to Bucharest, the capital of Romania, he transferred the orphans to a new orphanage he established there. Young boys and girls were thus provided with their physical and spiritual needs.

Long after the war was over, many Romanian Jews were still being jailed and tortured by the Communist regime. The Rebbe raised large sums of money to bribe officials and pay ransom to have the Jewish prisoners released. Suffering Romanian Jews knew there was one address where they could find solace and counsel — the Rebbe's home.

Most Jews wished to leave Romania, but the authorities made it nearly impossible. It took years, but finally, in 1959, with the political connections of Mr. Harry Goodman, President of Agudath Israel in England, Dr. Yaakov Griffel and other activists, the Rebbe was granted permission to leave Romania. After living in Belgium for a short time he came to America and settled in the Crown Heights section of Brooklyn.

From his home, the Rebbe continued working feverishly to free Jews from Romania. He became equally concerned for materially and spiritually impoverished Jews in Israel, and therefore established and led *Chessed L'Avraham,* the famous *tzedakah* and *chinuch* organization.

The Rebbe had been following Romanian politics and was aware that the government under the leadership of the dictator Nicolae Ceausescu (chow-ches-ku) was beginning to distance itself from Soviet policies. Romania had defiantly denounced the Soviet Union for its invasion of Czechoslovakia in 1968 and Ceausescu began asserting his insistence on full independence from the Soviet Union. Popular acceptance of his regime peaked and his contacts with the West multiplied.

In 1972 it was announced that Ceausescu would be coming to Washington to seek "most favored nation" status for Romania. At the time, if a Communist country wanted to export items to the United States, it had to pay extremely high tariffs; if it wished to import goods from America, it could not get credits. If Romania could achieve most favored nation status, its tarriffs on exports would be cut by 90 percent and it could obtain credits. Ceausescu saw this status as imperative for his country's economic growth and independence.

At that time the Rebbe had a list of sixty-five Jews who were suffering in Romanian prisons. He knew where each prisoner was and what hardships he was enduring. The Rebbe, who *davened* for the prisoners every day, wondered if there was a way that he could have key senators in Washington intervene in the discussions with Ceausescu and link the release of the prisoners to the granting of most favored nation status. Upon investigation, the Rebbe concluded that the best way to implement his plan was to speak with Senator Warren Magnuson, a Democrat from Washington State, who was an influential member on the Committee on Interstate and Foreign Commerce.

The Rebbe did not know anyone who knew Senator Magnuson, but he learned that Rabbi Shlomo Maimon of Seattle was a friend of the other senator from Washington, Henry (Scoop) Jackson, a known friend of Jews. Through his connections in the Democratic Party, Rabbi Maimon was able to make separate appointments for the Rebbe with both Senators Jackson and Magnuson.

It was then that the Skulener Rebbe called Reb Chaim Aryeh Spitz and asked him to take part in the senatorial meetings in Washington, D.C. Mr. Spitz, originally from Bistrita (Bistritz), in northern Romania, had become acquainted with the Rebbe in Bucharest shortly after the war. Their friendship flourished and continued when both moved to New York. The Rebbe did not know English and needed a trustworthy translator. He knew he could rely on Mr. Spitz. Honored at this opportunity, Mr. Spitz accepted immediately.

Throughout the train ride from New York to Washington, the Rebbe recited *Tehillim,* and he prayed that his mission be successful. By the time they came to the hotel there was a call waiting for the Rebbe, with the name of yet another Romanian Jew being held in prison.

The next afternoon, the Rebbe and Mr. Spitz were welcomed cordially into Senator Jackson's stately office. As the Rebbe began talking in Yiddish he started crying uncontrollably over the terrible plight of Romanian Jews, particularly the ones in prisons. He presented his idea of linking the release of prisoners to Romania's achieving most favored nation status. Senator Jackson listened intently as Mr. Spitz translated each of the sob-soaked words of the Rebbe. Jackson was deeply moved by the Rebbe's passionate concern. "I understand," he said softly, "I understand exactly what the rabbi is getting at."

Senator Jackson told the Rebbe that he had been to Buchenwald after the war and that he understood the plight and fright of the helpless and oppressed Jews. However, he explained, a senator could not intervene for sixty-six *individuals* regardless of how perilous their situation was. Something would have to be done on a larger scale.

Jackson was quiet for a few moments, as he cupped his hands over his sealed lips. He closed his eyes as thoughts swirled in his head. He finally opened his eyes and, peering at the two men sitting in front of him, he said softly but firmly, "Do you know what I'll do? I'll make it a law of the United States. I'll make it so that no Communist country in the world can get most favored nation status unless they liberalize their emigration laws and actually let people emigrate."

Henry Jackson didn't have to say more. The three men understood each other. If he could get such a law passed, it would be formulated so that any dictatorship wishing to do business with America would have to allow Jews to emigrate.

The Rebbe thanked Senator Jackson profusely. The Senator accompanied the Rebbe to Senator Magnuson's office, but when they were seated they were in for a disheartening surprise.

The Rebbe began the conversation and Senator Jackson continued it, but Senator Magnuson was inebriated and had difficulty following the discussion. Magnuson's legal assistant was angry that the receptionist had allowed the men into the office. Trying to minimize the embarrassment, the legal assistant assured the Rebbe that Magnuson would do what he could when he met with Ceausescu.

Scoop Jackson was a man of action, and that promise was not good enough for him. Seizing the opportunity, he asked the legal assistant to call the Romanian ambassador to the United States, Mr. Silviu Brucan, at once.

The call was made and Senater Jackson asked the ambassador to intervene on behalf of the sixty-six prisoners. Brucan asked that a list of the sixty-six people and their whereabouts be brought to his office. Within an hour, Reb Chaim Aryeh Spitz was at the ambassador's office with the requested information. [Remarkably, within months every single one of the sixty-six was released! Most of them went to live in Israel. Mr. Spitz is convinced that it was all due to the merit of the Rebbe's *tefillos* (prayers).]

That evening, the Rebbe and Mr. Spitz returned to New York and Senator Jackson began working on his promise. Jackson and Congressman Vanik of Ohio introduced an amendment to the trade bill on October 4, 1972 linking emigration to most favored nation status. It took two years to garner enough support in Congress to pass this amendment. Many in the business community opposed this amendment at congressional hearings for they wanted unencumbered access to the Communist financial markets. Secretary of State Henry Kissinger also expressed his doubts as to the advisability of this proposal, for it would limit his freedom of action in conducting foreign policy.

Ultimately the Jackson-Vanik Amendment to the 1974 Trade Reform Act became the law of the land, and in 1975 Romania was granted most favored nation status. However the Jackson-Vanik Amendment required that the most favored nation status had to be renewed on an annual basis. Thus every year the emigration policies of every Communist country would have to be re-evaluated.

The implementation of the Jackson-Vanik Amendment made one of the first cracks in the Soviet Iron Curtain. At first there was a trickle of Jewish emigration, but when Russia suffered a famine and had to purchase millions of tons of American grain, it was forced to allow tens of thousands of Jews to leave the country. The doors to freedom had been thrust open and the exodus of Jews from Russia soon reached monumental proportions. Over the next decade a million Jews were able to escape the shackles of Communism. More than 700,000 immigrated to Israel while another 260,000 came to America.

As emigration of Jews became a reality, the seeds of freedom that lay crushed and dormant for years in Russia began to sprout throughout the country. The cracks in the Iron Curtain widened as intellectuals and the common man dared think thoughts that were deemed impossible just months before. Eventually there was such upheaval that the Soviet regime, once thought to be the strongest in the world, toppled without a single bullet being fired. It is the opinion of many historians that the Jackson-Vanik Amendment significantly contributed to the collapse of world Communism, thereby changing the course of history.

Only a chosen few know that the idea of linking liberalization of emigration restrictions to trade with the United States was an offshoot of a concept first envisioned by the Skulener Rebbe. In his dedication to fellow Jews he had been hoping to have the sixty-six prisoners released from Romania. His actions (and *tefillos)* led to the freedom of multitudes such that even he could not have foreseen.

Chazal teach מְגַלְגְּלִין זְכוּת עַל יְדֵי זַכַּאי, *Benefit is imparted through one who is meritorious (Shabbos* 32a*).* One can only imagine how meritorious the Skulener Rebbe was considered in Heaven that he was allowed to be a vehicle that brought forth the release of a million Jewish souls, resulting in part in a resurgence of observance never before imagined. יְהִי זִכְרוֹ בָּרוּךְ, *May his memory be blessed.*

Greetings

When Moshe *Rabbeinu* and Aharon *HaKohen* were instructed to take a census of the Jews in the desert, they were told to count them בְּמִסְפַּר שֵׁמוֹת, *by the number of the names (Bamidbar* 1:2*).* The *Ramban* (ibid. 1:45*)* explains this ambiguous term to mean that Moshe and Aharon were not merely to approach the head of a household and ask, "How many are in your family?" Rather, they were to treat each individual בְּכָבוֹד וּבִגְדוּלָּה, *with honor and dignity.* Every person to be counted had to appear before Moshe and Aharon so that the great leaders would acknowledge him [by name] and give him an individual blessing.

We may be a people of millions but we are a nation of individuals. And every individual is entitled to respect and recognition.

Chazal (*Berachos* 17a) teach of Rabban Yochanan ben Zakkai: שֶׁלֹּא הִקְדִּימוֹ אָדָם שָׁלוֹם מֵעוֹלָם, אֲפִילוּ נָכְרִי בַּשּׁוּק, *No one ever greeted him first, even a gentile in the street* — such was his regard for another person. Rabbi Eliyahu Eliezer Dessler (*Michtav MeEliyahu* Vol. 4, p. 246) writes, "Picture who Rabban Yochanan ben Zakkai was. He knew all of Torah, *Mishnah, Gemara,* laws, Aggadic material, astronomical cycles, etc. He was the chief of the *Sanhedrin* at the time of the Temple's destruction. All the problems of Jewry rested on his shoulders and still there was *never* a time when he was so preoccupied that he forgot to greet any person first, even a gentile.

In this light, the following story told by Rabbi Moshe Aharon Stern (1925-1998), *Mashgiach* of the Kaminetzer Yeshiva in Jerusalem, is illuminating. As Shlomo *HaMelech* wrote: *Let a wise one hear and increase his learning (Mishlei* 1:5*).*

In Argentina there was a ritual slaughter complex, comprised of several buildings. There was a building where the animals were fed, a building where they were slaughtered and the meat packed and loaded onto trucks, and an office building with dressing rooms for the *shochtim.* The entire area was surrounded by a tall chain link fence and everyone entered through a wrought iron gate in the front, near the parking lot.

The owner, Yisrael (Izzy) Nachmal,* was a workaholic. He was the first one in every morning and the last one out every evening. He oversaw every aspect of his company, Ultimate Meats,* and made it a point to know every worker. The guard at the front gate, Domingo, knew that when Izzy left in the evening, he could lock the gate and go home.

One evening as Izzy was leaving, he called out to the guard, "Good night, Domingo, you can lock up and go."

"No," Domingo called back, "not everyone has left yet."

"What are you talking about," Izzy said, "everyone left two hours ago!"

"It is not so," Domingo said, "One of the *shochtim,* Rabbi Berkowitz, hasn't left yet."

"But he goes home every day with the other *shochtim,* maybe you just didn't see him," Izzy said.

"Believe me, I am positive he didn't leave yet," the guard insisted. "We better go look for him."

Izzy knew that Domingo was reliable and conscientious. He decided not to argue, but instead got out of his car and rushed back to the office building with Domingo. They searched the dressing room thinking that perhaps Rabbi Berkowitz had fainted and was debilitated. He wasn't there.

They ran to where the animals were slaughtered, but he wasn't there either. They searched the truck dock, the packing house, going from room to room. Finally they came to the huge walk-in refrigeration room where the large slabs of meat were kept frozen.

They opened the door and to their shock and horror they saw Rabbi Berkowitz rolling on the floor, trying desperately to keep himself warm. They ran over to him, lifted him off the floor and helped him out of the refrigerated room, past the thick heavy wooden door that had locked behind him. They wrapped blankets around him and made sure he was warm and comfortable.

Izzy Nachmal was incredulous. "Domingo," he asked, "how did you know Rabbi Berkowitz hadn't left? There are over two hundred workers here every day. Don't tell me you know the comings and goings of every one of them?"

---

*The name has been changed.

The guard's answer is worth remembering.

"Every morning when that rabbi comes in, he greets me and says hello. He makes me feel like a person. And every single night when he leaves he tells me, 'Have a pleasant evening.' He never misses a night — and to tell you the truth, I wait for his kind words. Dozens and dozens of workers pass me every day — morning and night, and they don't say a word to me. To them I am a nothing. To him, I am a somebody.

"I knew he came in this morning and I was sure he hadn't left yet, because I was waiting for his friendly good-bye for the evening!"

Rabbi Berkowitz's life was saved because of his genuine regard for another human being. The *Maharal* writes in regard to Rabbi Akiva's 24,000 students who perished because they did not honor each other: כַּאֲשֶׁר נוֹהֵג כָּבוֹד בַּחֲבֵירוֹ דָבָר זֶה הוּא עֶצֶם הַחַיִּים, *When you give honor and respect to another person, that is the essence of life (Yevamos* 62b*).*

In this respect, Rabbi Berkowitz gave *life* and so he merited life.

A Way to See Things

The very first credo in the first *Mishnah* in *Pirkei Avos* is הֱווּ מְתוּנִים בַּדִּין, *Be deliberate in judgment* (*Avos* 1:1). Though this admonition is addressed primarily to judges, it is applicable as well to all of us in our daily encounters with others. Each of us must "judge" and evaluate people and situations on a regular basis, and it behooves us to proceed with caution. (See *Avos D'Rav Nosson* 1:4.)

The following story is a case in point. Due to its sensitive nature the names and places have been changed.

In June of 1990, Rabbi Nachum Rosen accepted the position of rabbi at the Degel Yeshurun Synagogue in upstate New York. Rabbi Rosen was well aware that most of the members of the *shul* were elderly and that it would be a struggle to maintain a daily *minyan.*

Two decades earlier Degel Yeshurun had had a very active membership and was a focal point for Jewish affairs in the community. However many of the older members moved to the warmer climate of Florida or died and the younger people gravitated to non-Orthodox synagogues. Rabbi Rosen was hoping that his energy and enthusiasm would inspire the younger Jews of his community to join his congregation.

When Robert Lehman, a gentleman in his mid-20's, began coming to *shul* every morning, Rabbi Rosen was thrilled. He invited Robert to attend some of the *shiurim* (Torah lectures) that would be given throughout the week.

There was something strange about Robert's behavior, however. When he came to *shul* every morning, he would *daven* in the women's section. There were no women at the daily morning *minyan,* so Robert would sit behind the *mechitzah, davening* alone. Rabbi Rosen was tempted to ask Robert why he chose to sit where he did, as there were at least 200 empty spaces in the men's section of the *shul,* but the rabbi did not wish to antagonize Robert. He was the youngest congregant and the rabbi hoped to build a nucleus of new members around him.

Rabbi Rosen wondered what would happen on Shabbos when women *did* come to shul. He could not allow a man to sit in the women's section.

On Shabbos morning Rabbi Rosen peeked every few moments from his front seat to see if Robert had entered the women's sections which were situated on the right and left sides of the *shul,* with the men's section in the middle, between them. The *baal tefillah* was already up to *Baruch She'amar* and Rabbi Rosen still hadn't seen Robert. That was surprising because in the weekdays Robert had always been punctual.

Suddenly Rabbi Rosen had a thought and sure enough he was right. He looked up, and to his amazement Robert was *davening* in the balcony. Since there were women in the downstairs sections, Robert had gone upstairs to the balcony, which hadn't been used in years.

After *Shacharis,* before *krias HaTorah* (the reading of the Torah), Rabbi Rosen walked up to the balcony and wondered what he should say to this peculiar fellow. He approached Robert with a friendly smile. "We'd love to have you join us downstairs in the men's section, Robert," he said. "As you can surely see we have about 175 empty seats."

"Oh, rabbi," Robert replied. "You must think I'm strange, but really I'm not. You see I have a severe case of Retinal Pigmentosis. That means I am visually impaired and in my case I am already legally blind. (RP is a genetic disease, which causes progressive degeneration of the retina. It effects 1 in 4,000 people and the majority of patients become legally blind before the age of 60.)

"I can barely see the words in the *siddur.* Over the years I have tried to memorize as much of the *davening* as I could. I say the words out loud so that I can hear them, but I can't sit near anyone, for the sound of their *davening* confuses me, and my saying the words out loud would disturb them. So in the middle of the week, I *daven* in the women's section downstairs because no one is there and I have the whole section to myself. This Shabbos I had no choice but to come upstairs to the balcony so that I wouldn't disturb others and others would not confuse me.

"As a matter of fact, Rabbi, " Robert added, "I can well imagine that there may have been times in the last few days that you saw me in the street, and waved your hand or nodded your head in my direction and was surprised that I did not respond. That was not a display of disrespect, all it meant was that I did not see you!"

Rabbi Rosen was humbled and filled with remorse. "I'm so sorry," he said softly. "I had no idea of your condition. That was really insensitive of me."

"Rabbi, please don't feel that way," Robert said. "I should have told you about my condition. You did nothing wrong, how could you have known?"

> More often than not we are sure that our assumptions and judgments are right, because we believe we know everything there is to know about a particular situation. Time and again, as happened in the Degel Yeshurun Synagogue, there is more to a story than meets the eye.

A Time to Deliver

This touching story took place a number of years ago in one of the leading Jewish neighborhoods in Europe. By personal request, all names have been fictionalized.

Shimon Waller and his wife Shoshana had been married for seven years and had not been blessed with children. Their anguish was evident as they went from doctor to doctor, from medical facility to medical facility for advice and assistance. Rabbi Hillel Pincus, rav of the *shul* where the Wallers *davened,* counseled them with *hashkafah* (Jewish perspective) and gave them support and assurance of Hashem's Providence throughout their ordeal. The couple found strength in his genuine warmth and concern.

Sadly, Shimon's younger brother Peretz and his wife Penina, who lived in the same neighborhood and *davened* in the same *shul,* were experiencing the same painful situation. Peretz and Penina were married for five years but they too were without children. They too were brokenhearted and downcast, and Rabbi Pincus offered them, too, encouragement and reassurance.

In July of 1998 there was elation in the home of Peretz and Penina. After five years, they were going to have a child! They decided that for now they would not say a word about the pregnancy to anyone except their rav, so that the older brother and sister-in-law who were married longer would not feel despondent. Rabbi Pincus was overjoyed at the news and impressed by Peretz and Penina's sensitivity for Shimon and Shoshana.

A month later Shimon called Rabbi Pincus and asked if he could meet with him. Rabbi Pincus told Shimon that he could come whenever it was convenient. Rabbi Pincus wondered, had Shimon somehow found out about his younger brother and sister-in-law? Had Shimon and Shoshana gone through yet another procedure that failed? Or perhaps Shimon just wanted to talk about a totally unrelated matter. Rabbi Pincus' mind raced as he anxiously awaited Shimon's visit.

That evening both Shimon and Shoshana came to the rabbi's home. As they began to talk they could not hide their radiant smiles. "*Baruch Hashem,* there is finally wonderful news," said Shimon. "My wife and I are going to have a child."

Rabbi Pincus was ecstatic and embraced Shimon with joy. "But I have a problem," said Shimon, tempering the happiness of the moment. "How can I share this news with anyone? It will surely get to Peretz and Penina and they might feel so bad because of their own situation."

Rabbi Pincus thought for a moment and said, "Shimon, I know Peretz and Penina very well. They are special people and they love you so much. They will be thrilled to hear the news and he'll be so happy for you."

Shimon wasn't sure, "Do you really think we should be the ones to tell them?"

"Of course," said Rabbi Pincus. "Both of you should go to their home right now and tell them."

Shimon and Shoshana took the advice and went straight to the home of Peretz and Penina.

Within an hour, Shimon and Peretz, brothers in every sense of the word, were on the phone together with Rabbi Pincus sharing their mutual ecstatic delight and good fortune.

> Aside from the exemplary empathy that the brothers and sisters-in-law had for each other, one must admire Rabbi Pincus' handling of the situation — no breach of confidentiality, yet clever guidance to allow close families to share their joy.
>
> The prophet Daniel said: יָהֵב חָכְמְתָא לְחַכִּימִין, [*Hashem*] *gives wisdom to the wise* (*Daniel* 2:21). As the *Midrash Tanchuma* (*Vayakheil* 2) explains, Hashem gives wisdom to the wise, because only they know what to do with it! (See also *Midrash Rabbah, Koheles* 1:7 and *Berachos* 55a.)

Healing Powers

Shlomo *HaMelech* writes מַעֲנֶה רַּךְ יָשִׁיב חֵמָה, *A gentle reply turns away wrath (Mishlei* 15:1). Usually this directive is understood as advice to one who is the target of angry words or harsh feelings. Do not fight fire with fire, Shlomo *HaMelech* counsels. Instead use soft words and kind expressions, for they are apt to assuage the fury vented in your direction.

In this touching story we learn a new meaning to Shlomo *HaMelech's* words.

On a trip to England, I once met R' Asher Rutman* at a *minyan* in Oxford.* After *davening*, R' Asher introduced me to a boy he was holding around the shoulders. "This is my son, Chaim Baruch," he said proudly. "He is a living miracle!"

R' Asher proceeded to tell me the following story that moves him till this very day.

Two days after his son was born in July 1985, doctors told him that the infant would have to undergo a serious lifesaving operation. The child had been born with a rare illness and doctors feared for his life. The operation was scheduled for a Tuesday morning in the Buckingham Medical Center* north of London.

On Monday, R' Asher called the Manchester *Rosh Yeshivah*, Rabbi Yehudah Zev Segal, for a *berachah*. Rav Segal gave his warmest blessings and wished that the infant be well. For a good part of the day R' Asher and his wife recited *Tehillim* for the health of their son.

On Tuesday morning R' Asher came to the hospital early, as the infant was being prepped for the operation. While he was in the pediatric waiting room, the surgeon came in and announced that he would not be doing the surgery that day. "A life threatening emergency has come up with another patient and I must tend to that matter first," the doctor said emphatically.

"But what about my child," R' Asher protested, "he too has a life threatening situation."

"The other patient is in greater danger," snapped the doctor, "and we must turn our attention there. Your son will be operated on tomorrow."

---

*The name has been changed.

R' Asher was beside himself with worry and concern but it was obvious that the doctor was immovable. Though distraught with worry, there was nothing he could do. Then, he remembered, of all things, that he had to put money in the soon to be expired parking meter. "Besides all these problems, I could get a summons," he thought to himself.

When he went downstairs to the lobby to exit the hospital he noticed a cluster of Jews huddled together around someone. He approached the group and was surprised as he recognized his friend, Yankel Zweig.* A moment later he was more astounded when he saw that the man in the center of the group was none other than the Manchester *Rosh Yeshivah* himself, Rav Segal.

"What is the *Rosh Yeshivah* doing here?" R' Asher asked Yankel in amazement.

"I just picked him up from the train station," replied Yankel. "He arrived from Manchester and I was supposed to drive him down to Bournemouth (a vacation area), but when he got in the car he asked if I could bring him here to the hospital so that he could see you. When the *Rosh Yeshivah* came to the front door of the hospital," Yankel continued in a voice of awe, "he stopped in the doorway and said to all of us, 'Let us all say together, הִנְנִי מוּכָן וּמְזוּמָּן לְקַיֵּם מִצְוַת עֲשֵׂה שֶׁל גְּמִילוּת חֲסָדִים, *Behold I am prepared and ready to perform the positive commandment of doing beneficent kindnesses.'* That was the sole purpose of the *Rosh Yeshivah's* coming — just to give you encouragement."

R' Asher hurried to Rav Segal and exclaimed frantically, "The doctors won't operate today. They had a different emergency and so they are making us wait until tomorrow."

Rav Segal took R' Asher's hand in his hands, smiled understandingly and said softly, *"Dehr malach Rafael is gevehn haint farnumen. Morgen vett zein a besseren tug."* ("The angel Raphael [Hashem's angel of healing] was busy today. Tomorrow will be a better day!")

R' Asher held onto Rav Segal's comforting hands and smiled as he felt his tension and trepidation dissipate. If, indeed, as the *Rosh Yeshivah* said, Hashem's healing angel was occupied on this day,

*The name has been changed.

then those being operated on tomorrow surely had a better chance for recovery.

Rav Segal's מַעֲנֶה רַךְ, his sensitive caring sentence, accomplished יָשִׁיב חֵמָה — the elimination of R' Asher's anxiety.

How grateful we must be to the blessed individuals in our nation who know how to calm, comfort and console fellow Jews.

Incidentally, the child had his operation on the following morning, and today he is a fine, healthy boy learning, playing and running like all other boys his age.

On Friendship

Feivel Hauptman* of the Bensonhurst neighborhood of Brooklyn was a *talmid* in Mesivta Tifereth Jerusalem, on Manhattan's Lower East Side, for seven years. He became very close to the *Rosh Yeshivah* and *gadol hador*, Rabbi Moshe Feinstein (1895-1986). Feivel always consulted Reb Moshe on personal and spiritual matters, and Reb Moshe always made it a point to be attentive to his queries.

Eventually Feivel married a girl from Miami, and after two years of *kollel* study, they moved to Florida to join his father-in-law, Murray Wertig,* in the family business. The Wertigs were known for their charity, and less than a year after Feivel moved to Miami, the Wertigs agreed to host Reb Moshe at a parlor meeting to raise funds for his yeshivah.

The parlor meeting was well attended by local people and "snowbirds" from the north, who spent their winters in Florida. The attendees were awed to be in the presence of Reb Moshe. One of the guests was Zalman Plotnick,* an alumnus of the Telshe Yeshiva in Chicago, who had recently married and taught at a day school in Miami. Zalman loved to meet prominent Jews who came to Miami, particularly *roshei yeshivah* and *rebbes*, with whom he would share his latest *chiddush* (innovative Torah thought) and ask

*The name has been changed.

his latest *she'eileh* (halachic question), and from whom he would seek a *berachah* (blessing).

At the parlor meeting, Feivel and Zalman, who had never met before, struck up a conversation. Immediately, they became friends and within days they were inseparable. They began calling each other regularly and meeting whenever possible. Soon their wives knew that if they weren't home they were probably out together, learning or discussing a business venture.

Feivel and his wife had a family that kept increasing, but Zalman and his wife were childless. This situation became increasingly painful for both couples and they avoided discussing the topic. However when Feivel would go to New York to visit Reb Moshe, Zalman would always ask that Feivel mention him and his wife to Reb Moshe, for a blessing to have children.

Twice a year Feivel made his pilgrimage to Reb Moshe, and every time he would ask for a *berachah* for his close friends the Plotnicks. This went on for many years, and each time Reb Moshe would assure Feivel that eventually, with Hashem's help, Zalman and his wife would have children.

Five years after the Plotnicks were married, Feivel had the opportunity to be in New York. He went to the yeshivah to *daven* with Reb Moshe. After *Minchah,* Feivel approached Reb Moshe and said, "I hope the *Rosh Yeshivah* won't be upset with me, and I apologize if I am speaking in a manner that is not appropriate. I come from a *chassidic* background and sometimes when a *chassid* makes a request of his *rebbe* he is a bit more assertive. So I was wondering if perhaps this time the *Rosh Yeshivah* would be so kind as to promise my friend from Miami, *Zalman ben Rachel,* and his wife *Sarah bas Leah,* that they will have children. "

Reb Moshe looked at Feivel sternly and said, "For years, ever since you first came to me with their names, I have kept them in my *tefillos* constantly. The *Ribono Shel Olam* will help and they will have a child — soon!"

Feivel was astounded and overjoyed. Astounded that Reb Moshe had had the Plotnicks on his mind after all this time, and overjoyed at the confidence Reb Moshe had that there would be good news.

Ten months later, the Plotnicks had their first child — a girl.

And twenty years later, that girl became the daughter-in-law of Mr. and Mrs. Feivel Hauptman.

> To this day, Zalman has no idea about his friend's "assertiveness" in speaking to Reb Moshe. But who knows? Perhaps in the merit of Feivel's genuine concern for his friend, the Hauptman and Plotnick families became united forever, as today they share the same grandchildren.

A Time to Weep, A Time to Embrace

On a trip to England, I had the opportunity to meet R' Chaim Honig, of Stamford Hill, who related this deeply moving story. I told it to *mechanchim* (Torah educators) at a Torah Umesorah convention where the theme was: "Reaching the Mind, Spirit and Emotions." This story is a graphic example of that theme.

Reb Yisrael Klein, a saintly man in his 80's, passed away in Jerusalem. Reb Yisrael had been designated by the Belzer Rebbe as the *baal korei* (Torah reader) for his community and over the years he became beloved by the thousands who knew him and heard him read the Torah every Shabbos. Understandably a constant stream of people came to comfort the family during the *shivah*. Every visitor was known to at least one family member.

One evening during the *shivah* a gentleman walked in, tentatively scanned the room for a familiar face, but could not find one. He made his way forward to where Reb Yisrael's sons were sitting and sat down on a chair off to the side. He waited to be acknowledged and then said softly, "I came here tonight because I wanted to tell you a story about your father. I am religious today only because of him."

All who could hear this man's soft words turned their heads in peaked interest. "It was many many years ago," the man began, obviously pained by the memory of the episode. "I was a youngster, maybe 16 years old, in Auschwitz and I was starving. I was going from one garbage heap to another searching desperately for a scrap of food. I couldn't find a thing and I was terrified that I would die from hunger. As I was going from place to place I saw another fellow, a few years older than I, also searching for something. That fellow was Reb Yisrael.

"He came over to me and said, 'What are you looking for?'

" 'I'm starving,' I told him. 'I need some food — anything. Can you give me anything?'

"He looked at me with forlorn eyes and said, 'I, too, am looking for food, but I haven't found any.' Then he came close to me and took me in his arms and embraced me. 'This is what I can give you,' he said, 'a hug — because I love you. And I love you because you are a *Yid* and remember that the *Ribono Shel Olam* also loves you, just because you are a *Yid*.'"

The gentleman dabbed at his eyes as he struggled to continue. "After the war I went through many difficult times and my religious convictions teetered, but I always remembered his warm embrace and special words to me that day. That kept me going. Eventually I came to Israel and settled here. I remained religious only because of him."

The mourners nodded their heads in quiet awe. They hadn't known that story about their father — but they could believe it. Reb Yisrael always had the right words — and the caring heart to deliver them with passion.

The Man Who Came to Dinner

It was *Motza'ei Shabbos* in Flatbush and Mrs. Rochel Halpert's husband Moshe had left for the airport for a business trip to Belgium. About five minutes after he was gone the doorbell rang. Mrs. Halpert thought Moshe had returned to get something, but when she asked over the intercom who was at the door, the answer came back, "A *shaliach*."

Mrs. Halpert thought she misheard the man. "A *meshulach* (a fund collector)?" she asked.

"No," came the reply, "a *shaliach* (messenger)."

"I'm sorry but I can't open the door," Mrs. Halpert said. "My husband is not home. You can come back another time."

"I am not collecting money," the man said, "I have money for you."

Now that's a new twist, thought Mrs. Halpert. A clever way to get someone to open the door. She smiled nervously to herself. "I'm sorry, I can't open the door," she said through the intercom, not falling for the bait.

"But I really do have money for you," the man insisted.

"Well, if that's the case, you can leave it in the mailbox and I'll get it eventually," said Mrs. Halpert.

"Okay, if you insist," said the man. "But do make sure to get it. I will call you tomorrow."

A few minutes later, Mrs. Halpert peeked out the front window. The man was gone. Later that evening she had someone open the mailbox and sure enough there was a $100 bill there. Mrs. Halpert took the money and set it aside. She called her parents later that evening and they too were confounded by the mysterious money.

The next morning the phone rang. "Did you get the money?" a man asked Mrs. Halpert anxiously. "It was my responsibility to see that you get it."

"Yes I did," replied Mrs. Halpert, "but who are you and what is the money for?"

"Well, didn't you get married just before *Pesach,*" the man asked.

"Yes, I got married *Rosh Chodesh Nissan,* but that was six years ago!" said Mrs. Halpert.

"Well, the money is a wedding gift," said the man, "but I know I have to explain."

"I'm listening," said Mrs. Halpert curiously.

"You got married in Terrace on the Park (a wedding hall in Queens, New York) — is that correct?" the man asked.

"Yes."

"You might recall," the man continued, "that your family hired a bus to take your guests from Brooklyn to the wedding. The place where the bus was to pick up the guests was in front of the *Sefardishe Shul* on Fourteenth Ave. in Boro Park. That same night another family was also making a wedding in Queens, in a different wedding hall, and they also hired a bus to take *their* guests to the wedding. Coincidentally, the bus was to meet the guests in front of the *Sefardishe Shul* as well.

"One of the people invited to the other wedding, an elderly gentleman who lived alone, got on the wrong bus by mistake. He was a quiet man who always kept to himself so the fact that he didn't know anyone on the bus didn't surprise him.

"When he arrived at Terrace on the Park, he soon realized that he was at a wedding at which he knew no one. Obviously he was in the wrong place, but he was too embarrassed to say anything to anyone. Knowing that he had no other way to get home except with the bus that would be returning to Boro Park, he stayed for the evening and sat himself at one of the back tables and ate the meal.

"He made a note to himself to send you and your husband a gift. He wrote down both your names on a card, and when he got home he put it in a drawer planning to get to it in the near future.

"It was Nissan and he lost the piece of paper during the *Pesach* cleaning. He always felt bad that he hadn't sent you the gift, and he felt remorse especially for having eaten a meal that he hadn't really been invited to. He wanted to contact your parents to ask forgiveness but he didn't know who they are. Then last week he found the six-year-old piece of paper with the names of yourself and your husband. He was ecstatic. He called me and asked me to locate both of you so that he could give you the belated gift. But he also insisted that I ask you to ask your parents to forgive him for eating that meal.

"Mrs. Halpert, I want to fulfill my assignment. You now have the money, but I need you to call your parents and ask their forgiveness. Would you do that for this gentleman? I'll call you back tonight."

Mrs. Halpert was astounded at the honesty of the elderly gentleman and his commitment to his word and original intentions. She thanked the caller profusely for his efforts and that afternoon she called her parents who readily forgave the man.

A Blessing on Your Head

There are times when an opportunity presents itself for just a fleeting moment. In a flash it is here and then gone, never to be recaptured. How fortunate are those who "seize the moment" and make the most of it. Lives can be changed, friendships can be cemented and the moment cherished forever. This poignant story is a case in point.

Nachum and Hennie Rand* of Boro Park seemed to have everything. He had a wonderful job, they had a beautiful home, were charitable and could travel the world whenever they wished. But there was an emptiness — they had no children. The extent of their pain, anguish and heartache were comprehensible only to those who shared their fate.

After eighteen years of marriage they decided to adopt a young infant. The little girl, Naomi,* was beautiful and brought light to their home. Her smile was radiant, and her future was bright — or so the Rands thought. A little after her second birthday, the Rands noticed that their child was not attentive and hadn't yet begun to say words. They became concerned. Before long they had Naomi diagnosed and found to their dismay that she was autistic.

The Rands dedicated their lives to helping Naomi. They worked with her, gave her boundless love and undivided attention. She had a *neshamah* and they would nurture it however they could. It was an arduous task but they never gave up.

In 1997, Malka Traub,* a high school graduate from a girls school in Lakewood, New Jersey, came to live with the Rands. She had a job in Brooklyn, but commuting from Lakewood to Brooklyn was too strenuous, so she boarded with the Rands in Boro Park. In lieu of rent, she helped Mrs. Rand every night with the autistic girl.

Malka lived with the Rands for four years and could not help but be inspired and awed at the dedication, patience and affection the

*The name has been changed.

Rands had for Naomi. She witnessed levels of compassion and depths of understanding that she never had before and it affected her deeply. In turn, the Rands could not help but be grateful for Malka's assistance, warmth, and care.

In the summer of 2001, Malka got engaged and her family planned an autumn wedding. Naturally the Rands were invited. They knew that their autistic daughter, Naomi, would never get married. Malka's wedding would be the closest they would ever come to participating in the wedding of someone who had become part of their family.

At the wedding, Malka beamed as she sat on the *kallah's* chair, surrounded by her mother, mother-in-law, relatives and friends — and Mrs. Rand, who was there all the while, next to Mrs. Traub. Malka waited anxiously for her *chassan* to come into the room accompanied by his father and father-in-law, engulfed in a wave of friends singing and dancing to the thunderous music heralding the *badekken* — when he would put the veil over her face.

In the distance she could hear the band playing *Od Yishama.* The smiling women huddled around the *kallah,* both mothers trying to hold back their tears of joy. The precious moment was arriving. The singing, thumping dance steps and pounding music grew louder. They entered the room. The *chassan's* smile was radiant. He stepped forward and gently took the veil from on her head and brought it over her face.

Then Malka's father stepped forward and put his hands on her head and blessed her. That is always one of the moving moments of a wedding. Tears filled the eyes of many who watched this tender moment. Mr. Traub swayed as he expressed his deepest heartfelt wishes for his daughter. Mrs. Traub could hardly see out of her moist eyes. As Mr. Traub stepped back, he turned to Mr. Rand, who was standing alongside him. "Please bless my child," he said to Mr. Rand. "You and your wife helped make her what she is."

Startled, Mr. Rand came forward and extended his trembling hands over the *kallah's* head. He never thought he would do this in his life. Only fathers, grandfathers and occasionally great rabbis blessed *kallahs,* and now he too truly felt like a father.

With fervor and feeling he blessed the *kallah.* When he stepped back, he felt validated and significant. He and his wife had made a difference in Malka's life. They would always remember this tender, precious gesture and be forever grateful to the thoughtful father who allowed them to share this cherished moment with him.

Part C:

Achievement and Accomplishment

Transferred for Generations

The 613th and final *mitzvah* of the Torah is writing a *Sefer Torah.* This is deduced from the verse: וְעַתָּה כִּתְבוּ לָכֶם אֶת הַשִּׁירָה הַזֹּאת, *so now write this song for yourselves (Devarim* 31:19*). Rambam* writes that this commandment can be fulfilled by writing even a single letter of a complete Torah scroll. Since the lack of even one letter renders a scroll invalid, writing or correcting a single letter is equal to completing the entire scroll (*Hilchos Sefer Torah* 7:1*).* In order to fulfill this *mitzvah,* people engage a *sofer* (scribe) to write a Torah, or they purchase an existing scroll and leave the last few lines or words blank. Anyone who writes a letter or more to complete the scroll has performed the *mitzvah.*

Perhaps it is fitting that this was the final *mitzvah* that Moshe *Rabbeinu* transmitted to the Jews. There would soon be a new leader at the helm of *Klal Yisrael,* as Yehoshua was about to take the reigns of leadership. Presenting a *Sefer Torah,* especially when it is done by elderly people, has the symbolism of transmitting our heritage to the next generation. The ink may be fresh and the parchment new, but the ageless letters and words remain the same.

New environment? New circumstances? The laws, ideals, and philosophies remain the same. It is the essence of the transmission of Torah. In the following dramatic story we witness this transmission.

The Reichmann family of Toronto is known throughout the world for its integrity, philanthropy, and absolute faith in Hashem and His Torah. Despite the almost unfathomable wealth they had enjoyed, their priorities have remained steadfast, with religious commitment and family values always uppermost in their minds. This conviction stemmed from the patriarch of the family, who set standards for his future generations.

The patriarch was Shmayahu (Samuel) Reichmann. As Mr. Reichmann grew older, he wanted to have a *Sefer Torah* written on his behalf to fulfill the *mitzvah* that few Jews have the opportunity to fulfill, because the cost is great. (Writing a *Sefer Torah* today can cost well over $30,000.) In 1969 Mr. Reichmann commissioned a noted *sofer* in Bnei Brak to write a *Sefer Torah,* but the man was overworked and overburdened, and could not find the time to fully concentrate on the Reichmann project.

When Mr. Reichmann would have family members in Israel go to the *sofer* and urge him to complete the project, he would work on a few more *yerios* (sheets of parchment), but then he would get diverted with other things that he felt were more pressing. It was extremely frustrating, but the Reichmanns stayed with this *sofer* because of his reputation for beautiful handiwork.

Finally, in 1975, the Torah was completed and sent to Toronto in time for *Shavuos*. There could be no more appropriate time, for *Shavuos* commemorates Hashem's giving of the Torah at Mount Sinai. Plans were made for the Torah to be brought with pomp and ceremony on the first day of *Shavuos* to the Yeshivah Yesodei HaTorah. There would be a procession where the Torah would be carried, as family, friends and community members joined with song and dance. (See *Orach Chaim* 494:3, *Shaarei Teshuvah* note 7.)

The first day of *Shavuos* in 1975 was on a Friday. The day before, Mr. Reichmann, with the help of a local *sofer,* completed the *Sefer Torah,* by filling in the final letters. Ordinarily a calm and level person, Mr. Reichmann was visibly excited at the opportunity to present a *Sefer Torah* on *Shavuos.* On the first day of *Shavuos* the police closed off the blocks of Dalemount Avenue, where Mr. Reichmann lived. A meeting place was set up at the intersection of Dalemount and Fairholme Avenues. At about 9:50 a.m., about a hundred *balabatim* and children left Yesodei HaTorah and walked behind five men, each of whom was carrying a *Sefer Torah* and marching down

Fairholme Avenue toward the Reichmann home. They sang as they walked, regaling in the delight of the moment. At 9:55 a.m. Reb Shmayahu Reichmann, accompanied by his children and grandchildren, carried the new *Sefer Torah* from his home and walked majestically down Dalemount Avenue toward the crowd that would greet him at the designated corner.

At exactly 10 o'clock, just as planned, the two groups fused. Mr. Reichmann stood for a moment holding the Torah scroll — and suddenly turned to his son, Moshe, saying, "I don't feel well."

He handed the Torah to his son, collapsed on the spot and died!

The patriarch had delivered his message as he fulfilled the last *mitzvah*. He had transmitted the Torah to Moshe — and he and his siblings have bequeathed the message to their children and grandchildren that resonates in the family to this day.

On that very spot — where R' Shmayahu completed his *mesorah,* a yeshivah and *beis midrash* were built. It is appropriately called "Zichron Shmayahu."

One More Hello

Years ago people would talk of ordinary men and women who had *"emunah peshutah"* (simple uncomplicated faith). Often the so-called wise academians and bookish intellectuals were the ones with the most questions and the most doubts about religion. Frequently it was the unassuming Jew who had complete faith in Hashem and served Him with devotion and dedication. This is the type of Jew who is the hero of this story. There is much to learn from him.

In 1975, one of the more popular camps in the Catskills was Camp Kol Rina in Livingston Manor. It was owned and directed by the noted *talmid chacham* and psychologist, Rabbi Dr. Yaakov Greenwald of Monsey.

Camps are always looking for new ideas, so one evening the staff met to explore innovations in their summer program. They sought an activity that would create excitement and involvement, and that would enrich the religious life of the campers. One of the staff members was from England, where he had been a counselor in the Agudah boys camp. "We have a special day every summer called *Kiddush Hashem Day,*" he said. "Every bunk has to try and make a *kiddush Hashem* — each on his own level."

The staff thought it was a wonderful idea and they implemented it. One of the younger bunks put on a skit for the residents of a local nursing home; another bunk went to a shopping center where they helped people carry their packages to the parking lot; and a third bunk helped construction workers at a reservoir work site.

That summer Rabbi Hillel David of Brooklyn gave *shiurim* to staff members and Rabbi Lipa Geldwerth of Brooklyn was one of the *rebbeim* of the campers. Upon hearing the idea of *Kiddush Hashem Day,* Rabbi David said to Rabbi Geldwerth, "There is a *shul* here in Livingston Manor that I often drive by. It's always locked with rusty chains and looks as if it hasn't been used in years. I think it would be a beautiful thing if there could be a *minyan* in that *shul* one more time. Perhaps we could clean it up or even make some repairs and *daven* there. It would be a *kiddush Hashem.* I'm sure the builders of the *shul* were special people because it was built with twelve windows." [According to the *Zohar* there is Kabbalistic significance in building a *shul* with twelve windows (see *Orach Chaim* 90:4). Perhaps it symbolizes that Hashem accepts the prayers of all Jews, as represented by the twelve tribes.]

Rabbi Geldwerth agreed that it was a fine idea and enlisted the oldest bunk to carry it out. They were to get the local phone book and call people who had Jewish names like Adler, Cohen, Gibber, Goldberg, Kramer, Lichtman, Pfeiffer, Perlstein, Silverberg, and so on. Every man who answered the phone was to be asked if he would join a *minyan* that would be held on a designated day. The boys in the oldest bunk were already *bar mitzvah* and they would join the *minyan* too, so there would surely be at least ten people.

Rabbi Geldwerth made numerous calls and was able to locate the man who had the keys to the *shul*. A morning was chosen for everyone to gather there. That morning Rabbis David and Geldwerth, the boys of the oldest bunk plus a few older men from the area came to the *shul*. It was set back from the street and draped by tall trees that in years gone by had provided comforting shade for playful nursery children, giddy *bar-mitzvah* boys, handsome grooms, elegant brides, proud grandparents and saddened mourners.

One man wore a homemade cardboard yarmulke, another man was wearing only his *tefillin shel yad,* a third person sat bewildered staring blankly at an old *siddur.* There was one man, however, who had his own *siddur* and wore his *tallis* and *tefillin* as though he wore them every day, and was totally familiar with the *davening.* He was the one who had the keys to the *shul*. Rabbi David told Rabbi Geldwerth to ask him to serve as *baal tefillah* and lead the services. "Do you think he will want to?" asked Rabbi Geldwerth.

Rabbi David said, "I have been a rav for many years. I can tell who likes to *daven* before the *amud.*" Sure enough, when Rabbi Geldwerth asked the gentleman he readily accepted.

After the *davening,* Rabbi Geldwerth approached the *baal tefillah* and complimented him on his *davening.* The man, Mr. Izzy Brooks, told Rabbi Geldwerth that he had not missed a Monday or Thursday *minyan,* when they read from the Torah, since the First World War! "But isn't the *shul* closed?" asked Rabbi Geldwerth.

"Ever since our *shul* closed," Izzy said, "I drive twice a week to the *shul* in Liberty in my truck."

"But this *shul* seems so clean, almost immaculate," said Rabbi Geldwerth. "And what about the *Ezras Torah* calendar on the back wall. I see it's turned to the right page for this month. Who does that? When we drive by this *shul* it is always locked. What is the story of this *shul?*"

Izzy Brooks sighed and recounted the history of the *shul* with a mixture of pride and sadness. "In 1907 my father came with our family from the town of Suvalk (Lithuania) to Brooklyn. But the air pollution was too much for him so we moved to New Jersey. That wasn't good either so we came up here to Ferndale and then Livingston Manor."

In those days, Izzy explained, there were more than thirty farms owned by Jews in the area and that there was a *minyan* three times a day, as everyone took turns *davening* in different farms on a rotating basis.

Izzy continued. "After a while my father said that it's not right that we don't have a regular *shul* to daven in. He was a carpenter and so one day he and I began building this *shul*. It got finished in 1912. We had a *minyan* here every single day, throughout the First World War, throughout the Depression, until the Second World War.

"During the war many of the young boys were drafted into the army and it began getting hard to have the *minyan*. After the war, many of the boys did not make it back, and some of those who made it back were no longer religious and didn't care to come to *shul*. So we struggled with the daily *minyan*. Then we could have a *minyan* only on Shabbos. The last time we had a *minyan* on Shabbos was in 1955. From then on the *shul* is open only twice a year. Once on *Yom Kippur* and the second time ... on *Purim* — for the party." Izzy was embarrassed to reveal that the *shul* he loved was not even open on *Rosh Hashanah.*

"But the *shul* is so clean. We thought we might come in and clean it," said Rabbi Geldwerth. "And what about the calendar?"

Izzy felt self-conscious. The rabbis were listening, some of the boys had come over and were listening as well. "You see," he began slowly. "I am the only one with the keys. Every *erev Rosh Chodesh* I come here alone and wipe off all the dust from the tables, the chairs and the *Aron Kodesh* (the Holy Ark). Then, before I leave, I turn the page on the calendar to the right month. I do it because this is the place where G-d lives. You see, the *Ribono Shel Olam* still has His soldiers."

> Izzy Brooks never had yeshivah training. Yet his dignified care and concern for Hashem's dwelling place in this world educates us all. In that respect he was a sage after all.

Of Baltimore Bills and Denver Dollars

Parashas Terumah is the Torah portion that describes Hashem's request to Moshe *Rabbeinu* that Jews donate funds for the building of the *Mishkan* (Tabernacle in the desert). When the *parashah* was read in 1999, Rabbi Jonathan Aryeh Seidemann of Kehillah B'nai Torah synagogue in Baltimore, Maryland, told this story to his Shabbos afternoon *Chumash* class; the story involved his father-in-law, Rabbi Myer Schwab.

Rabbi Schwab is the founder and dean of the Bais Yaakov High School of Denver, Colorado. He is also responsible for the financial stability of the school, and in this role he often meets with philanthropists, to enlist their support. In the early 1970's there was a millionaire in Denver, an elderly gentleman named Max Rabinowitz* who had remained a *shomer Shabbos* even though most of his friends and family were not. He gave charity, but his parameters for giving were not in proportion to his wealth. He considered $500 a large donation, when in reality he could easily have given ten times that amount. His children were independently wealthy, he owned factories and real estate, but he could not part with large sums of money except for business investments. Indeed the most Max ever donated to the yeshivah of Denver or the Bais Yaakov was $500.

One morning as Rabbi Schwab was teaching a class, he was interrupted by his secretary. "I am sorry to disturb you," she said with urgency, "but you have an extremely important phone call."

Reluctant to stop the lesson, Rabbi Schwab asked the secretary if the call could possibly wait till later. "No," she said, "they are calling from the hospital."

Rabbi Schwab rushed to his office and picked up the phone. It was Max Rabinowitz. "Rabbi," he said. "I must see you right away."

Six months earlier, Max had asked Rabbi Schwab to get him a *siddur* that contained *Viduy* (the Confessional prayer recited on a

*The name has beed changed.

deathbed), and Rabbi Schwab had brought him Rabbi Yaakov Emdin's *siddur (Bais Yaakov).* Now, on the phone, Max pleaded with Rabbi Schwab to come immediately. "By this afternoon, it will be too late," Max said softly.

When Rabbi Schwab came to Max's room, the family was gathered at his bedside. After Rabbi Schwab greeted all those present, Max asked everyone to leave the room. Slowly and carefully, Rabbi Schwab recited with Max the poignant words of *Viduy.* When they finished, silence enveloped the room. Then Max said softly, "I remember when I was a little boy there was a *maggid* who came to our town. He spoke of the importance of giving charity and he mentioned over and over the expression צְדָקָה תַּצִּיל מִמָּוֶת, *Charity rescues from death.* Before my end I would like to fulfill that *mitzvah* and be clear with G-d. I have prepared two checks: one for your Bais Yaakov and the other for the yeshivah (Toras Chaim in Denver). Please take them out of the drawer and deliver them."

Rabbi Schwab thought hopefully that perhaps his budgetary problems for the year might be over. He opened the top drawer of the cabinet and took out the two checks. He could not believe his eyes. Each check was for $500.

Rabbi Schwab stared at the checks and was incredulous. "Max," he exclaimed, "you have the opportunity to acquire a share in *Olam Haba* (The World to Come) as you never did before. Our Bais Yaakov is now housed in trailers. We need a building. Max, give us $50,000 and we'll put your name on the building as an everlasting testimony to your charity. You'll be helping hundreds of girls who are the future mothers of our people. This is your last chance."

Max thought for a long moment and then said in Yiddish, "*Glaib mir, mine hartz vill, und mine kup farshteit, uhber der hant lust zich nisht efenen.*" ("Believe me, my heart wants [to give the charity] and my head understands [that it is the right thing to do] — but my hand refuses to let itself be opened.")

Max died that night forever bereft of the opportunity of magnanimous eternal reward.

Days later Rabbi Schwab defined this episode. He said, "In discussing a man's reluctance to give charity, the Torah warns, לֹא תְאַמֵּץ

אֶת לְבָבְךָ וְלֹא תִקְפֹּץ אֶת יָדְךָ, *You shall not harden your heart or close your hand (Devarim* 15:7*).* The Torah says that there are two parts to the *mitzvah* of *tzedakah,* the heart and the hand. A man can understand that his financial help is needed and that a situation is indeed dire, but if he is not trained from his earliest years to open his hand to benefit others, he will find it all but impossible to part with his money."

When Rabbi Seidemann finished this story, he said to his congregants, "A person has to have a special merit to give charity. Max could have earned eternal reward for his philanthropy, but he passed up the chance. We, while we are on this world, should not lose the opportunity when its presents itself. "

After the class, one of the attendees, Mrs. Gretta Golden, said to Rabbi Seidemann, "Rabbi you told this story in the past. You mentioned it at a Shabbos *Chumash* class three years ago!"

"And you remember it from then?" asked Rabbi Seidemann, surprised and complimented that someone would remember something that he had said years ago.

"Oh yes," she said, "I remember that story so well. It made such an impression on me. And Rabbi," she added, "I should really tell you a story about that story."

Mrs. Golden was employed by the world-renowned Johns Hopkins Hospital in Baltimore, where she was a marketing representative of international services. She headed the Israeli unit. Since Johns Hopkins is one of the finest hospitals in the world, it attracts patients from around the globe.

Just two weeks after Mrs. Golden first heard the story from Rabbi Seidemann, an Israeli family came to Johns Hopkins with their 8-year-old son who needed major surgery. They brought along all the boy's medical files and explained to Mrs. Golden that they could not afford to pay for the operation the child so desperately needed.

As she leafed through the boy's files, his father said that a few months earlier a relative of theirs had suggested that they write a letter to a certain Jewish philanthropist who had been written up in *The New York Times*. "You have nothing to lose," said the relative, and indeed they found someone to write a letter in English, explaining their child's desperate situation. A few weeks later the family received a reply from the philanthropist wishing their son a complete recovery but adding that he could not help financially. This letter was in the file along with the medical records.

Mrs. Golden read and reread the letter and thought of the story she had heard from her rabbi. That night she composed a letter to this philanthropist, explained the nature of her work and detailed the situation of the little Israeli boy. She finished the letter with the story about Max Rabinowitz and his inability to give charity even at the end of his life.

Mrs. Golden's final sentence in the letter was, "Don't let that man be you."

Two weeks later Johns Hopkins received a check of over $40,000 from that philanthropist to cover the entire cost of the operation!

When Rabbi Seidemann told me these stories he said, "You can never tell what happens when you tell an inspirational story. I told the story of my father-in-law once and look how an Israeli family was helped. And I never would have known about it except that I told the story a second time three years later. Stories can be so motivating."

I agree.

The Maximum From the Minimum

The commitment and level of adherence that parents show in their performance of *mitzvos* is frequently an indication of how their children will fulfill those same *mitzvos*. The sacrifice parents make to perform a particular *mitzvah* often leaves an indelible impression on their children. This memorable story told to me by Rabbi Shlomo Jakobovits, principal of the Eitz Chaim network of schools in Toronto, is a case in point. Rabbi Jakobovits' brother was the late Rabbi Lord Immanuel Jakobovits, Chief Rabbi of the British Empire.

In the 1930's the Jakobovitses lived in the Neuklon section of Berlin. Their father, Rav Yoel, was a noted *talmid chacham* and a respected *dayan* (rabbinical judge). Whenever the family had to relocate to a new apartment, Rav Yoel would inspect the balcony to see if there were any impediments to a kosher *succah* such as a balcony directly overhead, or tree branches covering his own balcony. This would invalidate the *succah,* for the *s'chach* must lie directly beneath unobstructed sky (see *Orach Chaim* 626).

Furthermore, Rabbi Jakobovits always had a clause inserted in the lease specifying that he could build a *succah* on the balcony. Although he knew that German landlords would not be keen on having a visible Jewish object such as a *succah* built on their property, he also knew their mentality: Germans would not renege on a signed agreement. A contract was a contract.

In October of 1938, virulent storm winds of anti-Semitism were rampant. Every day Jews would hear about their brothers and sisters being carted off to the concentration camps in Dachau and Buchenwald. At that time the general consensus among Jews was that their brethren were merely being imprisoned; no one could have imagined the horrifying atrocities that were in store.

Nazi storm troopers roamed the streets of Berlin and Jews could be dragged off at any time to be sent away. However, *Succos* was approaching and it was unthinkable for Rabbi Jakobovits to eat his *Yom Tov* meals outside a *succah.* His balcony on the third floor faced the street below and was glaringly visible to all passersby. If Heaven forbid Nazi soldiers saw the *succah,* they could charge upstairs, ransack the premises, and cart the family off to police headquarters — or worse.

Rav Yoel considered his options. He closed his eyes in thought and then had an idea. He measured the height of the surrounding wall of the balcony. It was a little more than forty-four inches —

approximately eleven *tefachim* (handbreadths). The minimum permissible height of a *succah* is ten *tefachim,* approximately forty inches (*Orach Chaim* 633:2). Rav Yoel could build a *succah* ten *tefachim* high, cover it with *s'chach* and still be below the forty-four inch height of the wall. No one would be able to see his *succah* from the street.

The Jakobovitses were concerned that their neighbors on higher floors might inform Nazi authorities about the *succah,* but Rav Yoel was willing to take that perilous chance. Aside from his determination to fulfill the *mitzvah,* he had always been on good terms with the upstairs neighbors. He prayed they would not betray him.

His prayers were answered. Rav Yoel indeed built a *succah* that was all of ten *tefachim* high (forty inches!), and today, more than sixty years later, Rabbi Shlomo Jakobovits recalls with pride how his family crawled on their knees into that tiny *succah* on the balcony on Elizabeth Ulfer Street and ate all their meals sitting on pillows, observing Hashem's commandment in an unforgettable manner.

The very next month, in November 1938, the Nazi barbarians rampaged Jewish communities on the infamous afternoon and evening forever to be known as *Kristallnacht.* Throughout Germany and Austria, hundreds of synagogues and Jewish homes and businesses were looted and burned. Afterwards, tens of thousands of Jews tried to escape the clutches of the savage Nazis. Most Jews could not leave, but the Jakobovits family was granted Hashem's protection and was able to flee.

Succos commemorates Hashem's sheltering of Israel during their travels in the wilderness for forty years after having left Egypt (see *Vayikra* 23:43). Perhaps it was the Jakobovits' adherence to the *mitzvah* of *Succah* under such dangerous circumstances that merited their shelter and refuge.

David *HaMelech* wrote: כִּי יִצְפְּנֵנִי בְּסֻכֹּה בְּיוֹם רָעָה יַסְתִּרֵנִי בְּסֵתֶר אָהֳלוֹ, *He will safeguard me in His shelter on the day of distress, He will conceal me in the concealment of His tent (Tehillim* 27:5*). Metzudas David* comments: בְּיוֹם בּוֹא הָאוֹיֵב

הִסְתִּירֵנִי בְּסוּכָּתוֹ וְלֹא יָכְלוּ לִי, *On the day the enemy came, He protected me in His succah, so that they could not defeat me.*

A *succah* offers protection — in more ways than we sometimes imagine.

Shortly after his escape, Rabbi Jakobovits began reciting the רִבּוֹן כָּל הָעוֹלָמִים (*Master of All Worlds*) prayer every Friday night after *Shalom Aleichem.* Though German Jews do not customarily recite this prayer, he decided to do so because he was so grateful for his fortunate escape and so moved by the words that expressed his feelings: מוֹדֶה אֲנִי לְפָנֶיךָ ד׳ אֱלֹקַי וֵאלֹקֵי אֲבוֹתַי עַל כָּל הַחֶסֶד אֲשֶׁר עָשִׂיתָ עִמָּדִי וַאֲשֶׁר אַתָּה עָתִיד לַעֲשׂוֹת עִמִּי וְעִם כָּל בְּנֵי בֵיתִי, *I thank you, Hashem, my God and the God of my forefathers, for all the kindness You have done with me, and which you will do with me, and with all my household.* That supplication remained a poignant Friday night ritual with him for the rest of his life.

Covenants

In the late 1940's an elderly gentleman came from *Eretz Yisrael* to deliver a letter to Rabbi Chaim Shereshevsky from his father, Rav Yosef, who lived in Jerusalem. Reb Chaim was a highly regarded *talmid chacham,* known already in the Mirrer Yeshiva when it had been in Poland and Shanghai. After the war he came to New York where he was a *mechanech* in yeshivos and Bais Yaakovs for close to four decades.

Reb Chaim was thrilled to get the letter and invited the elderly gentleman for some cake and coffee. In conversation, the man told a remarkable story. In subsequent years Reb Chaim would tell the story often. I thank his brother-in-law R' Moshe Heller for sharing it with me.

During the early 1900's Rabbi Yosef Chaim Sonnenfeld (1848-1932) served as Chief Rabbi of Jerusalem. He lived in the Old City but would travel anywhere to perform a *bris.* He had learned *milah* from his *rebbi,* Rav Avraham Shaag (1801-1876). (See ArtScroll's *Guardian of Jerusalem,* pp. 210-211.) One day, Reb Yosef Chaim was asked to perform a *bris* on an infant whose parents lived in one of the poverty-stricken areas of the city. On the designated day, he made his way to the neighborhood of the young couple. He knew there would be very few people at the *bris,* for the family had no money to tender a *seudah* (festive meal) afterwards.

As Reb Yosef Chaim entered the courtyard of the apartment complex he heard a baby cry. The sound was coming from the building where the *bris* was to be. He followed the voice and knocked on the door.

A young woman answered the door. "*Mazel tov,*" said Reb Yosef Chaim. "I am here to do the *bris* for your son."

"*Oy, Rebbi,*" sighed the woman. "I only wish you were in the right house!"

Seeing the great rabbi unexpectedly, the woman started crying. "*Rebbi,* I have been married so many years and my husband and I have no children. *Rebbi,* please bless me." Then she added, "The child is next door; it's my neighbor who had the baby."

She turned away, wiping her tears in embarrassment for her brazenness in asking the great *tzaddik* for a *berachah* (blessing). She was ashamed that she had broken down and had revealed her plight.

Reb Yosef Chaim felt terrible that he had been the cause of the woman's anguish. By walking into the wrong apartment he had inadvertently brought forth her sad situation.

Reb Yosef Chaim said softly and compassionately, "I give you a *berachah* that I should come back to your home next year and it won't be a mistake. It will be for a *simchah.*"

A year later, the woman had a little boy, and Reb Yosef Chaim was called to perform the *bris.* It was the only child the woman ever had.

The old man sitting in the Shereshevsky home, said, "I know that every word in the story is true. My mother was that woman and I am that child!"

Unfortunately, some of the world's greatest *Roshei Yeshivah* have to leave their study halls to collect funds for their institutions. Ideally, they should be able to remain with their *talmidim*, teaching and guiding them, unperturbed by financial burdens. However, often it is only their personal prestige and presence that encourage people to donate generously, so they are compelled to be "on the road."

Yet, precisely because they must travel abroad, the public has an opportunity to come face to face with Torah greatness. Perhaps this is why Hashem ordained that this be their fate. The multitudes of Jews who live far from a yeshivah atmosphere draw inspiration from the visits of these great Jews whom they would otherwise never see. Whether it was Rav Meir Shapiro (1887-1934) or Rav Boruch Ber Leibowitz (1870-1941) in earlier generations, or Rav Aharon Kotler (1881-1962) and Rav Yitzchak Ruderman (1900-1987) more recently, the encounters with them were always memorable.

For the *Roshei Yeshivah* themselves, however, it is never easy. I once heard that the Ponevezher Rav, Rabbi Yosef Kahaneman (1886-1969), the great founder of the Ponevezher Yeshiva in Bnei Brak, Israel, once remarked that every time he knocked on someone's door to raise money for his yeshivah, he secretly wished that the person would not be at home. This would spare him the embarrassment of having to ask someone for funds.

Raising money, even for a universally accepted cause, is often tinged with humiliation and uneasiness. It is not pleasant to have to ask others for money. One can imagine the reward in store for those who greet fundraisers with warmth and respect. The following story told by Rabbi Yitzchak Zilberstein at his *Chumash shiur* in Bnei Brak (*Tuv'cha Yabi'u,* Vol. 2, p. 247) is a case in point.

Rav Elchonon Wasserman (1875-1941) often traveled to raise funds for his yeshivah, Ohel Torah in Baranovich. One of the people he visited regularly was the wealthy philanthropist, Reb Binyamin Beinish Dennis of Charkov, whose home was adorned with beautiful furniture, draperies and carpeting. Reb Binyamin Beinish always welcomed Rav Elchonon warmly and responded generously.

One winter night, Rav Elchonon made his way to Reb Binyamin Beinish's home. There had been a raging snowstorm a few days earlier followed by a dreary, pelting rain. The streets that evening were filthy with blackened slush. Rav Elchonon's boots, trousers and coat were dirtied by the high, wet muck. Knowing that his boots would soil the expensive carpeting in the Dennis home, Reb Elchonon decided to enter through the back door. The kitchen was tiled rather than carpeted, so it could be mopped easily.

Reb Elchonon knocked on the back door. When Reb Binyamin Beinish saw him, he understood immediately why the great sage had not come in through the front entrance. "Reb Elchonon," Reb Binyamin Beinish called out. "You've ruined my two daughters!"

"What are you talking about?" Reb Elchonon replied. "I don't know your daughters. I never even saw them. What do you mean I ruined them?"

"All their years I have told them, time and again, that there is nothing more important than *kavod haTorah* (honoring the Torah). The carpeting, the couches, the curtains — they are all nothing, just superficial trimmings. I beg you, come through the front, tread through the living room with your dirty shoes and sit on my couch with your soiled coat. I want my daughters to see that it is you and your Torah I honor, not the household furnishings. Wall to wall carpet is meaningless compared to wall to wall *kavod haTorah.*"

Reb Elchonon had no choice but to come in through the front entrance, tread through the living room with his muddy shoes, and sit on the couch with his wet coat. Reb Binyamin Beinish made Reb Elchonon feel comfortable, served him tea and after an animated conversation, gave Rav Elchonon his customary large donation.

Many years later, after having escaped from Communist Russia to a temporary dwelling in Hamburg, Germany, Reb Binyamin Beinish and his family came to live in Petach Tikvah, Israel. There, he once said to his dear friend, Rabbi Yitzchak Greenberg, "Today I no longer have any money. During the Communist Revolution the Bolsheviks robbed everything I had and forced me to flee the country. But two precious diamonds they could never steal from me. Those diamonds are my wondrous sons-in-law, who became the *Roshei Yeshivah* of Telshe (Rabbi Avraham Yitzchak Bloch who married Rasya Dennis and his brother Rabbi Zalmen Bloch who married Luba Rachel Dennis). They taught Torah to multitudes. That is real wealth."

Indeed, *Chazal* teach: דְּמוֹקִיר רַבָּנָן הָווּ לֵיהּ חֲתַנְוָותָא רַבָּנָן, *One who honors Torah sages will have sons-in-law who are Torah sages (Shabbos* 23b*).* The Dennis daughters, Rasya and Luba Rachel, together with their esteemed husbands, built Torah families of prominence and majesty. Each of them had two daughters who married *Roshei Yeshivah* who blazed the trail of Torah learning in America, bringing to these shores the highest levels of *hasmadah* (diligence), *yegiah* (toil), *amkus* (depth) and *havanah* (understanding) of Torah.

Rebbetzin Rasya's daughter Rachel married Rav Baruch Sorotzkin (1917-1979) and her daughter Chaya married Rav Aizik Ausband. Rebbetzin Luba Rachel's daughter Shoshana married Rav Mordechai Gifter (1917-2001) and her daughter Naomi married Rav Pesach Stein.

This great Torah dynasty, which reestablished the Telshe Yeshiva in Cleveland, Ohio, sprouted its first roots in an atmosphere created in Charkov, where a wealthy father taught his children what *real* wealth was. Generations later, thousands throughout the Torah world are the beneficiaries.

Courtroom Drama

In the spring of 1999, Rabbi Mattisyahu Salomon, the *Mashgiach* of Beth Medrash Govoha in Lakewood, New Jersey, came to Kew

Gardens Hills and spoke about the significance of *tefillah.* He posed the following question:

"The *Shulchan Aruch* (O.C. 124:7) writes: לֹא יָשִׂיחַ שִׂיחַת חוּלִין בְּשָׁעָה שֶׁשְּׁלִיחַ צִבּוּר חוֹזֵר הַתְּפִילָּה וְאִם שָׂח הוּא חוֹטֵא וְגָדוֹל עֲוֹנוֹ מִנְּשׂוֹא, *One should not make idle conversation or discuss mundane matters while the shaliach tzibbur is repeating the Shemoneh Esrei, and if one does speak, he is a sinner, and his transgression is too great to bear.*

"The powerful expression: גָּדוֹל עֲוֹנוֹ מִנְּשׂוֹא, *this transgression is too great to bear,* is not found anywhere else in the entire *Shulchan Aruch!"* exclaimed Rabbi Salomon. "Not by the laws of *kashrus* (kosher food), nor by the laws of *chillul Shabbos* (desecration of the Sabbath). We find the expression only once in the entire Torah and that is when Cain, after committing the first murder in history, pleads with Hashem for forgiveness, and exclaims, גָּדוֹל עֲוֹנִי מִנְּשׂוֹא, *Is my transgression too great to bear?"* (*Bereishis* 4:13).

How then can the *Shulchan Aruch* proclaim that talking during the recitation of the *Shemoneh Esrei* is such an enormous transgression? Doesn't this seem to be an exaggeration? I was intrigued by this question and days later I thought that perhaps the *Shulchan Aruch's* wording can be understood with the following illustration.

Imagine a solemn courtroom where a man is on trial. As the lawyer pleads his client's case, the client begins chatting and joking with a friend. Noticing the client's lack of attention and interest, the judge becomes furious, thinking, "If he doesn't care what the lawyer says on his behalf, why should I care?"

The judge is patient and waits for the defendant to be quiet. However, another few moments go by and the client waves to a passerby and then answers a call on his cellphone, all while his lawyer is still trying to defend him. The judge becomes even more irritated and roars to the client, "Get out of my courtroom! I will have nothing to do with you! If you don't care about your case, I certainly don't care!"

The *Shemoneh Esrei,* particularly the section of requests, is phrased in the plural: וְחָנֵּנוּ ... דֵּעָה בִּינָה וְהַשְׂכֵּל, *Endow* ***us*** *graciously [with wisdom];* וְקָרְבֵנוּ ... לַעֲבוֹדָתֶךָ, *Bring* ***us*** *back [to your service];* סְלַח לָנוּ, *Forgive* ***us;*** רְפָאֵנוּ, *Heal* ***us;*** בָּרֵךְ עָלֵינוּ ... לְטוֹבָה, *Bless* ***us*** *[with pros-*

*perity]; שְׁמַע קוֹלֵנוּ, Hear **our** voice.* Thus, the *shaliach tzibbur* is in a sense our lawyer as he pleads to the Supreme Judge on our behalf.

If we make idle conversation and show a lack of interest in our "lawyer's" words, it is understandable that the Judge will separate Himself from the case and thereby break His connection with us. If that happens, and our connection to Hashem is severed, Heaven forbid, then that is indeed גָדוֹל עֲוֹנוֹ מִנְשׂוֹא, a *transgression too great to bear.*

No wonder the *Mishnah Berurah* (ibid. note 26) cites the *Shelah HaKadosh* who writes that conscientious people hold their *siddur* during the repetition of the *Shemoneh Esrei* and follow the *shaliach tzibbur* word for word. It shows interest, and will pay dividends.

On the Money

Rabbi Avraham Asher Zimmerman (1915-1996) was a highly regarded *posek* (halachic authority). Born in New York, he traveled to Europe in 1933 to study under the legendary Rabbi Elchonon Wasserman (1875-1941) in Yeshiva Ohel Torah in Baranovich. Reb Elchonon regarded the young American *masmid* (diligent student) and his parents, R' Yosef Yehoshua and Shaina Rachel, so highly that he stayed in their Williamsburg home when he visited America in 1939.

Reb Asher was a man of impeccable integrity whose rulings were decisive, firm and uncompromising. He remained home throughout the summer, not taking a vacation, so that there would be at least one rav in the community who was available to answer *halachic* questions. He was a revered rabbi, a noted *Rosh Yeshivah* for over forty years, first in Yeshiva Rabbeinu Chaim Berlin and then in Yeshivas Birkas Reuven, and he served as a chaplain at the Brookdale Medical Center in Brooklyn for more than twenty years.

The following incident is testimony to his meticulous honesty. In his later years Rabbi Zimmerman was once hospitalized in

Brookdale. During his stay there, a doctor checking Rabbi Zimmerman found something that needed immediate attention, but could only be done at Maimonides Medical Center, several miles away. The doctor instructed that Rabbi Zimmerman be transferred to Maimonides at once. Attendants went to the rabbi's room and informed him that he was being transferred immediately.

"Wait a minute," exclaimed Rabbi Zimmerman. "Don't you see that I'm wearing a Brookdale hospital gown? Who is going to bring it back from Maimonides? To take a gown from a hospital is *geneivah* (stealing)! Unless you promise to bring the gown back here you'll have to wait until I change to street clothes."

The astonished attendants knew that the transfer had to be done without delay, so they promised Rabbi Zimmerman they would indeed bring the gown back to Brookdale. Only then did Rabbi Zimmerman agree to the transfer.

The following story about Rabbi Zimmerman was told by his son, Reb Eliyahu, who repeats it with awe.

After Rabbi Zimmerman passed away, his family was discussing his financial matters. His wife, Mrs. Miriam Zimmerman, recalled, "Years ago someone approached Daddy for a $5,000 loan but we didn't have the money to lend him. Daddy lent him $1,000 and told him that he would cosign a loan for the other $4,000. Henoch Rimler* agreed to lend the fellow the $4,000 only if Daddy would cosign the loan. It is years since that loan took place. The fellow paid us back a mere $100 of the thousand he owes us, and he never gave a penny to Mr. Rimler. I think we should give some money to Mr. Rimler because the loan is long overdue." The Zimmermans knew that the lender did not have the means to pay any money back.

A discussion ensued. At first it was suggested that the family would pay Mr. Rimler $1,000 to begin payment of the loan. After

*The name has been changed.

more discussion, however, it was decided to pay the entire amount. "Mr. Rimler has waited long enough," one of the children said, "it's only right that we should pay off the entire loan."

A few days later Mrs. Zimmerman and one of her children went to Mr. Rimler's home. "I've come to pay back the loan that my husband cosigned for several years ago," said Mrs. Zimmerman.

"I never asked you for the money," protested Mr. Rimler. "Your husband was a *tzaddik.* He knew as I did that the fellow he co-signed for would most likely not pay the loan, but I gave the fellow the money anyway because I knew how much it meant to your husband. You don't have to pay me. It's years already and I just about forgot the whole thing," said Mr. Rimler.

"But I insist on paying," said Mrs. Zimmerman. "My husband was a man of his word and if he said he would be responsible for the money he would have kept his word. I know that he would want me to pay you."

Mr. Rimler knew that Mrs. Zimmerman was right. Rabbi Asher Zimmerman was a man of the utmost integrity. His self discipline in *halachic* matters was firm and uncompromising. Mr. Rimler knew that if Rabbi Zimmerman were alive he would have no choice but to accept the money.

Reluctantly he took the money from Mrs. Zimmerman. As she was about to leave Mr. Rimler called out, "Wait, don't you want the IOU that your husband wrote?" (Once a loan is paid it is forbidden for a lender to keep the *shtar* of the loan in his home for he might be tempted to, or erroneously try to, collect the loan again.)

"I guess you're right," said Mrs. Zimmerman. "Do you still have it?"

"I think I know where it is," said Mr. Rimler. "I haven't looked at it in years."

When Mr. Rimler found the IOU and gave it to Mrs. Zimmerman, they read it and were astounded. Rabbi Zimmerman had written, "I accept responsibility to pay $4,000 if the loan is not paid by the borrower. I will try and complete all payments by *erev Rosh Chodesh Elul* 5759."

Incredibly, that day was *erev Rosh Chodesh Elul* 5759.

No one had remembered that he wrote a date by which the loan would be paid. Only by Hashem's orchestration had the Zimmermans paid back the loan just in time.

David *HaMelech* writes: ה׳ אֹהֵב צַדִּיקִים, *Hashem loves the righteous (Tehillim* 146:8*)*. In His love for Rabbi Zimmerman, Hashem saw to it that his honesty remained intact even after his passing.

The next verse written by David *HaMelech* is equally telling: יָתוֹם וְאַלְמָנָה יְעוֹדֵד, *He encourages orphan and widow* (ibid. 146:9). Indeed, the Zimmermans were comforted and inspired that their actions, though unintentional, were timed so incredibly.

A Cup of Blessing

Every year during the Nine Days (the period from *Rosh Chodesh Av* until *Tishah B'Av*) a gathering of thousands of women is held in Jerusalem to foster *ahavas Yisrael* and unity. It is known as the *Shemiras HaLashon Kinus* (Assembly for Safeguarding Proper Speech). Local and international speakers inspire the assembled during these solemn days, when Jews the world over focus on the loss of the Second *Beis HaMikdash,* due to *sinas chinam* (baseless hatred) (see *Yoma* 9b).

In 1998, Dayan Chanoch Ehrentreu of London spoke eloquently of the importance of being sensitive to the feelings of others. To bring home his point, he told the following compelling story. I had first heard the story two years earlier from Rabbi Shmuel Baron of Jerusalem. Dayan Ehrentreu graciously filled in the details for me in a subsequent phone call to his home in England.

It was Friday afternoon in *Kislev* 1951 and there was a pall of sadness in the home of Rabbi Eliyahu Dessler (1892-1954) in the Zichron Meir section of Bnei Brak. His wife, Rebbetzin Bluma, had passed away the Friday night before and now he was sorrowfully preparing for his first Shabbos alone.

An endless flow of people had come to be *menachem avel* Rabbi Dessler during the week of *shivah.* He was the revered *Mashgiach* of the Ponevezher Yeshiva and known throughout the Torah world for his piety and the depth of his *mussar* thoughts. The *Chazon Ish,* Rav Avraham Yeshayah Karelitz (1878-1953), had referred to him as the *gadol hador* in *kochos hanefesh,* the generation's leader in elucidating human potential. Now, an hour before Shabbos, the apartment was nearly empty. One of Rabbi Dessler's primary *talmidim* was setting the Shabbos table.

As the tablecloth, cutlery, *challos, kos* (*Kiddush* cup) and Shabbos candles were set on the table, Rabbi Dessler whispered to his *talmid,* "Put back that *Kiddush kos* and take out the other one that is on the shelf."

The *talmid* was surprised. It seemed like such a mundane matter. What difference did it make what *kos* would be used. The *talmid* knew that this was not the time to ask his *rebbi* to explain. Nevertheless, he remained curious. He knew that there was a reason for anything his *rebbi* did. He was the quintessential *baal mussar* and *halachic* Jew, and he had a rationale for every action. After the *seudah* the *talmid* asked the question.

Rabbi Dessler told the following story. Years later Dayan Ehrentreu heard it from the *talmid.*

Some history is in order. At the bequest of Rabbi David Dryan, the *shochet* in Gateshead, England, Rabbi Dessler came to that city in Northern England to found the famous *kollel,* which he led from 1941 until 1948. (For a detailed history of this era, see ArtScroll's *Rav Dessler,* by Yonason Rosenblum.) When the Ponevezher Rav, Rabbi Yosef Shlomo Kahaneman (1886-1969) met Rabbi Dessler on one of his fundraising trips to England, he was so impressed that in 1946, when the *Mashgiach* of Ponevezh, Rabbi Abba Grosbard, passed away, he offered the position to Rabbi

Dessler. At that time Rabbi Dessler felt that his many responsibilities in England did not permit him to leave, but shortly after *Pesach* in 1949, the Desslers indeed settled in Bnei Brak, and he assumed the position as *Mashgiach*.

For all the years the Desslers had been married, since the spring of 1920, Rabbi Dessler always made *Kiddush* on a *kos* that he and his wife had received as a wedding gift from Rav Chaim Ozer Grodzinsky (1863-1940), who had received the *kos* as a wedding present from Rabbi Yisrael (Lipkin) Salanter (1809-1883), his first wife's grandfather.

On their first Shabbos in Bnei Brak, Rabbi Dessler used a different *kos*. Noticing that he had not used the familiar family *kos*, the rebbetzin asked him about it.

Rabbi Dessler explained that because they now lived in Bnei Brak whose spiritual guide was the *Chazon Ish*, it was proper to follow his *halachic* opinions. According to him, a *Kiddush kos* had to be larger than the one they had used until now. Rabbi Dessler therefore wanted to use the larger *kos*.

The rebbetzin respectfully disagreed. She maintained that if their *kos* had been used by such *gedolei hador* (Torah giants of a generation) as Rabbi Yisrael Salanter and Rabbi Chaim Ozer Grodzinsky, then it should be good enough for them, as well. Rabbi Dessler acquiesced, and from then on until she passed away, he used the family *kos* he had used in England.

Only now, after her passing, did Rabbi Dessler begin to abide by the ruling of the *Chazon Ish*.

Telling the story in Jerusalem, Dayan Ehrentreu expounded on Rabbi Dessler's extreme sensitivity, and used this story as a model lesson in *middos tovos* (exemplary mannners).

At times people have asked me, "If Rabbi Dessler was so sensitive to his wife's feelings, shouldn't he have continued to use the *kos* she treasured after her death?"

The answer lies in another episode that took place the morning of her funeral. A relative, Rabbi Simcha Zissel Schapiro, noticed that Rabbi Dessler was polishing his shoes before he left for the funeral. Rabbi Schapiro was astounded. Rabbi Dessler explained, "She was always meticulous that my clothes should be spotless before I left the house, so I am fulfilling her will."

When she was alive he acquiesced to her wish regarding the *kos* because there were other *gedolei hador* to rely on, and thus *shalom bayis* tipped the scale. But afterwards he could not do so in good conscience when it conflicted with the *Chazon Ish.*

A Greek Tragedy

This moving episode, which I first heard from my brother-in-law, Rabbi Mishel Teitz of Montreal, speaks to all of us. The *Mishnah* (*Avos* 2:1) cautions us to be careful in everything that we do because, עַיִן רוֹאָה *An eye sees.* The *eye* refers to Hashem's constant vigilance of mankind. Hence, nothing we do escapes Him.

What many of us fail to realize is that often, totally unbeknownst to us, people are observing us as well, and our actions can make indelible impressions.

In September 2000, R' Shaul Tzvi (Tommy) Czeisler was sitting *shivah* for his 87-year-old father, R' Shmuel. The mourners were in R' Shmuel's home on Bedford Rd. in Montreal. One morning a Greek gentleman, a total stranger, walked in and made his way to where Tommy was sitting. Before Tommy could say anything to him, the fellow pointed and said, "You are a champion!"

The gentleman introduced himself and said that he lived directly across the street. "I am retired," the man said, "and I don't have to get up at 5:30 in the morning. But a number of years ago I was up one morning and I saw how you came to pick up your father. I watched how you held his hand gently and helped him down the front stairs. I watched how you walked him to your car to take him to the synagogue. I could not get over how you treated him with such dignity.

"I got up the next morning and watched again how you treated him with such loving care. No one in our Greek community does this. I made it a point to get up every morning just to watch how you came for your father and how you cared for him. That daily scene carried me through the entire day." The gentleman became choked with emotion, but continued, "But now that he died, where am I am going to get my inspiration? What am I going to do now?"

And with that he burst into tears and ran out of the room and out of the house.

A *kiddush shem Shamayim* of the first order.

The Necklace

In the spring of 1990, Mrs. Tamar Hoffner* of London attended the wedding of the son of one her husband's business associates. The wedding was beautiful and most of the guests, who were enjoying every moment, stayed quite late. As Mrs. Hoffner and her husband Yehudah were leaving the wedding she noticed something sparkling on the floor. When she bent to pick it up she was astounded to see that it was a beautiful diamond necklace.

She immediately showed it to her husband, who expressed surprise that no announcement had been made about the lost piece of expensive jewelry. The Hoffners went to the caterer's office and told the manager about their find. He announced it over the public address system, but no one came forth to claim it or even to inquire about it. The Hoffners told the parents of the *chassan* and *kallah* that if anyone called to say they lost a necklace, they should contact them at once and it would be returned. They were sure that they would be called in a matter of days.

Mr. and Mrs. Hoffner felt uneasy leaving the hall with the necklace, but they were determined to do anything required by *halachah* to get it back to its rightful owner. When a few days went by with no calls, they spoke to Rabbi Henoch Padwa (1908-2000), one of the

*The name has been changed.

esteemed *dayanim* (rabbinical judges) in London to seek his counsel as to their obligations to inform people about the necklace.

Rabbi Padwa told them that they must put up signs in the London *shuls* announcing that an expensive item was found at a local wedding. Rabbi Padwa also told Mrs. Hoffner that she should wear the necklace at any *simchah* she attends, so that women would notice it and perhaps recognize it either as their own or belonging to a friend. (See laws of *Aveidah U'Metziah, Choshen Mishpat* 259.) Mr. and Mrs. Hoffner made signs immediately and posted them in many *shuls* throughout London. Though uncomfortable about it, Mrs. Hoffner wore the necklace at numerous weddings and festive occasions. Whenever she was complimented on its beauty she would explain that the necklace wasn't hers, but she was following the *psak din* (religious ruling) of Rabbi Padwa.

The signs were up for a few months, and still no one called to claim the necklace. Rabbi Padwa suggested that the Hoffners place an ad in London's Orthodox Jewish newspapers, such as the *Jewish Tribune,* which was read primarily by the type of people who attended the wedding. The ad in the newspaper explained that a precious item was found at a wedding in the spring of 1990. Still no claims. After a while, they discontinued the ad and the signs came down. Mrs. Hoffner put the necklace in a safe place and stopped wearing it. Within a year the incident was forgotten. The necklace lay in its hiding place for close to ten years!

On the fifteenth day of *Av,* in August 2000, Rabbi Padwa passed away. There were many *hespedim* (eulogies) as speaker after speaker extolled the virtues of the beloved *dayan*. [One speaker told how in 1951, the Tshebiner Rav, Rabbi Dov Berish Weidenfeld (1879-1965), insisted that Rabbi Padwa leave Vienna and go to London to serve the community.] The Orthodox papers were filled with accounts of the eulogies.

As Mrs. Hoffner read the eulogies, she recalled Rabbi Padwa's *psak* of ten years before. It was more than nine years since she had worn that necklace. Perhaps it would be a merit to his soul if she followed his advice once again, she thought. Indeed, in a few weeks she would be attending another wedding.

She took out the necklace, dusted it, polished it, and made a mental note to wear it. The evening of the wedding, it glistened and stood out. During the dancing, a lady she didn't know began conversing with her. She remarked, "That necklace of yours is magnificent! Years ago, I had one just like it."

"You had a necklace that looked like this?" Mrs. Hoffner asked incredulously.

"Yes, I did," the woman said sadly. "I came from my home in Israel to a wedding here in London, and when it was time to go back home, the necklace was nowhere to be found. I had no idea where I had lost it and I was horrified because I treasured it so much."

"Do you remember the name of the families whose wedding you attended?" asked Mrs. Hoffner.

"Of course, I do," the woman said, "It was the Berman and Silver wedding. I was a childhood friend of the *kallah's* mother. I was only in London for a few days, and this is the first time I am back since then."

Now Mrs. Hoffner understood why no one had responded to the signs in the *shuls* or the ads in the papers. The woman had already returned to Israel!

"You may not believe this," said Mrs. Hoffner slowly as she removed the necklace, "but this is yours. I wore it only so that someone might recognize it." The Israeli woman gasped.

Mrs. Hoffner then detailed to the flabbergasted woman the whole episode and the *psak* of Rabbi Padwa. "I haven't worn this in nine years," Mrs. Hoffner exclaimed excitedly. "Only because Rabbi Padwa was *niftar* did I even think to wear it again!"

The women embraced with tears and joy — the Israeli woman because her long-lost heirloom was finally back and Mrs. Hoffner because she had merited to fulfill the *mitzvah* of *hashavas aveidah* (returning a lost item). The women marveled at the *psak* of Rabbi Padwa and agreed that he merited a special Heavenly reward.

A few days later, before she left for Israel, the woman called Mrs. Hoffner to thank her again for her diligence.

And I thank Rabbi Chaim Horowitz of Antwerp for remembering the story and sharing it with me.

A Prince of a Priest

The ideal way to serve Hashem is through unbounded love for His Torah and *mitzvos.* The following episode speaks for itself in its depiction of a man's attitude toward *mitzvos* and *maasim tovim* (good deeds).

Moshe Kohn, a businessman in Amsterdam, was known for his punctiliousness in *mitzvah* observance. Because he was a *Kohen,* however, he could not participate with the *Chevrah Kaddishah* (Burial Society) when they performed a *taharah* (the preparation of a body for burial), nor could he assist in burying a fellow Jew who had passed away. The sanctity of a *Kohen* is such that he is prohibited by Torah law to be in close proximity to a deceased person (see *Vayikra* 21:1-3).

One day Mr. Kohn heard that the *kehillah kedoshah* (Jewish Community) of Amsterdam had purchased a new plot of land that was to be used as a cemetery. Immediately he went out and dug the first grave!

In his ardent desire to perform the *mitzvah* of burying the dead, a *mitzvah* for which Hashem Himself is extolled (see *Devarim* 34:6 *and Sotah* 14a), Mr. Kohn quickly performed a segment of the *mitzvah* while he still could. Had someone already been buried in that plot of land, it would have had the status of a cemetery and he would have been prohibited from being there.

Bagged

Reb Shepsil Gutfarb* of Jerusalem is an exceptionally pious man who is meticulous in his *mitzvah* observance. People are inspired by his learning and *davening* and moved by his kindness and thoughtfulness to his neighbors and friends.

One afternoon in May 2001, in the middle of the Hebrew year 5761, Reb Shepsil came home from a long day of teaching at one of

*The name has been changed.

the community *chadarim* (religious elementary schools). He went to the refrigerator to get an apple. There were two of them before he had left that morning — but, to his surprise, they were both gone.

"No apples left?" he asked his wife Chaya. "I was sure I saw some here this morning."

"I'm sorry," Mrs. Gutfarb said, "I gave them to the *ozeret* (cleaning lady) who left just a few minutes ago. She said she was hungry and she had a long way home by bus. So I gave her the apples."

Reb Shepsil's mouth dropped open in alarm and disbelief. *"Peiros Sheviis!"* he exclaimed.

The Torah dictates that every seventh year be observed as a Sabbatical year in the Land of Israel. The year is known as *Sheviis* or *Shemittah.* The produce of that year, known as *peiros Sheviis,* has special sanctity and its use is regulated. Even the disposal of the remains of *peiros Sheviis* are governed by special laws. The *ozeret* was a non-Jewish Romanian woman and Mrs. Gutfarb was not permitted to give her *peiros Sheviis* (see *Rambam, Hilchos Shemittah V'Yovel* 5:13).

Reb Shepsil was frantic. It was the *Shemittah* year and he and his family had tried to be so careful observing its laws. Now they inadvertently had made an error. His wife told him that in order for the *ozeret* to get home she normally took a local bus to the *tachanah merkazit* (central bus terminal) and then boarded a second bus to her home in Mevaseret. He ran downstairs, dashed toward the bus stop, and was told that a bus had picked up passengers 10 minutes ago. He waited impatiently for the next bus but when an available taxi drove by he hailed it and had the driver take him to the bus terminal. He prayed softly that he could reach the cleaning lady before her bus left for Mevaseret.

When he got to the station, he ran towards the Mevaseret bus. He boarded the bus and said to the driver, "I'm looking desperately for someone who may be on this bus. I'm not traveling, please allow me to go through the bus and check out the passengers. I'll get off right afterwards."

The bus driver nodded his approval. Reb Shepsil started down the center aisle and then he saw the woman near the back. *"Aifoh hasakit? Aifoh hasakit?"* ("Where is the bag? Where is the bag?"), Reb Shepsil shouted.

The woman's mouth dropped open in alarm and disbelief. Her eyes widened with terror. "Don't call the police! Don't call the police," she exclaimed in a panic. And with that she took out a small bag from her purse and gave it to Reb Shepsil. It contained the jewelry she had stolen from the Gutfarb home.

Before she had left that afternoon, the Romanian woman had taken two bracelets, a necklace and a pair of earrings from Mrs. Gutfarb's jewelry box. Had Reb Shepsil not run after her for the *peiros Sheviis* he would never have gotten the jewelry back as she may never have returned to work for the Gutfarbs.

And yes — Reb Shepsil also made sure to get back the apples.

Signs of Swiftness

I have been blessed with the opportunity to be a *mohel* for more than thirty years and I have participated in numerous *brissen* that were especially moving and inspirational. Two particular instances that occurred in 1999 were remarkable because of the unusual dedication of the fathers.

In February 1999, Ivan Kralnitzky* called me to perform the *bris* for his newborn son. A recent émigré from the Soviet Union, Ivan lived in Manhattan, and struggled with his English. I therefore repeated and spelled twice every item I needed him to purchase for the *bris* (gauze pads, ointment, diapers, wine, etc.). Ivan and his wife Natasha* were not *shomer Shabbos* but they wanted the *bris* to be performed according to *halachah*. I explained to Ivan that since his baby was born on a Tuesday afternoon, the appropriate time for the *bris* of his son was the following Tuesday.

Ivan insisted that the *bris* be done late in the afternoon; he did not want to miss a day of work and his family and friends could not come in the morning or early afternoon. I told him that as long as

*The name has been changed.

we did the *bris* before sundown, it would be proper. I *thought* he understood everything I said.

Frankly, I was happy that he was having a *bris* for his son altogether. After all, he did not have a religious upbringing, he knew very little about *Yiddishkeit*, and he had seen few *brissen* throughout his life. However, as *Chazal* teach: כָּל מִצְוָה שֶׁקִּיבְּלוּ עֲלֵיהֶם בְּשִׂמְחָה כְּגוֹן מִילָה עֲדַיִין עוֹשִׂין בְּשִׂמְחָה, *Any commandment that [the Jewish people] accepted upon themselves with joy, such as circumcision ... they still perform with joy (Shabbos* 130a*).* Hence, today tens of thousands of Jews like Ivan, who observe very little if anything, still make it a point to have a *bris* performed on their newborn sons.

The *bris* was scheduled for 4:30 p.m. on Tuesday afternoon and I arrived at Ivan's uptown Manhattan apartment at 4:15 p.m. As I was standing outside the door I was surprised at how quiet everything seemed inside. Usually there is a perceptible din coming from the festive conversations of family and friends at a *simchah.*

I rang the bell wondering if perhaps they had decided to have the *bris* somewhere else and forgot to tell me. (That has happened more than once.) The grandmother opened the door and when I introduced myself she said, "Please come in and speak to my daughter."

Natasha was sitting on the couch cradling her newborn son. When she realized who I was, she exclaimed, "I knew my husband had it wrong! I told him last night to call you because I was sure he had it scheduled on the wrong day! He told everyone to come tomorrow at 4:30."

Obviously Ivan had misunderstood the calculation of how to count the eight days for the *bris*. "Where is your husband now?" I asked Natasha.

"I'll get him on the phone," she replied, embarrassed and upset.

I pictured Ivan in his office somewhere in downtown Manhattan. I realized that not only had I made the trip to Manhattan from Kew Gardens for nothing, but that I would have to make the same trip tomorrow to do the *bris* that should have been done today.

"Ivan," I said on the phone with forced pleasantness, "I thought I had explained that the *bris* was today, but I see there was some miscommunication. Perhaps I should have explained it better."

"Rabbi," he said, "I am sure it was my fault. How much time do we have left?"

"What do you mean?" I replied.

"I'm working out in the gym a few blocks from my house. You told me it has to be before sundown, right? When is sundown? If we still have time, you get everything ready and I'll run right over."

"And we'll do the *bris*?" I asked, not believing that a non-observant person would be willing to do the *bris* without anyone there and have to do some embarrassed explaining to his family and friends when they came to his home the next day.

When I told him that we still had 20 minutes before sunset he reiterated that I should get everything ready and he would be there in time.

Within 10 minutes Ivan came running into the apartment in his gym suit. I explained to Ivan that as the only male there beside myself he would have to be *sandak.* He smiled nervously as I told him to wash his hands thoroughly.

The *bris* was done and the only people present were Ivan in his gym suit and sneakers, Natasha and her mother, dressed in simple housecoats, and myself. (At least I was dressed for the occasion.) Ivan and I embraced after the *bris* and I told him how special he was. I also said that I would be back tomorrow at 4:30 when his guests would arrive. I asked him not to tell anyone what transpired.

On Wednesday afternoon, when the guests assembled, we brought out the newborn infant and I explained to everyone what had gone on the day before. Family and friends could not help but be inspired by Ivan's commitment and dedication to having his son's *bris* done at the right time.

> *Bris milah* is a sign of the covenant that Hashem made with Avraham *Avinu* (see *Bereishis* 17:11). Ivan's diligence was a sign of *Klal Yisrael's* timeless passion for this *mitzvah.*

In October 1999, I was called to perform a *bris* for a family in Woodmere, N.Y., but the parents, Ezra and Yaffa Patner,* could not schedule it because their baby was yellow and had a very high bilirubin count. A high bilirubin count can be an indication that the child's liver may not be functioning adequately. Since the liver helps produce clotting factors in the blood and it is imperative that the blood clot after a *bris*, the *halachah* is that if there is even a slight suspicion that the liver is not functioning properly, it is forbidden to perform the *bris* (see *Yoreh Deah* 263:1).

I assured Ezra that I would be in constant contact with the baby's pediatrician and that together we would determine when the *bris* could take place. For a few days the infant's condition remained the same and then on the sixth day the bilirubin level went up. Having the *bris* on the eighth day did not look promising.

On the seventh day, the jaundice condition improved only slightly and the baby's pediatrician estimated that it would be safe to do the *bris* on a Thursday morning, the ninth day of the child's life. He felt strongly that the baby would not be ready by the eighth day.

A responsible *mohel* never performs a *bris* against a doctor's advice. Hence there was no choice — the *bris* would be delayed by a day. (At times, *mohelim* are even more stringent than doctors, and will delay a *bris* even if a doctor feels the child is medically ready.)

Based on the pediatrician's recommendation, the *bris* was scheduled for Thursday morning. On Wednesday afternoon on my way home from a *bris* in New Jersey, my wife called me in the car and said, "Mr. Patner of Woodmere is trying desperately to reach you. Can I conference you with him?"

When we were connected, Ezra spoke anxiously.

"My wife just came home from the pediatrician and he says that surprisingly the baby is perfectly okay. I wasn't expecting her to go to the doctor, but now that the baby is okay, we must do the *bris* today. Are you available?"

"I'm in New Jersey," I replied, "I can't get to Woodmere by sunset."

"But we really must do the *bris* if the baby is healthy. Isn't that so?"

*The name has been changed.

"You're right," I said. "I could try to get you another *mohel*."

I knew he was expecting more than a hundred people at the *bris* so I asked, "Are you going to be able to notify anyone that the *bris* is taking place?"

"No," he said. "There is no time to make all those calls. It'll just be my wife, her mother and the baby."

"What about you?" I asked incredulously. "Aren't you there?"

"No," he said, exasperated, "I'm in my office in Manhattan, there is no way I can get home in time."

"You're not going to be at your own son's *bris*?" I exclaimed.

What Ezra then said was classic. "This is the first *mitzvah* in my son's life — it has to be done right. Throughout Jewish history people risked their lives so that their sons would have a proper *bris* (see *Shabbos* 130a). It's more important to me that my son know all his life that he had his *bris* on the proper day than it is for me to be there."

I was able to find a *mohel* and the *bris* was done that afternoon a few minutes before sunset in the presence of just the infant's mother and grandmother.

The next morning the people came to *shul* expecting a *bris*, bagels and lox. They got the bagels and lox and an inspiring story.

> Hashem said to Avraham *Avinu:* וְאַתָּה אֶת בְּרִיתִי תִשְׁמֹר אַתָּה וְזַרְעֲךָ אַחֲרֶיךָ לְדֹרֹתָם, *You shall guard My covenant — you and your offspring after you throughout their generations (Bereishis* 17:9*).* Ezra Patner is one of the noble guardians.

Write On

Rabbi Chaim Kanievsky, one of the greatest Torah scholars of our generation, reviews the entire *Talmud Bavli, Talmud Yerushalmi, Shulchan Aruch, Midrash and Tanach* every year! In order to complete *Talmud Bavli* in one year, one must study about seven and a half *blatt* a day, but Reb Chaim studies eight *blatt*, so that he does not feel the pressure to rush his studies during the final month, as he nears completion of *Shas* for that year. Reb Chaim completes his daily eight *blatt* by sunrise every morning, in time to *daven* with the *netz* (sunrise) *minyan.*

In the autumn of 2001, Reb Chaim suffered a stroke. While recuperating in the Mayenei Hayeshua Hospital in Bnei Brak, he began physical therapy. His therapist asked Reb Chaim to write something on a blank sheet of paper, in order to accustom the great sage to using his hand and fingers.

Reb Chaim is the author of over a dozen *sefarim,* so writing is an integral part of his life. Slowly and painstakingly he wrote in Hebrew, יְקוּם פֻּרְקָן מִן שְׁמַיָּא, *May salvation arise from Heaven* (the opening phrase of the prayer for those who uphold the Torah, recited after the Torah reading on Shabbos).

The therapist was impressed by Reb Chaim's choice of words, which were obviously a prayer for his recovery. But the therapist was surprised, as well. "I have been doing this work for years," he said to Reb Chaim. "Every single patient that I ever had always wrote his name when I first asked him to write something. This happened every time without fail. Why did the rav not write his name?"

Rav Chaim looked out at the therapist from under his thick bushy eyebrows and said with simplicity and sincerity. "*Chazal* teach that a person should not write his name on a blank sheet of paper, lest a dishonest person find it and write above the signature that the undersigned owes him money, and then he would be liable!" (See *Kesubos* 21a.)

Who would have thought of this except for Reb Chaim?

Bread, Butter and Business Values

Shimon and Chana Hartstein* moved to Boro Park after having lived in *Eretz Yisrael* for three years, where Shimon studied in the Beis HaTalmud *Kollel*. After they had settled in, they began shopping at an Eighteenth Avenue grocery a few blocks from their apartment. The proprietors were an elderly couple, Harry and Ethel,*

*The name has been changed.

Holocaust survivors who had struggled for years to make a success of their modest store. Now, after many years, it was well stocked, well organized, and doing a thriving business.

Shimon had just started a new job and Chana was home with the three children, so they could not always pay their bills on time. Harry was understanding and allowed them to shop on credit. Shimon's father always exhorted him never to be more than a week overdue with his grocery payments: "The grocer has a right to make a living and he needs your money to pay his bills. You must be diligent in your payments."

Shimon would have loved to pay his bills on time but it wasn't always possible. At times the bill would be two or three weeks overdue, but neither Harry nor Ethel said a word about it. As the Hartstein family grew, the size of their grocery bills increased proportionately. At times the bills were more than a month old, but Harry never complained. He realized that the Hartsteins had other bills besides his.

One day near the end of June, Shimon said to Chana, "We must pay the grocer before we go off to the mountains for the summer. We can't make him wait for two months until we get back."

At the time the bill was quite substantial, but Shimon managed to put together the necessary funds and went to pay. He carefully counted out the money and handed it to Harry. It was a little more than $1,200. Harry thanked him, and the Hartsteins were off with their children to a bungalow in the Catskills.

When they returned from the mountains in September, Shimon went to the grocer to stock his empty refrigerator and kitchen cabinets at home. As Harry was checking him out, he said to Shimon, "You have quite a bill left over from before the summer."

Shimon was taken aback. First, Harry usually didn't mention anything about the bill, and second, Shimon had made it a point to pay his bill before he and his family had left for the summer. "Excuse me," said Shimon "but there is a mistake here. I know for sure that I paid the bill in June, before we left for the mountains."

"My records show that you didn't pay it," Harry said. "I don't remember your coming in with that kind of money."

Shimon was incredulous. He knew he had paid the bill, but there was nothing he could say to convince Harry of his error. Shimon realized that he should have either taken the sheet on which the balance had been recorded or at least made sure that Harry ripped it up or marked it "paid."

Shimon explained to Harry that he didn't have nearly enough money with him on hand to pay such a sizeable bill but that he would get back to him. The Hartsteins consulted with rabbinical authorities, sure that they would get a ruling in their favor, but the matter was not simple.

After much discussion Shimon decided he would pay the grocer again. He did not want to keep any money that could possibly belong to someone else. Furthermore, Shimon rationalized that by paying his "bill," he would assure that Harry would continue giving credit to others.

After Shimon paid the grocer he never shopped there again.

Years went by, the Hartsteins moved to a new area, and with time the memory of and resentment over the incident faded into the past. It was one of life's trying situations that everyone seems to experience at one time or another. The spectrum of life has many shades and this was one of the darker ones.

Twelve years later, Shimon was sitting at home when his wife told him, "There is an elderly woman on the phone, and she insists on speaking only to you."

Shimon picked up the phone and announced himself. "Hello," the woman on the phone said in a voice that cracked. "Is this Mr. Hartstein?"

"Yes, that's me," Shimon replied, "Whom am I speaking to?"

"Maybe you remember the name Weingott?" the woman asked.

Shimon tried to recall where he had heard that name before. "You remember," she interrupted his thoughts, "we used to have a grocery store on Eighteenth Ave. where you used to come in?"

Shimon remembered the store and he recalled that everyone referred to the owners as Harry and Ethel. He had forgotten that their last name was Weingott. "I am Ethel Weingott and my husband Harry died last week and the *shivah* just finished," the lady said. "For the last number of years my husband suffered from Alzheimer's. It got so terrible that we had to close the store. I remember very well years ago when you came in after the summer and you claimed you paid your bill before the summer. My husband said that you didn't pay, but I thought you did. He was so firm about it that I couldn't argue with him. I realize now that it was just about that time that his Alzheimer's was beginning to set in. He truly forgot that you paid him. So now I want to pay you back the money I owe you."

Shimon was stunned. "Please, please," he stammered. "It happened so long ago, I forgot about it already. It is so kind of you to call, but I forgave your husband years ago. Don't worry. You don't have to pay me. But if you want to, you can give the money to *tzedakah*."

"Mr. Hartstein," Ethel Weingott said, "it's your money. You give it to *tzedakah* if that's what you want to do."

And that's exactly what happened. She came, she paid ... he took and he gave.

מִי כְּעַמְּךָ יִשְׂרָאֵל, Who is like Your people Israel?

When I was discussing the *halachic* ramifications of this story with Rabbi Kalman Epstein, *Rosh Yeshivah* of Yeshiva Shaar HaTorah in Kew Gardens, N.Y., he related an incident that took place with his renowned father, Rabbi Zelik Epstein, the senior *Rosh Yeshivah* at Shaar HaTorah.

When Reb Zelik lived in Williamsburg he shopped at Flaums, the famous appetizing store. One day he purchased a small item and paid Mr. Flaum for it. Mr. Flaum gave him change as if he had been given a $1 bill.

Rav Zelik said, "Excuse me, but I gave you a $20 bill."

"Oh, I am so sorry," said Mr. Flaum. He gave Rabbi Epstein the appropriate change.

When Rabbi Epstein came home, he put his hand in his pocket and to his surprise he took out a $20 bill. He realized then that he had actually given Mr. Flaum only $1. He rushed back to Mr. Flaum and said, "I am so sorry, I made a mistake. I thought I gave you $20, but it was really $1."

"I knew that," replied Mr. Flaum with a smile.

"If you knew that, then why didn't you say anything?" asked Rabbi Epstein.

"I would never contradict a rabbi," replied Mr. Flaum with utmost sincerity.

Some grocers provide more than food — they provide moral sustenance.

In light of the above I was happy to hear the following story from Rabbi Reuven Mendlowitz, a *kollel* fellow living today in the Har Nof section of Jerusalem. The story is about his grandfather, the person he was named for.

Reb Reuven, the brother of the legendary Reb Shraga Feivel Mendlowitz (1886-1948), was a grocer in the Williamsburg section of Brooklyn. On the day of the funeral of Reb Shraga Feivel, thousands of people gathered at Mesivta Torah Vodaath on South Third Street to pay their final respects to the man who was an architect of Torah in America. (The funeral procession had made its way from Monsey, where it had begun in Bais Medrash Elyon.) On the way to his brother's funeral, Reb Reuven was walking to the Mesivta when suddenly he went into a grocery along the way.

The people who were walking alongside Reb Reuven were taken aback. What could be so important to divert his attention from the matter at hand? In respect of Reb Reuven's piety no one said anything. When he was asked about it during the *shivah,* the answer he gave symbolized the special nature of the Mendlowitz family.

There was a poverty stricken man who came to Reb Reuven's grocery every morning for bread and milk for his family. Reb

Reuven never charged him but to preserve the man's dignity he wrote the amount due on a balance sheet that he knew — and the poor man knew — would never be claimed. It was an unspoken pact between them.

"During *shivah* my store will be closed," explained Reb Reuven, "and this man will have to go to the other grocer for his family's bread and milk. I wanted to be sure that the grocer wouldn't charge him so I went in to assure him that I would cover the cost!"

> If that's what the grocers of that generation were, one can only imagine how extraordinary the Torah leaders were.

Royal Toil

R' Chaim Honig of Stamford Hill in London has an engraving business. Every day people come to his shop to have items engraved; sometimes it is a *bar mitzvah* boy's name on a *Kiddush* cup; sometimes a *chassan's* initials on cufflinks; sometimes it is an inscription on a plaque intended for an honoree at a *shul* or school dinner.

Recently, R' Chaim was commissioned to do something he had never done before. A Jewish organization wanted a large, decorative *mezuzah* case to be enclosed in an elaborate silver setting; it would be presented to Her Royal Highness, Queen Elizabeth of the British Commonwealth. A message in both Hebrew and English lettering was to be ornately engraved, decorated and surrounded by a magnificent floral design.

R' Chaim had been engraving such items for more than a decade, yet as he began to set up the machinery for the letters for this assignment, it took him more than two hours to line, realign, measure and remeasure every letter until he was convinced that the result would be perfect. It took another hour to get the floral pattern in place. Never had he been so meticulous.

As he worked, he marveled at his own painstaking concentration and deliberation. It was then that he remembered the following Talmudic teaching: חֲסִידִים הָרִאשׁוֹנִים הָיוּ שׁוֹהִין שָׁעָה אַחַת וּמִתְפַּלְּלִין

כְּדֵי שֶׁיְּכַוְּונוּ אֶת לִבָּם לַאֲבִיהֶם שֶׁבַּשָּׁמַיִם, *The early pious people would tarry for one hour and [then] pray, in order that they might direct their hearts to their Father in Heaven* (*Berachos* 30b).

"I always wondered what they did during that hour," says R' Chaim. "However, as I became aware of my own behavior in this instance, I understood that when one is about to make a presentation to royalty, the preparation and vigilance necessary to achieve perfection are time consuming. Those righteous people knew that their prayers were an offering to the מֶלֶךְ מַלְכֵי הַמְּלָכִים (the King of Kings), thus they spent a long time making sure they understood each word, were positive of the pronouciations, and sure of the intent they had to have with every word they would say."

How do we prepare for our *davening*?

A Ready Remedy

Rabbi Yitzchak Zilberstein, a noted *posek* in Israel, is the rav of the Ramat Elchanan neighborhood in Bnei Brak and son-in-law of *HaGaon* Rabbi Yosef Sholom Eliyashiv. His weekly *shiurim* in *halachah* and *Chumash* are attended by hundreds of people. At a *Chumash shiur* he repeated a story told by Rabbi Simcha Kaplan, the rabbi of the holy city of Tzefas.

When Rabbi Kaplan was a young man studying in the Mirrer Yeshivah in Poland, the *talmidim* would rent rooms and have their meals with families near the yeshivah. One Friday morning, R' Simcha overheard his landlady say to her husband, "Are you going to the next town for anything before Shabbos?"

When her husband said that he was, she cautioned him, "Hurry and make sure you are back by *chatzos!* (midday). Take care of everything that has to be done for Shabbos by then. You know how important it is."

R' Simcha was surprised. The next town wasn't far away and it was still early morning. Why was she so worried? And what was so crucial about being back by midday? R' Simcha was even more bewildered when he saw the woman standing by the window as noon was approaching, anxiously awaiting her husband's return.

R' Simcha couldn't contain himself. "Why are you so concerned?" he asked her. "Your husband is an *ehrlicher Yid* (a religious Jew). There is no way that he will do anything to endanger the sanctity of Shabbos. And besides, the next town is not far away and Shabbos doesn't start for a few hours."

The woman sighed and said, "Let me tell you a story that happened many years ago."

For many years after she and her husband were married, they were childless, which saddened their lives. Finally they had a son, and he was the only child they ever had. When he was a youngster he became seriously ill. She and her husband took him from doctor to doctor, but no one could help them.

The woman then took her son to Vienna, which was known for its fine specialists. She brought her son to many professors (as doctors were known in those days), but they gave her little hope that her son could be restored to good health. As a matter of fact, the general consensus was that his days were numbered.

She paced the streets of Vienna quietly weeping, preparing for the trip back to Mir. One afternoon, a gentleman saw her crying and asked her what was wrong. When she told him her story, he said, "If you are traveling back to Mir, why don't you stop off on the way in Radin. Go to the Chofetz Chaim. Maybe his blessing will do what doctors can't."

The distraught mother was ready to try anything, and so, broken and contrite, she went to Radin and asked to see the great sage. The Chofetz Chaim was already elderly and his family tried to keep people away from him, but because of her desperate plight, they allowed her in. She cried and poured out her heart to the great *tzaddik*. He said, "What can I do? I am old man. When I was young I had the strength to fast for the sick people of *Klal Yisrael*. I can't do that anymore."

The woman burst into tears as her last hope seemed to float away in the wind. She stood before the great sage crying and pleading. A family member of the Chofetz Chaim came in and whispered something in his ear. The woman could hear that he was saying something about this being an only child and that the family was suffering terrible anguish.

The Chofetz Chaim suddenly stood up from his chair and said firmly, "I will give you two resolutions. If you accept them both, I guarantee that your son will have a full recovery."

"*Rebbi*," she said emphatically, "I will do anything you tell me to do."

She expected him to ask her to fast for many days or to undertake some stringent behavior. She waited anxiously for the Chofetz Chaim to speak. When he did, she was astonished and astounded by what he told her.

"First," he said, "you must promise to put the Shabbos tablecloth and the *leichter* (candelabra) on the table by Friday before *chatzos*." She was relieved. That didn't seem too extraordinarily difficult. She waited for the next resolution.

"Second, from the moment that the candles are supposed to be lit Friday night (i.e. the posted time on the calendar) — not the time that you actually light candles — no member of your household may do any work."

The woman finished her story by saying, "Of course my husband and I accepted these conditions and within a short time our son was cured. The doctors in Vienna could not believe it. That is why I am so anxious to have everything ready for Shabbos by midday."

The Torah exhorts us: וּשְׁמַרְתֶּם אֶת הַשַּׁבָּת כִּי קֹדֶשׁ הִוא לָכֶם, *You shall observe the Shabbos, for it is holy to you (Shemos* 31:14*).* The word שמר can also mean *to wait for,* or *anticipate.* When Yaakov heard of his son Yosef's dream of supremacy over his brothers, the Torah says, וְאָבִיו שָׁמַר אֶת הַדָּבָר, *his father [Yaakov] waited for the matter (Bereishis* 37:11*). Rashi* (ibid.) comments, "He was waiting and looking forward to the realization of the dream." Perhaps, then, the verse regarding *observing Shabbos* also alludes that we should *look forward* to Shabbos.

When Rabbi Zilberstein told the story of Rabbi Simcha Kaplan and his landlady's accepting the Chofetz Chaim's resolutions, (see *Tuv'cha Yabi'u,* Vol. 1, p. 311), he stressed the importance of not leaving Shabbos preparations for the last minute. If one is frazzled and stressed by the time Shabbos arrives, one cannot be in the frame of mind to create the atmosphere of holiness and tranquility of Shabbos.

The *Aruch HaShulchan (Orach Chaim* 262:5, citing *Gittin* 52a*)* notes that the *Satan (*i.e. the *Yetzer Hara* or Evil Inclination*)* vigorously attempts to cause disharmony in the home *erev* Shabbos so that people will not enter Shabbos with the proper frame of mind. Rabbi Dovid Cohen suggests that perhaps the *Satan* has success in causing conflict *erev* Shabbos, for he successfully enticed Adam *HaRishon* to sin on the first *erev* Shabbos, thereby causing "conflict" between Adam and Hashem and setting a precedent for the future (*Maaaseh Avos Siman LeBanim,* Vol. 3, p. 105).

Rabbi Yaakov Kamenetsky (1892-1986) said, "In America we have gained Shabbos, but lost *erev* Shabbos." He meant that although American Jews are not faced with the choice of working on Shabbos or losing their jobs, our hectic lifestyle and multiple obligations keep us occupied until the very last minute before Shabbos.

The Chofetz Chaim taught that this hectic pace ruins Shabbos. Having the table set by *chatzos* on Friday creates an atmosphere; the total cessation of work by all members of the household at candle-lighting time assures it.

On-time Arrival?

The Talmud (*Berachos* 47b) teaches: לְעוֹלָם יַשְׁכִּים אָדָם לְבֵית הַכְּנֶסֶת כְּדֵי שֶׁיִּזְכֶּה וְיִמָּנֶה עִם עֲשָׂרָה הָרִאשׁוֹנִים, *A person should always awake early [to go] to the synagogue, so that he should merit to be counted among the first ten.* The Talmud explains that the ten who arrive first to the synagogue receive (Heavenly) reward equal to the reward of all those who come afterwards.

The *Maharsha* (ibid.) explains that the *Shechinah* (Divine Presence) arrives where people pray only after a quorum of men has gathered. Hence only the first ten to arrive in the synagogue deserve credit for bringing the *Shechinah.* Those who come later get Heavenly recompense for praying in the presence of the *Shechinah,* but the first ten are rewarded for affording them that opportunity. *Chazal* (ibid.) teach that this reward is equal to what everyone else there receives for praying in the presence of the *Shechinah.*

In light of the above, the following story is quite sobering.

In Milwaukee* there was a young man who owned a furniture* store. One morning in the store he noticed that smoke was coming up between the wooden slats of his parquet floor. He ran to the basement to see if there was a problem, and when he opened the door to go downstairs his worst fears were confirmed.

A fire was raging and smoke was filling most of the basement. He tried desperately to put out the fire with a fire extinguisher, but it was to no avail. By the time he ran back upstairs, the fire had spread to the first floor. Curtains, tables, desks, beds, and night tables were all aflame. He ran to call the fire department and then returned to his store, only to watch helplessly as the place burned to a shambles.

All the fire department could do was hose down the adjacent store to make sure the fire didn't spread. The furniture store was gutted. It would be months before its owner could open for business.

A few days after the fire, this young man came to *shul* and said to a friend of mine, "You know, a few days before the fire, a fellow came over to me in *shul* and said, 'You come to *shul* every day, but why do you always come late? You are never there when they start *davening*!'

"I answered him, 'What's the difference? At the end I come!' Now I realize — the fire department also came at the end. But it was too late. Hashem wanted to show me that when I said, 'At the end I come,' so the fire department, too, could say, 'At the end we came.'"

*The name has been changed.

We should be honest with ourselves. If we come late to *davening* it is almost impossible to catch up with the *baal tefillah* and yet say every word properly. If we are late, we may miss the recitation of *Kaddish* numerous times, and latecomers hardly have the opportunity to say *korbanos*.

"At the end I come" can be potentially disastrous.

Life Cycle

The phone rang at 3 a.m. The sudden piercing ring in the stillness of the night frightened Rabbi Moshe Faskowitz, rav of the Torah Center Synagogue in Hillcrest, New York, as he leapt from bed to answer the phone. His heart raced as he wondered what emergency could have warranted a call at this hour.

"Is this Rabbi Faskowitz?" an elderly woman asked apologetically.

"Yes," he replied, "and who are you? Is everything all right?"

"Rabbi, I am so sorry to call in the middle of the night, but I have been searching for you for the last three hours. I don't know if you remember me. My name is Mrs. Worthington* from Canarsie."

Rabbi Faskowitz tried to think as quickly as one could at 3 o'clock in the morning. He had lived in Canarsie years ago and so he strained to recall the name. Surprising himself, he suddenly flashed back to an incident he hadn't thought about in years. "Are you the woman that I gave the ride to about fifteen years ago?"

"Yes, that's me," she said, sounding relieved but exhausted.

How could he forget it? One afternoon in the winter of 1986, he was driving on Ralph Ave. in Brooklyn as windswept sleet and rain sliced the air. Huddled under the awning in front of a kosher supermarket was a middle-aged woman laden with bags of groceries, hesitant to walk out in the rainstorm without an umbrella. He pulled alongside the curb and called out to the woman,

*The name has been changed.

"Hello, I am Rabbi Faskowitz of the Young Israel. Can I offer you a ride home?"

"That would be nice," said the woman, "but I am not Jewish so maybe you don't want to take me."

"I am a rabbi and I'm glad to help anyone," Rabbi Faskowitz replied with a smile. "Please get in the car. I'll help you with your packages."

The woman settled into the back seat of the car with her groceries, introduced herself by name and thanked the rabbi profusely. A conversation ensued and Rabbi Faskowitz asked, "Tell me, if you are not Jewish why do you shop in this kosher food market?"

"The food is not for me," she replied. "I live in an apartment house, and there is an elderly Jewish couple on my floor. Both of them are invalids. They can't get out to buy their own food, so once a week, I go out and buy what they need. I know they eat only kosher food so I shop at the store where I know everything is kosher."

Hearing this, Rabbi Faskowitz was doubly delighted to have helped this considerate woman. He drove her home, helped her with the groceries and complimented her generosity.

Now in the middle of the night, Mrs. Worthington was on the verge of tears. "Rabbi," she said, "the man I brought food to all these years died yesterday. There is no one to bury him. He has no children and his wife died a few years ago. I remembered that you were from a synagogue in Canarsie and I have spent a few hours trying to find you. It took a while till I got your name and then finally someone told me you had moved to Queens. I just got your number from the operator so please forgive me for calling so late. You are the only rabbi I know. If you don't help, the man will be buried by city authorities in Potters Field (a cemetery for the destitute and for unclaimed bodies). I know he would want to be buried in a Jewish cemetery. Do you think you could help?"

Rabbi Faskowitz was astounded at the kindness, consideration and perseverance of this woman. He quickly called Coney Island

Hospital in Brooklyn, where the police had taken the body and where it was being temporarily held in the morgue until someone would claim it. After numerous calls to authorities later that morning, Rabbi Faskowitz was able to get the body released for a Jewish funeral service and burial.

No one attended the funeral at the Hebrew Free Burial cemetery in Staten Island except Rabbi Faskowitz. It was sad, simple, and solitary. Tears welled in Rabbi Faskowitz's eyes as he eulogized the gentleman softly to himself, and said, "You must have been an אָדָם כָּשֵׁר, *worthy* (lit. kosher) *man,* because by the virtue of כַּשְׁרוּת, *kosher food,* you merited קְבוּרַת יִשְׂרָאֵל, *Jewish burial.*" Then in silent dignity the man was laid to eternal rest.

> *Chazal (Avos 4:2)* teach: מִצְוָה גוֹרֶרֶת מִצְוָה, *One mitzvah leads to another mitzvah.* Isn't it remarkable that this dictum holds true even after a lapse of fifteen years? Perhaps it was because, מְגַלְגְּלִין זְכוּת עַל יְדֵי זַכַּאי, *Benefit is imparted through one who is meritorious (Shabbos* 32a*)* that Rabbi Faskowitz's kind gesture many years before on that stormy day in Brooklyn made him praiseworthy. Additionally it undoubtedly encouraged Mrs. Worthington to continue her kindness. Hence, Rabbi Faskowitz became "deserving" — and thus merited to perform the ultimate חֶסֶד שֶׁל אֱמֶת (genuine charitable deed) — burying a מֵת מִצְוָה (an abandoned corpse).

Tables (Re)turned

In the early 1930's, Rabbi Yaakov Yisrael Berger, a noted *talmid chacham,* was the rabbi of the Shomer Shabbos *Shul,* a small congregation in downtown Cleveland, Ohio. He earned a meager $18 a week from the *shul,* and if he performed a wedding or funeral he might recieve an extra dollar or two. To supplement his inadequate salary, he was forced to seek work in businesses or factories. But such jobs — even if he was hired — rarely lasted for more than a week. In the America of those days, it was common for Orthodox

Jews to be fired at week's end for not coming to work on Shabbos. Rabbi Berger managed to put bread on the table for his wife Faige and their seven children, but no one could consider him wealthy by any stretch of the imagination.

Yet, in a sense, he was a millionaire. For in an era where most Jewish parents lost their offspring to the excitement and opportunities that secular America offered, Rabbi Berger's children were Torah committed, totally observant Jews. Two of his sons, Avraham and Yerachmiel, were attending Yeshiva Torah Vodaath in Brooklyn. Avraham eventually returned to Cleveland where he was the rabbi of the Ahavas Yisroel Congregation for more than thirty years.

One day Rabbi Yaakov Yisrael Berger received a letter from his sister Rivka in Rava-Mazeweczka, Poland. Their sister Yocheved had just become engaged but the poverty was such that they did not have any money for the necessary dowry. Rivka pleaded with her brother to raise funds for his sister Yocheved, so that the family could go through with the wedding.

Rabbi Berger considered his options. No one he knew had substantial funds that they could part with, yet the *mitzvah* of *hachnasas kallah* was of paramount importance. He didn't have any funds to speak of — but he did have furniture. He gathered his children and told them of his decision. He would bring their expendable furniture to the local pawnshop and use the proceeds to help defray the costs of the wedding in Poland. In time, when he was able to save up enough money, he would redeem the furniture.

The children were incredulous. Would their father actually give away his bookcases, dressers and movable cabinets for a *kallah* about 5,000 miles away? To Rabbi Berger, though, there was no question. A sister was in desperate need. How could he dare *not* sacrifice for this important need? Years later a daughter recalled that the day the trucker came and took out the furniture there was a pall of sadness in the home resembling *Tisha B'Av.*

Now bereft of most of its furniture, the Berger home appeared to have shed much of its personality. Walls that had not been visible suddenly stared with emptiness at all that transpired in the home. The house, which now seemed bigger, also seemed diminished.

Rabbi Berger assured his family that he would redeem all the furniture, item by item, as soon as he had the money. The children were pacified but skeptical. Where could he possibly get those funds? It would take years! Though despondent, they were nevertheless proud of what their father had done. They understood that if the tables were turned and *they* needed help, they would be eternally grateful to their benefactor.

A week after the furniture was gone, a member of Rabbi Berger's congregation approached him and said, "I, too, would like to send my two sons to Torah Vodaath, but I know they are far behind in their studies compared to boys their age in the yeshivah. Perhaps two of your boys could tutor my two sons in order to bring them to the level they would need to be accepted by Torah Vodaath. I'm ready to pay them well for their time." Rabbi Berger had two sons at home: Yosef, who became one of Rabbi Yaakov Yitzchak Ruderman's first *talmidim,** and Moshe. Rabbi Berger was sure his boys would accept the challenge.

The Berger family decided that the "new found" income would go directly to the pawnshop to get back the family's furniture. The two Berger boys began tutoring immediately and as they were paid they handed the money to their father who made weekly payments to the proprietor of the pawnshop. Over a period of months, the Bergers were able to reclaim all the furniture they had given up, and the lonely walls and rooms were full again.

A discussion then ensued in the Berger home as to what they might do with the extra money that would be coming in from the future tutoring. All the children had suggestions.

One day shortly afterwards the father of the boys being tutored approached Rabbi Berger. "I am very pleased with the progress my

*In 1925, Rabbi Yehudah Heshel Levenberg (1885-1938) founded the first Lithuanian-style yeshivah in America — where only *limudei kodesh* and no secular studies were taught. The *Mashgiach* of the yeshivah was Rav Sheftel Kramer. The yeshivah began in New Haven, Connecticut, but Rabbi Levenberg moved it to Cleveland in 1929, when he accepted the position of rabbi of two different synagogues. During the yeshivah's tenure in Cleveland, Rabbi Yaakov Ruderman, son-in-law of Rav Sheftel Kramer, joined the staff and began saying *shiurim*. In 1933, Rav Ruderman moved to Baltimore where he founded Yeshivas Ner Yisroel. Yosef Berger, one of the *talmidim* in Rav Ruderman's *shiur,* followed his *rebbi* to Baltimore.

boys are making," he began. "I'm thinking that perhaps now is the time to send them to New York so that they can be tested for entrance into Torah Vodaath. What do you think? Are my sons ready?"

Rabbi Berger, who was following the boys' progress, was very honest. "You are right," he replied. "I think your boys are doing remarkably well. Let them go off to the yeshivah and may they have *hatzlachah.*"

Incredibly the amount of money earned from the tutoring was the exact amount the Berger family needed to reacquire its furniture. The tutoring came to an end, and so did any additional income.

Recently, Rabbi Berger's great-granddaughter, who teaches in two seminaries in Jerusalem, told her classes the story of her great-grandfather. She added the following appropriate thought which is a lesson for all of us. The *Baal HaTurim (Shemos* 30:12*)* writes that the Hebrew word וְנָתְנוּ, *and they shall give,* is a palindrome (a word that reads the same forwards and backwards), to signify that those who give charity need not worry that they are losing anything. To the contrary, they will be rewarded and get back all they have given — which is exactly what happened in the Berger home.

The teacher then called to tell me the story and to inform me that she first heard the *Baal HaTurim's p'shat* on one of my tapes. I felt personally gratified because the teacher is my daughter-in-law, Mrs. Genendel Krohn, who named her first son, my grandson, Yaakov Yisrael, after her great-grandfather, Rabbi Berger.

Part D:

Heavenly Harmony

Orchestrations

Quite often we are convinced that if only things would go the way we want them to, everything would work out perfectly. At times we get frustrated and even angry when things don't go smoothly: A missed call, a missed bus, a missed opportunity can send us into a frenzy. We should remember, however, that the loss of time, the loss of an object, the loss of money — all of it is calculated by the One Who orchestrates our lives — the *Ribono Shel Olam* Himself. Sometimes we are fortunate to "hear the music," to understand that events blend together to create a symphony; other times, in our limited vision, we see events as a cacophony of random sounds and noises that seem to have neither rhyme nor reason. Then it becomes a matter of faith, implicit trust in the *Ribono Shel Olam* that everything happens for a reason.

The Talmud (*Berachos* 60b) relates that Rabbi Akiva was once traveling. With him were his donkey, a rooster and a candle. Night was falling and Rabbi Akiva expected to be someone's guest in a town on the way, but no one invited him or allowed him into their homes. He was thus compelled to sleep outdoors. Rabbi Akiva accepted his situation and said: כָּל דְּעָבִיד רַחֲמָנָא לְטַב, *Whatever the Compassionate One does is for the good.* He found a spot in the woods outside the city and made himself comfortable for the evening. He kept a candle lit so he could avail himself of its light. Soon a wind blew out his candle.

What good could there be in being forced to spend the night alone, in eerie surroundings and in total darkness? Perhaps Rabbi Akiva had the same question, but he also had faith. He was sure there was a reason even if he didn't know it. Soon afterwards a cat came and ate his rooster. The rooster was his "alarm clock"; how would he get up on time the next morning? Then a lion came and devoured his donkey! How could he travel? How would he carry all his belongings if not on the donkey's back? Again he said: כָּל דְּעָבִיד רַחֲמָנָא לְטַב, *Whatever the Compassionate One does is for the good.*

In the morning Rabbi Akiva learned that a gang of marauders had plundered the city the night before. Many people were hurt and robbed. Had Rabbi Akiva's candle remained lit, the robbers may have spotted him. Had his rooster crowed or his donkey brayed, his whereabouts would have become known and he could have been harmed. Once again Rabbi Akiva said: כָּל דְּעָבִיד רַחֲמָנָא לְטַב, *Whatever the Compassionate One does is for the good.*

Rabbi Akiva made this statement of faith twice, even before the fortuitous ending of the episode. Even when things looked bleak, Rabbi Akiva was sure that there was a reason, that there had to be some good in his seeming misfortune. Indeed, we are taught in the *Shulchan Aruch*: לְעוֹלָם יְהֵא אָדָם רָגִיל לוֹמַר כָּל מַה דְּעָבִיד רַחֲמָנָא לְטַב עָבִיד, *A person should always* (even before an incident plays itself out) *be in the habit of saying, "Whatever the Compassionate One does is for the good"* (*Orach Chaim* 230:5).

On a trip to England in January 2002, I heard two different stories, in two different cities, that carried this same message, one that should apply in our daily lives.

Rabbi Yehudah Leib Wittler is a *rebbi* in one of the yeshivos in Gateshead, England. One of the students, Tuli,* misbehaved constantly and was a bad influence on his classmates and others in the dormitory. Tuli lived too far away to travel back and forth every

*The name has been changed.

day to yeshivah, but his behavior made it impossible for the yeshivah to let him remain in the dormitory. The administration now wanted him expelled permanently.

After discussing the matter with his wife, Rabbi Wittler told the administration that the third floor in his home had two small rooms that were vacant. Rabbi Wittler wanted to give Tuli one more opportunity to succeed. Tuli would live in the Wittler home in his own apartment. They would give him some independence in the hope that he would mature. Rabbi and Mrs. Wittler felt they could control the amount of influence Tuli would have on their children. They would provide his meals, but he would be responsible for getting to yeshivah on time.

One late Friday afternoon Rabbi Wittler was on the way to *shul* with his 5-year-old son Avraham. Suddenly the little boy said, "*Oy, Tati*! I forgot my Shabbos *kappel* (yarmulke)."

"Run home and get it," said Rabbi Wittler. "I'll wait right here till you get back."

They had only walked a block, so Rabbi Wittler could watch his son scamper home. Little Avrom'eleh ran home and up to his parents' room where the yarmulke was kept. He turned on the light to find it, located it, snapped it on his head and ran out in a hurry because he knew his father was waiting. In his rush, he forgot to turn off the light.

Later that night after the family had eaten the *seudas Shabbos* and the Wittlers were ready to retire for the evening, they saw that the light to their room had been left on. It didn't take much to figure out that Avraham had forgotten to shut it when he rushed back to get his Shabbos yarmulke. It was already late and very few gentiles if any would be walking the streets, and no gentiles lived on the block. There wasn't anyone who could be summoned to shut the light.

Try as he could, Rabbi Wittler could not fall asleep with the bright light. He went back downstairs and began learning a new *sefer* that piqued his interest, but after a half hour his eyes began closing. Yet he could not fall asleep. Suddenly he thought of an idea — the second small room on the third floor next to Tuli! It was empty and dark and it even had an old bed in it.

Rabbi Wittler went up to the third floor, put a fresh sheet on the mattress and tried to fall asleep. He caught a few winks but he was restless. He could feel the springs of the thin mattress digging into his back. He twisted and turned, trying to make do with a difficult situation.

As he closed his eyes to catch a few more winks, he heard a crackling sound. He tried to focus on where it was coming from. Then he smelled smoke! He ran out of his room and saw that the smoke was coming from Tuli's room next door. He opened the door and saw Tuli lying on the floor surrounded by a fire on the carpet. Rabbi Wittler yelled out at Tuli and grabbed him from the floor. Together they ran downstairs.

Tuli had wanted to read before going to sleep and before Shabbos had taken a lamp and bent it downward facing the floor to illuminate the book he would be reading. He fell asleep while reading and the lamp fell to the floor and heated the carpet until it caught fire.

Rabbi Wittler awakened his wife and together they grabbed all their children and ran out of the house. By this time the third floor was engulfed in flames. The fire brigade came shortly afterwards and put out the fire, but not before extensive damage was done to the roof and third floor. More important than anything else, however, no lives were lost and no one was hurt.

Rabbi Wittler has told this story many times. Each time he ends it by asking the same question. Was it really terrible that my son left the light on in my room? That was the only reason I ended up on the third floor and had the opportunity to smell the smoke before the fire spread.

What seemed like a bothersome inconvenience actually was the catalyst for rescue of a family. Sometimes we get answers immediately, other times it takes longer.

(And speaking of rescue, today Tuli is a young married *kollel* fellow learning in Bnei Brak, Israel — having been *saved* by the Wittlers.)

Mr. Zvi Kahn of Golders Green, a London neighborhood, gives *bar mitzvah* lessons. He teaches boys how to read the Torah and the

Haftarah, how to be the *chazzan,* and how to deliver a *dvar Torah* (Torah thought) in the synagogue or at a reception. Mr. Kahn's reputation as a masterful teacher preceeds him, so his clients include a wide gamut of boys coming from all sorts of families, Orthodox as well as non-observant.

In the winter of 1998, Mr. Kahn was contacted by a non-observant family, the Robinsons,* to prepare their son Shawn for his *bar mitzvah.* Mr. and Mrs. Robinson were not antagonistic to Orthodoxy, just ignorant. Neither of them had had a formal Jewish education, but their friends had celebrated the *bar mitzvahs* of their sons, so they were doing the same. All they wanted was that Shawn be able to recite the blessings at the Torah reading and make a little speech at the reception.

It sounded simple enough. After a few weeks of lessons, the Robinsons asked Mr. Kahn if he would grace them by attending the Sunday afternoon reception. Mr. Kahn said he would be happy to attend, but he would do so only if the food was kosher.

"What does one thing have to do with the other?" Mr. Robinson asked. "We don't keep kosher at home, so why should we have a kosher celebration outside the home?"

"When I teach the boys," replied Mr. Kahn, "I give them the total package. Becoming a *bar mitzvah* boy is not merely a 13th birthday celebration, it is a time for commitment. We don't only study the blessings and the speech. I explain the concepts of *mitzvos,* we discuss Sabbath observance and rules and guidelines of *kashrus.*"

"That's fine," said Mr. Robinson, "but that does not obligate me to make a kosher affair."

"Certainly not," said Mr. Kahn respectfully. "But then you must appreciate that I am not obligated to attend a non-kosher *bar mitzvah* affair which is totally against all I have been teaching your son."

"I can respect that," said a disappointed but obstinate Mr. Robinson.

Over the next few months, Shawn (who enjoyed Mr. Kahn calling him Simchah, his Hebrew name), became inspired by his teacher. He told his parents that he wanted Mr. Kahn to be able to attend his *bar mitzvah.* The Robinsons knew what that meant —

*The name has been changed.

they would have to have a kosher affair. They were not happy with that prospect for it would mean that some of their favorite foods could not be served. Reluctantly they capitulated to their son's request and called Mr. Kahn.

Mr. Kahn could tell from the conversation that the Robinsons were not enthusiastic about the change of plans, but they asked him to recommend a kosher caterer. Mr. Kahn suggested they call Mr. Josh Bleier* of Royal Kosher Catering.*

Weeks went by and the issue of the kosher catering did not come up again. Every once in a while Mr. Kahn wondered if indeed the Robinsons had called Royal Kosher. He was hesitant to bring up the matter for fear that it might look as though he were questioning their integrity. Yet the question gnawed at him.

On the Sunday morning of the *bar mitzvah,* Mr. Kahn decided to call Josh Bleier and see if indeed he was catering the event. He called Mr. Bleier at home but there was no answer. He called a half hour later and again no answer. This time he left a message on the answering machine that he needed to be called back immediately.

He waited impatiently but received no call. He tried every 20 minutes and each time hung up in frustration at not reaching anyone. He decided to call the office of Royal Kosher, and there, too, all he got was an answering machine. He couldn't understand how a catering outfit could be working at an affair and not have a way of being contacted.

Now Mr. Kahn began debating whether he should go to the reception altogether. If it wasn't going to be kosher, he would have to walk out and that would be insulting. He certainly couldn't stay there he reasoned, for it would be a *chillul Hashem* for someone in his position to sit at a table where non-kosher food was being served. If he didn't go, however, and the affair was kosher, the Robinsons would be upset that the Orthodox teacher had lied to them about his coming, and that would be an even bigger *chillul Hashem.* Mr. Kahn tried Mr. Bleier's home and office one more time and again he reached no one.

By 1:00 p.m. Mr. Kahn decided that he would go to the *bar mitzvah*. It was the lesser of two evils if he had to leave. At least the Robinsons would see that he made the effort.

---

*The name has been changed.

As he walked into the hall where the *bar mitzvah* was taking place, Sandy Pilberg* of Prince Prestige Caterers* came running towards him. "Zvi," he said excitedly, "it's only because of you that this *bar mitzvah* is kosher. What a *zechus* you have that no one here today will eat *treif!*"

Zvi Kahn was perplexed. "Sandy, what are you doing here? Isn't Josh Bleier catering this event?"

"No," replied Mr. Pilberg. "I think he has two jobs out of town. And when this family called him months ago he told them he would not be available and referred them to me for the job. When they called me, they told me they didn't keep kosher but they were doing it only for you! You don't realize how influential you are."

Zvi was amazed. What if he had reached Josh Bleier and was able to ask him if he was catering the Robinson *bar mitzvah*? Josh would have said that he wasn't and Zvi would have wrongly concluded that the Robinsons didn't call after all. An office as busy as the Royal Kosher office could not be expected to remember who had and who had not called, especially if they weren't doing the job.

Not reaching Josh Bleier or his office was frustrating and irritating, but it was the reason Mr. Kahn avoided a *chillul Hashem.*

> Do we hear the music of the symphony of our lives? Maybe we have to tune in a little better.

On Golden Paths

Ever since his father Jack (Yankel) died, Tully Gold has made it a point to visit his mother every morning on his way to work. Tully lives in Flatbush; his mother lives in Belle Harbor, a small Queens neighborhood with pretty homes and manicured lawns sandwiched between Jamaica Bay and the Atlantic Ocean.

Yankel Gold and his wife settled in Belle Harbor in 1964, where he eventually moved his Madelaine Chocolate Novelties company

*The name has been changed.

and became a prominent member of the Jewish community. He was a prosperous businessman and beloved philanthropist who supported numerous causes, especially the Belz institutions in New York and Israel, as he had grown up with Belzer *chassidus* in Europe before the War.

Tully had been working for his father for more than a decade and he ran the business after his father passed away. Every morning he would drive from his home in Flatbush, over the Marine Parkway Bridge into Belle Harbor, stop at his mother's home for a coffee and take the small bagged lunch that she lovingly made for him.

One morning as Tully was driving in Belle Harbor on Cronston Ave. on the way to the factory, he noticed a hearse at the corner of 129th Street in front of Yeshiva Mercaz Hatorah. Standing behind the hearse was Rabbi Moshe Lerer, one of Belle Harbor's community leaders and activists, along with a group of *bachurim* from the yeshivah. They were about to accompany the hearse and pay final respects to the *niftar* (the person who had passed away).

Tully wondered if the *niftar* was someone he knew. His mother hadn't said anything about a death in the community. He parked his car, crossed the street, and walked toward the hearse.

Rabbi Lerer noticed Tully and exclaimed with astonishment, "I can't believe you're here. You actually belong here!"

Tully was taken aback. Who was the *niftar* and why did Rabbi Lerer think Tully belonged there?

As they walked behind the hearse with the *bachurim* behind them, Rabbi Lerer said, "The man who died was a tragic, lonely figure who spent years in hospitals for his mental condition. Over thirty years ago your father started the *Chevrah Kaddisha* (burial society) in Belle Harbor and got me involved. In the beginning he did everything. He did the *taharos* (ritual cleansing of the *niftar*), the arrangements for the funeral, and at times even the burial. We saw all kinds of situations. One day he said to me, 'Rabbi Lerer, I am giving you money and I want you to hold onto it. Some day there will be someone who can't afford *tachrichim* (burial shrouds) or the cost of a funeral or even a plot to be buried in. I want you to be able to take care of it without delay.'

"I'm using your father's money for this funeral, because the *niftar* had nothing. Had your father been alive today he surely would have been here with me. The *Ribono Shel Olam* orchestrated your schedule so that you would be here to take his place. What a great *zechus* for you and your father!"

As Tully walked silently behind the hearse he thought to himself, "My father always taught us what do with our money. Turns out he's still teaching us."

Building on a Foundation in Mexico

The negotiations were taking much longer than expected. Two representatives of a real estate conglomerate were trying to complete the purchase of an office building in downtown Mexico City, but the lawyers were belaboring the details slowly and meticulously. Every office had to be inspected, the insurance policies verified, and the terms of payment specified to the last penny. Jacobo Sherem, the managing partner of the owners' group, was desperate to complete the transaction. With every passing moment, he was becoming more impatient and exasperated.

An architect by profession, Jacobo had been trying to sell this particular office building for months, so that he could finally turn a profit on his investment. He had designed, bought and sold buildings in the past, but this building on Calle Presa Salinillas had been his biggest investment, and so far it had been a losing proposition for his group. Due to the depressed financial climate in Mexico, most of the office space was unoccupied.

As the hours passed, Jacobo became increasingly nervous. The buyers had told him unequivocally that they were leaving Mexico on the first plane out the next morning, which was Saturday. They would not delay their trip. If they could complete the purchase that day, that would be wonderful; otherwise they would cancel the negotiations and move on to prospective deals in other countries.

It was the late hour of the day, Friday, that was putting pressure on Jacobo. For the last year he had been attending evening study classes in the Aram Tzovah *Kollel* in the Polanco section of Mexico City. He studied Torah a few nights a week, but he was not as yet *shomer Shabbos* (Sabbath observant). After many discussions and much introspection and inspiration from *avreichim* (*kollel* members) at Aram Tzovah, Jacobo and his wife Sophia were inching closer to total commitment to Shabbos observance. Jacobo had already started going to *shul* every Friday night and his office was closed on Shabbos, but he and Sophia were not yet complete Sabbath observers.

Frustrated at being so close to, yet so far from, fulfilling his dream of selling the building, Jacobo looked at his watch and saw that there was less than an hour and a half to Shabbos. Reluctantly he told the prospective buyers that the negotiations would have to continue Sunday or Monday — he had to leave and close his office. The buyers threatened that it was now or never, for they were flying out of the country the next day. But Jacobo would not budge. Shabbos was coming. He hadn't missed a Friday night in *shul* in weeks and he wasn't going to miss tonight. The buyers were incredulous that Jacobo would scuttle a deal that would lift him out of the financial doldrums, but he would not be moved.

The parties to the negotiations bid each other a final farewell, and Jacobo went home to prepare for Shabbos. He couldn't help but second guess himself. Had he acted correctly? There would be other Shabbosos when he would be in the synagogue, but now he might never be able to sell this building that was becoming an albatross around his financial holdings. He tried to enjoy the Shabbos, but it was difficult. An internal debate raged in his mind. He was proud of his commitment but he wondered if it was worth the price.

Two weeks later, early Thursday morning, September 19, 1985, (during the *Selichos* of *Aseres Yemei Teshuvah)* Mexico was struck by the greatest tragedy in its history. In a matter of seconds, a monstrous, rumbling earthquake gashed and shook Mexico City, toppling buildings, swallowing homes, wreaking havoc and bringing instantaneous death to thousands of people! Within 24 hours, as the country staggered to adjust to the shock and magnitude of the Thursday tragedy, an aftershock staggered the city. The number of people killed in these earthquakes reached a shocking 4,541. Another 14,236 were injured and 2,637 required hospitalization.

In the downtown district there was utter devastation. People searched in vain for relatives and friends, but it was mostly for naught. The destruction, mayhem and sorrow was beyond imagination. Yet, amidst all the devastation, one building remained standing — the one Jacobo couldn't sell. Its windows were blown out and some of the facade of the building had peeled off, but remarkably it was structurally sound.

The Mexican government had to regroup. Aid and rescue efforts had to be directed and coordinated. People needed the assurance that the government was functioning and accessible. Thus within days of the earthquakes, Jacobo's building, conveniently located downtown, was checked for its strength and stability. When it passed inspection, the government bought most of the offices in the building and the remaining space was sold to large corporations who had lost their offices when other buildings collapsed or were deemed unsafe. Jacobo's extraordinary profit was far beyond what he would have made had he sold the building weeks before.

The deals for his building propelled Jacobo into a category of wealth he never imagined. The *Hashgachah Pratis* (Divine Providence) of the Shabbos not allowing him to sell the building propelled him into being a total Sabbath observer.

Jacobo and Sophia never told the story to anyone. Word got out that their building was sold to the government, but no one in the community knew about the frantic Friday negotiations two weeks before the earthquakes, and Jacobo's decision to close his office for Shabbos.

Years later, in the palatial lobby of his new magnificent office building, Jacobo and Sophia tendered a grand party in honor of his first completion of a Talmudic tractate, which he had studied for several years with Rabbi Shea Deutsch (now teaching in Lakewood, N.J.) at the Aram Tzovah *Kollel*. There, in the presence of rabbis, community leaders and friends, Jacobo told the story that changed his life.

As Jacobo showed aerial photos taken from governmental helicopters of his building standing alone among the ruins, one saw the isolated structure symbolizing the predicament of the *baal teshuvah*. Rising alone among people who are in spiritual ruins, he remains unfazed by the whirlwind of *apikorsus* (heresy) and apathy toward authentic *Yiddishkeit* that swirls around him. The *baal teshuvah* stands tall because he is firmly connected to the foundations of his heritage.

Curbside Handling

The Talmud teaches: לְעוֹלָם יְהֵא אָדָם זָהִיר בִּתְפִלַּת הַמִּנְחָה שֶׁהֲרֵי אֵלִיָּהוּ לֹא נַעֲנָה אֶלָּא בִּתְפִלַּת הַמִּנְחָה, *A person should always be diligent with regard to the Minchah (afternoon) prayer, for Elijah (the prophet) was answered through the Minchah prayer (Berachos* 6b *and I Kings* 18:36*).*

The *Tur* (*Orach Chaim* 232) states that there is abundant reward for those who pray the afternoon *Minchah* service, for it requires special concentration and fortitude to remove oneself from midday involvements and focus attention on prayer. This is unlike the *Shacharis* (morning service) or *Maariv* (evening service) prayers when one has not yet started or has already finished his ventures for the day.

The following story, which took place during a *Minchah* in Lawrence, New York, made a deep impression on the participants, who recognized it as an example of *Hashgachah Pratis* (*Divine Providence*).

It was a hot, sweltering day in July 2001. The stifling, thick, humid air caused everyone outside to sweat profusely as temperatures climbed over 100 degrees. The men coming to daven *Minchah* at Beth Sholom in Lawrence, an affluent area in New York's Nassau County, weren't concerned with the weather, for they drove to their air-conditioned *shul* in their air-conditioned cars, having come from their comfortably air-conditioned homes. They had to confront the torrid heat only for the few steps it took to walk from the *shul's* parking lot to the entrance on Broadway and Washington.

On that day, however, the *shul* was locked. The custodian was usually there to open the *shul* and set the temperature long before anyone got there, and if he wasn't there the *shammas* (sexton) had the key. On this late Tuesday afternoon, for some unknown reason, neither the custodian nor the *shammas* was there.

The men, in their various shades of casual Lawrence dress, stood around making small talk, waiting for some relief. Beads of perspiration began running down their cheeks. Finally someone said, "Gentlemen, it's getting late. We'll just have to *daven* right here on the lawn."

Someone called out *"Ashrei"* and the *minyan* began. Most men knew *Minchah* by heart. One fellow took out a small *"Mincha* and *Marriv"* from his pocket; another fellow actually had the *Shemoneh Esrei* scrolled on his Palm Pilot.

The *baal tefillah* was just starting *Kaddish* when a silver SUV (Sports Utility Vehicle) pulled up in front of the *shul*. Some men glanced at the new arrival, but none of them recognized the car.

The driver exited the car and walked around the front of the vehicle, toward the sidewalk alongside the lawn where the men were about to begin *Shemoneh Esrei*. Suddenly, without warning, the man fell to the ground. Some thought that he may have slipped, but as he lay motionless, several men dashed over to help him. He was unconscious.

There was a doctor among the *mispallelim* and he immediately began attending the fallen man. He had had a heart attack and his life was in danger. The doctor told his friends to call Hatzalah (the Jewish emergency medical unit) and within minutes they were on the scene.

A crowd gathered around the unknown man who still lay motionless. People watched with concern as the man was gently placed on a stretcher and taken to the waiting Hatzalah ambulance. Within 10 minutes the police came and began their investigation. One of the officers asked if there was anyone else in the car — no one had even thought about that.

A police officer went to the ambulance and searched through the victim's pockets. He found a set of car keys and a remote to unlock the doors. He rushed to the vehicle and to his horror he saw a 2-year-old child, drenched in sweat, harnessed in a car seat in the back.

The officer unbuckled the child and took him out into the fresh air. The onlookers gasped, realizing that he could have suffocated in the intense heat of the closed car.

Later that evening the news spread that the gentleman was recovering and that he would be fine. One of the Lawrence men brought the child back to his grateful mother, who could only thank Hashem a thousand times over that the *shul* was locked, something that had never happened before. For it was only because the men were on the front lawn — where they saw the man fall — that a horrifying double tragedy was averted.

A Cycle in a Cemetery

There is a custom to visit and pray at the grave sites of parents and ancestors before *Rosh Hashanah,* as a prelude to the awesome days of *Aseres Yemei Teshuvah* (the Ten Days of Repentance) between *Rosh Hashanah* and *Yom Kippur.* (See *Orach Chaim* 581:4.) The *Mishnah Berurah* (ibid. note 27) writes that prayers at cemeteries where *tzaddikim* (righteous people) rest are more apt to be accepted. Prayers are offered to Hashem (not to the deceased) that one should merit Heavenly compassion in the merit of the *tzaddikim.* The following remarkable story took place before *Rosh Hashanah* in 1999, at the Syrian-Sephardic section of a cemetery on Staten Island, New York.

Every year Rabbi Shmuel Amon, rabbi of the Sephardic Congregation Shaare Tefillah in Eatontown, New Jersey, and his wife Gene visit the grave site of her late mother, Mrs. Sylvia Serouya, before *Rosh Hashanah*. They usually go on a Sunday, which is more convenient for both of them, but on Sundays — especially before *Rosh Hashanah* — the narrow cemetery roadways are always crammed with the cars of people who come to pray and pay respects to their loved ones. In Elul of 1999, the Amons found it difficult to go on a Sunday and went on a Tuesday afternoon instead.

It seemed strange to drive quickly on the narrow cemetery roads and right up to the grave site. The Amons were the only ones there and the area was eerily quiet. The endless symmetrical rows of gray headstones lent an air of sadness, because each monument bespoke a life that was no more, a story that had come to a sad end.

The Amons were reciting *Tehillim* quietly when they noticed a small funeral procession in the distance, on the way to an open grave site nearby.

It was obvious that the mourners were not observant; the yarmulkes perched on the men's heads sat like stiff, uncomfortable triangles, balancing in the soft wind. The Amons watched as a coffin was removed from the hearse and placed alongside the open grave. Suddenly one of the men motioned to Rabbi Amon to join their group. Rabbi Amon assumed that either the mourners needed help with reciting *Kaddish* or they needed a tenth man to complete a *minyan*. It turned out that they needed both, and he was more than happy to assist.

As the coffin lay on the ground, Rabbi Amon asked the mourners, "Aren't you going to bury the person?"

"We just want to say *Kaddish*," said one of them. "The cemetery workers will lower our father into the ground and cover the coffin."

"But that's not the way it should be done," Rabbi Amon protested. "The coffin should be lowered into the grave and covered by Jews."

"Rabbi, we are not religious," was the curt reply. "Let's get the *Kaddish* done and leave it to them. That's what they get paid for."

Rabbi Amon realized that he could not convince them to comply with *halachah*. He was able to persuade them to assist in lowering the coffin into the grave, and then helped them with the *Kaddish*. After the mourners left to go home, Rabbi Amon approached the gravediggers who were waiting alongside their tractor, ready to sweep the mound of earth over the coffin. "Do you mind if I take care of the burial myself?" he asked.

"You can do it," one of them said. "It's a slow day we're not going anyplace."

For the next half hour, Rabbi Amon scooped earth with an old hardwood-handled shovel. His back hurt but he continued his lonely toil, for he was convinced that the deceased man, left alone by his family, was in the category of a *mes mitzvah* (a corpse whose burial is not being attended to; see Responsa of *Maharatz Chayes* no. 26).

In the silence of the cemetery, Rabbi Amon felt elated, elevated and grateful that he had this rare opportunity — right before *Rosh Hashanah*. He remembered the Talmudic teaching (*Sotah* 14a) that it is a *mitzvah* to emulate Hashem's attributes. *Chazal* give numerous examples: "Hashem visited the sick (Avraham *Avinu*) — you too should visit the sick; Hashem buried the dead (Moshe *Rabbeinu*) — you too should bury the dead." How fortunate he was to be able to emulate Hashem in this way at this time of the year.

He wondered who this man was and why, despite his family's disinterest, he merited to have a Jewish burial. Had he done something extraordinary so that at the very last moment he was fortunate to be buried according to Torah law?

Before Rabbi Amon and his wife left the cemetery, he bent down to read the identity marker over the grave. He had buried a man named Manny Haleb.* The rabbi went to the office and asked for the family's address. During the next few days he made some inquiries and was stunned at what he found out.

In the late 1960's and early 1970's many Syrian families were able to flee their country and come to America. The families settled in various communities throughout the United States; Rabbi Amon's parents had settled in Seattle, Washington, where they raised their children and struggled to make a living. Young Shmuel attended the Seattle Hebrew Day School but was not sure where he would attend high school. Rabbi Sholom Rifkin

*The name has been changed.

and Rabbi Shlomo Maimon of Seattle decided to extend the day school to a ninth grade to assure that the boys would have at least one more year of *limudei kodesh* before going to a public high school.

In June of 1964, a boy in his early teens came back to his hometown of Seattle and gave a stirring talk to the graduating ninth graders. They all knew him because he had attended their school for years. He told them what a wonderful year he had had in Yeshivas Ner Yisroel in Baltimore, and he encouraged his friends to take the same bold step he had, and come to Ner Yisroel, where their minds and hearts would be opened to new levels of Torah and *yiras Shamayim.* The young speaker, Yissocher Frand, was so convincing and inspiring (even then!) that six of the seven ninth graders followed his lead and went to Ner Yisroel the next September. One of them was Shmuel Amon.

When Shmuel arrived in Ner Yisroel, he saw that he wasn't the only Syrian boy in the yeshivah. Under the direction of Rabbi Naftali Neuberger, Ner Yisroel had opened its doors to immigrant young men, to give them opportunities they never had before. Very few of those boys could pay tuition, however, as their parents struggled to establish themselves in their new country. To defray the cost of their studies, a group of successful Syrian businessmen undertook to sponsor the Syrian *talmidim.* Manny Haleb was one of the sponsors.

Remarkably, the man that Rabbi Shmuel Amon buried according to *halachah* was one of those who helped pay for his Torah education! Shmuel studied in Ner Yisroel for ten years, from 1964 until 1974, and became a teacher and rabbi, first in Denver and then in New Jersey. By providing funds for Shmuel's education, Manny had helped give Rabbi Amon the opportunity to learn and teach Torah until this very day. Though Manny fell on hard times and eventually became an almost forgotten man — Hashem remembered. He thus orchestrated that Manny's beneficiary would perform the final *chessed shel emes* (kindness without expectation of a reward) for his benefactor. And with that act, a cycle of *chessed* was completed.

The View From Chicago to Chevron

At the Agudath Israel convention in 2001, Rabbi Moshe Chodosh, *Rosh Yeshivah* of Yeshivas Ohr Elchonon in Jerusalem, told me a story of horror and heartache that occurred in *Eretz Yisrael*. In the summer of 1929, Reb Moshe's parents, the esteemed *Mashgiach* Rabbi Meir Chodosh (1898-1989) and his wife, Rebbetzin Tzvia Leah, witnessed the horrific events which affected them for the rest of their lives.

Reb Moshe's purpose in telling the story was not merely to share history. He wanted to relay the sensitivity, temperament and perspective of numerous people touched by the events. I am grateful to Rabbi Aryeh Zolty of Jerusalem who provided dates and details of this painful episode, which involved a close relative. Additional information was culled from *Hamashgiach*, the biography of Rabbi Meir Chodosh, written by his daughter, Rebbetzin Shulamis Ezrachi.

In the 1920's, members of the Chovevei Zion (lit. lovers of Zion) organization traveled throughout the world encouraging Jews to support those living in the New *Yishuv* (settlement) in Israel and to consider immigrating there.

One of those who traveled from *Eretz Yisrael* to the United States was Rabbi Yaakov Volk of the Shaarei Chessed neighborhood of Jerusalem. He was a dynamic, eloquent speaker who inspired his listeners with his passionate love for *Eretz Yisrael*.

Shortly after *Succos* in 1927, Rabbi Volk spoke in various *shuls* in Chicago. One of his speeches was attended by one of the wealthiest Jews in Chicago, Mr. Yerachmiel Wexler.

Rabbi Volk's words were mesmerizing and exhilarating. After Shabbos, Mr. Wexler met with Rabbi Volk. Mr. Wexler said that he would consider investing in *Eretz Yisrael* and, if things worked out well, he would even consider settling there. Over the next few days, they held lengthy and detailed discussions, and by week's end Mr. Wexler was filled with anticipation and excitement.

In March 1928, the entire Wexler family took an ocean voyage to Israel. Mr. Wexler traveled throughout the land, purchasing valuable real estate and seeking business opportunities. He also looked for a place where his family could settle. Reb Yerachmiel was so taken by the land that soon it was no longer a question *if* he would immigrate, rather *when* he would immigrate.

The Wexlers visited the town of Chevron and the famed yeshivah Knesses Yisrael that had relocated from Slabodka, Lithuania in 1924. At the time there were 200 *talmidim* in Knesses Yisrael, fifty of whom were Americans.

The Wexlers' 16-year-old son Yaakov became enamored of the *talmidim* (students) in the yeshivah.

A number of *talmidim* spoke to Mr. Wexler about letting Yaakov join the yeshivah. They assured him that they would keep an eye on him, help him find *chavrusos* (study partners) and make sure he felt comfortable in his new surroundings. Having become enthralled with *Eretz Yisrael* and recognizing Yaakov's eagerness to study in Chevron, Mr. Wexler agreed.

The family returned to America, and Yaakov, now in Chevron, grew in his Torah studies and *yiras Shamayim* as never before. He was a humble, caring person who shared his wealth with numerous impoverished boys in the yeshivah. He became beloved by his peers and admired by his teachers. On *Rosh Hashanah* 5689 (1928), he was so moved by the atmosphere in the *beis midrash* that he said to one of his *rebbeim,* "Until this moment I had no idea what *davening* was all about."

After four months in the yeshivah, Yaakov's aunt wrote him, asking about his life and welfare in the yeshivah. He wrote back, "If you consider life to mean luxuries and amusements, then I am devoid of all that, but if you consider life as I understand it today, I am most fortunate and thrilled to be part of this life."

While the intensity of learning continued uninterrupted within the confines of the yeshivah, the streets in nearby Jerusalem simmered with Arab hatred, as Arabs and Jews were often involved in bloody skirmishes and confrontations. There were those in Chevron who were convinced that no matter what happened elsewhere in the rest of the country, no harm would befall the Jews who lived in the town of the Patriarchs and Matriarchs. Arabs and Jews did business together in Chevron and socialized in the streets. If any place was safe, it was the sacred town of Chevron.

The sense of security was nowhere stronger than in the home of the popular bank manager and *rosh hakahal* (leader of the Jewish community), Mr. Eliezer Don Slonim, known to everyone as Lazer Don. Mr. Slonim was well connected politically. He dealt with Arab merchants every day, and was involved in all communal affairs. His father, Rabbi Yaakov Yosef Slonim, was the official rav of Chevron.

One Thursday morning, Rebbetzin Tzvia Leah Chodosh and her friend Rebbetzin Wolinski overheard Arabs joking in the marketplace. Rebbetzin Wolinski, who understood Arabic, heard one of them say, "Those women are buying for Shabbos but they don't realize they won't even be alive on Shabbos."

Frightened, the two women thought it would be prudent to go with their husbands to Jerusalem for Shabbos. They discussed it with their husbands and together the four of them went to the Anglo-Palestine bank where Lazer Don was in the middle of a meeting with seven Arab merchants.

The Chodoshes and Wolinskis took Mr. Slonim aside and told him what they had overheard. Mr. Slonim went back to the meeting and repeated their story to the seven Arabs. They laughed and told him that they themselves would protect him if anything happened. They assured him that all would be quiet. Mr. Slonim confidently told the two couples they could stay for Shabbos.

Nothing would be further from the truth. The savage Arabs betrayed their friend. On Friday morning, August 23, 1929, the infamous Chevron pogrom began. Marauding and plundering Arabs attacked Jews in the street, and ransacked homes and stores. They ran into the Knesses Yisrael building and killed Shmuel Rosenholtz in the *beis midrash*. Shmuel had been known as the *masmid* of the yeshivah.

The British authorities did little if anything to stop the fighting and killing. Friday night Mr. Slonim announced that his house would be open to anyone who sought protection. All night, yeshivah *bachurim* and people of the community streamed to the Slonim home.

On Shabbos morning, August 24, after provocative and inflammatory speeches by the Arab *Mufti* (leader), Arab mobs yelling "Jihad!" brutally attacked and murdered Jews throughout Chevron with a vengeance. As a wild, armed mob marched on Lazer Don's home, he came out of his house brandishing a gun. He was killed instantly.

The Arabs ran through his home, room to room, searching for Jews, brutally killing anyone they found. Among the unfortunate people who were killed in Mr. Slonim's house was the beloved *bachur* from Chicago, Yaakov Wexler. The blossom that was Yaakov was torn from its roots.

By the time the savage brutality ended, sixty-seven Jews had been killed, among them twenty-four yeshivah *bachurim*. Reb Meir Chodosh and his wife Tzvia Leah, who were at different ends of the Slonim home, were beaten and left for dead. They survived only because others who were killed fell on top of them and shielded them.

A pall of sadness and melancholy shrouded *Klal Yisrael*. It was a devastating time for the yeshivah and a defining moment for the Jews in the *Yishuv*. The yeshivah left the town and moved to the Geulah section of Jerusalem and was renamed Chevron. It still carries that name.

Life would go on, but those who survived would remain scarred forever. And those who had any association with the events would try to make sense of their existence.

A while later, the Chodoshes had their first child, a boy. They named him Aharon David after one of the yeshivah *bachurim* who had been killed in Chevron, Aharon David Epstein, also from Chicago. He was a cousin to Rebbetzin Chodosh. When the rebbetzin was asked why she would name a child after one who had perished so horribly, she answered, "Because I know that it will always be a source of strength to his mother that a child was named for her son." Rav Aharon David Chodosh is today the *Mashgiach* in Yeshivas Mir in Jerusalem.

Rabbi Volk, the noted speaker, made other trips to America but he never went back to the *shul* in Chicago where the Wexlers *dav-*

ened. He could not face his friend Yerachmiel Wexler, for he knew in his heart that it was he who had perked the family's interest in *Eretz Yisrael*, an interest which had ultimately brought their dear son Yaakov to Chevron.

In 1930, Rabbi Volk was in a *shul* in New York City and was taken aback when he saw Mr. Wexler. "We miss you in Chicago," exclaimed Mr. Wexler, as he greeted Rabbi Volk warmly. "We used to enjoy your talks. Why haven't you come back?"

Rabbi Volk's face became flushed. At first he couldn't talk and then, barely raising his head, he said hesitantly, "To tell you the truth, Reb Yerachmiel, I feel terribly guilty about your son. I know that I had a part in your coming to *Eretz Yisrael* and in Yaakov's staying in Chevron ..." His voice trailed off. He could not face his friend.

"You are wrong for feeling guilty," said Mr. Wexler. "Just the opposite. You saved my son. If indeed there was a Heavenly decree that he should die at the age of 17, he could have died in New York in a car accident, or in Chicago from illness. But because of you he came to *Eretz Yisrael* and died because he was learning Torah in Chevron. He died only because he was a Jew and there can be no nobler death than that."

Rabbi Volk was awed that a bereaved father could have such thoughts, and moved and grateful that he shared them so openly.

Yerachmiel Wexler eventually moved his family to Israel, where he raised his extraordinary children. His daughter Esther married Rabbi Betzalel Zolty, who later became the distinguished rav of Jerusalem.

Their son Reb Aryeh Zolty told me of a wrenching incident that happened in 1995 when he was sitting *shivah* for his mother. An elderly gentleman came to the Zolty home, accompanied by his middle-aged son. The man was out of breath, having labored up three flights of steps. None of the mourners recognized him, but once he was acknowledged he began speaking softly.

"Surely you heard of the name Yaakov Wexler," he said slowly. He didn't have to explain. They knew that Yaakov was their mother's older brother. The mourners nodded their heads.

"When your grandfather Reb Yerachmiel came to Chevron more than sixty years ago, I was the American boy who convinced him to let Yaakov stay in the yeshivah. It was on my reassurances more than anyone else's that your grandfather consented to go back to America without him. I have felt so horrible all these years after what happened to him during the pogrom. Did your mother ever say anything about it; did your grandfather ever say anything about it?"

Reb Aryeh repeated to the saddened gentleman what his grandfather had said to Rabbi Volk, that if Yaakov was destined to die, there could have been no more noble place than the yeshivah surroundings of Chevron.

Tears came to the visitor's eyes as he said softly, "בָּאתִי לְנַחֵם וְנִמְצֵאתִי מְנוּחָם, I came to console but I became consoled."

> אָבִינוּ מַלְכֵּנוּ עֲשֵׂה לְמַעַן הֲרוּגִים עַל שֵׁם קָדְשֶׁךָ, Our Father, our King, act for the sake of those who were murdered for Your Holy Name.

A Song of Scorpions

Rabbi Yaakov Haber has served Jewish communities in numerous capacities. He was rabbi of the Saranac Synagogue in his hometown of Buffalo, N.Y., for ten years, and National Director of the Australian Institute of Torah in Melbourne for six years. When he returned to the States, he became the National Director of Jewish Education for the Union of Orthodox Rabbis (O.U.) and is currently the rabbi of the Beis Torah Congregation of Monsey, N.Y., where he succeeded the founder of the congregation, Rabbi Berel Wein.

At the *bar mitzvah* of my nephew Yochanan Sofer, in Far Rockaway, N.Y., Rabbi Shlomo Menachem Sofer of Australia told me a remarkable story about Rabbi Haber. He saw from my reaction that I questioned its veracity. Two years later at a wedding in Bnei Brak, Rabbi Sofer told the story again, and he added, "Call Rabbi Haber, he will confirm that every word is true."

He was right. I thank Rabbi Sofer for his persistence and Rabbi Haber for providing more facts.

It was the first night of Chanukah and Rabbi Haber, with his wife, Bayle, at his side, was about to light the menorah. The Habers, who lived in the Unsdorf section of Jerusalem, were expecting their first child. They were delighted to begin their married life in Israel. R' Yaakov was studying at Yeshiva Torah Ore, where he enjoyed a close relationship with the *Rosh Yeshivah*, Rabbi Chaim Pinchus Scheinberg.

There was a knock on the front door. The Habers were not expecting anyone and their surprise turned to astonishment when they opened the door and saw a bedraggled, disheveled middle-aged man. His hat was turned askew, his clothes were filthy and his face unshaven. His right eye seemed locked shut, making him look like a pirate who misplaced his eye patch.

"Do you think you might have a meal for me?" he asked politely.

The Habers looked at each other and then back at the poor visitor. It was Chanukah, Hashem had blessed them with much good, and they could only imagine how lonely the fellow must feel. He didn't look dangerous, just sad. Why not share their bounty with others?

"Yes, come in," said Rabbi Haber. "We're going to eat after I light the menorah. Please join us."

The man tried to smile but his effort failed. He seemed to grimace as he thanked them softly. As he walked past the Habers into the dining area, they could smell the stench of his clothes that probably hadn't been washed in weeks. They would not go back on their word. He could stay for the meal and they would endure it.

He said his name was Beinish* and he seemed pleasant though he didn't talk much about his personal life. He did mention that he lived alone and that he had fallen on hard times. The meal went by uneventfully as Rabbi Haber discussed some spiritual aspects of

*The name has been changed.

the festival. However before Beinish left, he asked the Habers if he could come back again. They assured him he could.

Over the next few weeks Beinish began coming with increased frequency and soon the Habers found themselves hosting him on Shabbos and a few times in the middle of the week. Mrs. Haber didn't mind washing the soiled clothes that Beinish would bring her every few days, but when he started coming in mid-afternoons while R' Yaakov was in the yeshivah, it became uncomfortable. The Habers hinted to Beinish that it was better that he come in the evening, but he said that it was often hard for him to do so. He came and went as he pleased.

The Habers were scheduled to move to the Romemah neighborhood, where apartments were more affordable. They wondered if they were obliged to tell Beinish when and where they were moving. Rabbi Haber asked a *she'eileh* (religious ruling) and was told that he need not reveal his new address or even tell Beinish that he was moving, so they moved to Romemah and didn't hear from Beinish again.

The Habers settled in their new quarters and had their first child. A few weeks later, Rabbi Haber noticed a scorpion sprinting across his dining room floor. He caught up with it and made sure it would never come back.

There are 1,300 species of scorpions worldwide, and some of the most dangerous are in the Middle East. Only one species in the Unites States and almost twenty others worldwide have venom potent enough to be dangerous to humans. Israel is home to the most deadly of all scorpions, the Palestine yellow scorpion, whose sting can be fatal to children. Rabbi Haber wasn't taking any chances.

A few days later a number of scorpions scooted across the floor. Rabbi and Mrs. Haber were frightened. Scorpions could be lethal. Soon scorpions came every day, so the Habers placed blankets over their infant's crib to prevent them from crawling in. They called an exterminator, who made two visits, but eventually he announced, "There is nothing more I can do here."

The Habers were devastated. If the exterminator couldn't eliminate the scorpions, how could they? The strange thing was that no one else on the block had this problem.

The final straw came one Shabbos morning. Rabbi Haber awoke to his wife's screams. She was standing on a chair pointing to a corner of the room where scorpions ran alongside the baseboard. Rabbi Haber hurried to get his *Mishnah Berurah,* for he knew that one may not kill a scorpion or any other insect on Shabbos, unless one is positive that it is one of the life-threatening species.

Rabbi Haber jumped atop another chair, scanning the *Mishnah Berurah (Orach Chaim* 316:10), desperately trying to decide which kind of scorpion he was permitted to kill and which he would have to leave scampering around to its pedipalps' delight.

After that harrowing Shabbos, Rabbi Haber went to see his *Rosh Yeshivah,* Rabbi Scheinberg. "*Rebbi,*" he began, "my wife and I have been going through this terrible experience with scorpions roaming our apartment. It is frightening and dangerous. Have we done anything wrong? How should I view this spiritually? Why is this happening?"

Rabbi Scheinberg is a world famous *posek* (halachic authority) and *Rosh Yeshivah* to thousands of *talmidim* in Israel and the United States. In the years that Rabbi Haber had studied under Rabbi Scheinberg and in the decades since then, never had he heard his *Rosh Yeshivah* base a halachic decision or practical advice from the source he quoted.

"Let's take a look at *Perek Shirah,*" said Rabbi Scheinberg.

> The theme of the six chapters of *Perek Shirah* is that everything in Creation has a role to play in Hashem's plan. To illustrate what that role is, *Perek Shirah* assigns a verse from *Tanach* to every being in the world, from huge mountains to tiny ants. The *sefer* is very ancient. Some say it was composed by King David, some say by King Solomon, and some say by Rabbi Yehudah HaNasi. (It is first mentioned in *Yalkut Shimoni, Parashas Bo* 187:11. For an in-depth commentary and historical background of *Perek Shirah* see Rabbi Nosson Slifkin's *Nature's Song.*)

Rabbi Scheinberg took out a *sefer* that had *Perek Shirah* and turned to Chapter Six, which contains the "songs" of creeping creatures, such as the snake, snail and ant. He pointed to the entry on scorpions. עַקְרָב אוֹמֵר טוֹב ה׳ לַכֹּל וְרַחֲמָיו עַל כָּל מַעֲשָׂיו, *[The scorpion says:] G-d is good to all, and His mercy is upon all His handiwork (Tehillim* 145:9*).*

Rabbi Scheinberg turned to Rabbi Haber and said, "We don't know the purpose of scorpions in this world. Even though some of them are lethal, the *Ribono Shel 0lam* has compassion on scorpions and supplies them with food and with what they need to survive. Perhaps you failed to show compassion to someone. The scorpions song is one of *rachmanus* (mercy) and that's what we must adapt in our lives."

Rabbi Haber was stunned! Suddenly the picture was becoming clear. In a sense he had abandoned Beinish, the poor man who had been relying on him and his wife. As he left Rabbi Scheinberg, he knew he had to find Beinish somehow, somewhere.

Beinish had said he lived somewhere in the Geulah neighborhood. Rabbi Haber walked through the legendary streets named after Biblical prophets, which recalled ancient Jewish history and holiness. Rechov Yecheskel, Rechov Chagai, Rechov Ovadyah ... but Beinish was nowhere to be found. Days went by and Rabbi Haber felt anxious. He couldn't spend so much time searching for Beinish — he had come to Israel to study — but the scorpions were still invading his apartment.

One day as he was on a bus coming down Rechov Strauss toward Kikar HaShabbat, the square where Geulah meets Meah Shearim — he spotted Beinish. He quickly got off the bus and ran over to the destitute man who seemed to be walking aimlessly. "Reb Beinish, we miss you and we need you! When can you come again?"

Beinish smiled and said, "I miss you, too. Tell me when and where I should come."

Rabbi Haber gave Beinish his new Romemah address, and that night Beinish came for supper. That was just the start; once again he began coming regularly. Beinish was the Haber's frequent guest, but the scorpions were gone. Not one returned!

This went on until the Habers moved from Israel as Rabbi Haber accepted his first rabbinical position in his hometown of Buffalo, New York.

The introduction to Perek Shirah is noteworthy. ... *"And Rebbi said: Anyone who involves himself with Perek Shirah in this world — I testify that he is destined for the World to Come ... he merits to learn and to teach, to observe and to fulfill [mitzvos] ... his studies are established in him, and his days are lengthened."*

An exact description of Rabbi Chaim Pinchus Scheinberg.

Part E:
Mentor's Messages

Without Reservation

The following story is from the most incredible I have ever heard. Its impact is striking because it blends empathy, insight, validation, and genuine love for a fellow Jew. One pauses with awe at its surprise ending. Let us begin.

In the 1960's Ben Richards* grew up in the Canarsie section of Brooklyn hating city life. He was a voracious reader of books on nature and dreamed of living on a farm where he could witness the seasonal flowering of the earth, nourished by life-giving rains, the warming sun and the freshness of daily dew. He yearned for the music of songbirds, the evening chatter of crickets, and the tranquility of sheep grazing in the meadows. To Ben, life meant the rebirth of spring with its vivid yellows and greens bursting forth along acres of land, transforming into brilliant oranges, browns and reds, and finally shedding its vibrancy for the silent sleep of winter as land and trees became blanketed with snow.

Ralph and Nostrand Avenues in Canarsie weren't doing it for him. The fumes of the buses, the carbon copy houses, the endless rows of stores repelled him. He had to leave city life. In his view, urbanized Brooklyn, or for that matter urbanized anywhere, was not the way life was meant to be lived.

That his parents were Orthodox Jews meant little to Ben. He had no use for Judaism. He was a "free spirit," with no desire to be encumbered by rules and regulations that controlled every aspect of his life. He needed his freedom. He wanted his space. And so at age 17 he left home and traveled 2,000 miles westward to live a

*Name has been changed.

totally different life, experience a totally different culture, and carry on with a totally different mindset. He joined the Blackfeet Indian Reservation in the northwestern mountains of America, bordering Glacier National Park.

While at the reservation he enrolled in the local university where he majored in wildlife biology. His primary teacher on the reservation was an old man named Whitecalf. Ben stayed at Blackfeet for a while and then joined another reservation in nearby South Dakota. Eventually he became accepted as an equal. For years he tilled the soil, ate his own produce, and worked alongside his adopted family members. He knew their culture, understood their language and respected their traditions. He participated in powwows — festive gatherings of celebration — dressed in traditional Indian garb.

In his constant quest for truth and the meaning of life he sought out "wise men who had knowledge of the Heavens." He learned that in the higher elevations of Ogallala, South Dakota, there was a woman on a small reservation, the matriarch of the Sioux Indian Society, who had legendary foresight and insight. To reach her he would have to travel across prairies and over hills where there were no roads and no signs, but to Ben it was not only worthwhile but imperative. Whatever it would take, he had to hear her wisdom.

He traveled alone for two days not sure he was heading in the right direction. Late one afternoon he could see the outlines of a small camp in the distance. There were people up ahead and he hoped the sagacious woman was there. He trekked toward that outpost, and was told by an old sun-baked shepherd that he had reached his destination.

The woman, Elva Onefeather, lived with her children in a twelve foot square tarpaper shack. Some of the children slept in a dilapidated 1941 Ford automobile. It seemed to Ben that some of the children, who always seemed to be dressed in shredded clothes, were retarded. He wondered if malnutrition was the cause. She brushed her children's hair every morning with a brush made from porcupine thistles.

He stayed in the area for two weeks and attended ceremonies and celebrations. Finally he approached the wise woman who spoke English and asked her about her Indian heritage.

She refused to answer him. "You are not one of us," she said. "You can never be like us, you don't belong here."

"But I have lived on reservations for years. I know your culture, I know your language, I practice your customs, and I feel part of ..."

She interrupted him. "If you were Christian, I could understand. But you are a student of the Holy White Rock Man," whom she referred to as the Wah-Kinyan-Sapa.

Ben assumed she was referring to Moshe *Rabbeinu*. (Years later he understood that the "holy rock" was a reference to *Shemos* 33:22 וְהָיָה בַּעֲבֹר כְּבֹדִי וְשַׂמְתִּיךָ בְּנִקְרַת הַצּוּר, *When My Glory passes by, I shall place you in the cleft of the rock.)*

"You are not one of us," she admonished him. "Go back to your roots. That's where you belong."

Ben was dumbfounded. He was being rejected. After all the time and effort he had invested in this lifestyle, he was being labeled, by a revered personality no less, as an outcast. Was he now to go back to city life? Jewish life? To the life he had run away from? The rejection hurt him but it made him rethink his world. Until then he had assured himself that his search for the ideal life had been successfully accomplished. Now his confidence was shaken.

Within days Ben packed his 1952 Chevy pick-up truck and together with his dog, Chika, began his long journey eastward. He made his way to Brooklyn and began asking old acquaintances for names of people or organizations who might give him guidance. He was given a list of names and consulted each of them.

He came away from his visits feeling that the people he had spoken to either lacked authenticity or were self-promoting and narrow-minded. None shared his global vision. He had one name left on his list. If it didn't work, he would go back west. The name was Rabbi Shlomo Freifeld (1926-1990), *Rosh Yeshivah* of Yeshiva Shor Yoshuv in Far Rockaway.

Ben, who had a long ponytail, drove out to Far Rockaway in his pick-up truck. He parked on Central Ave. in front of the yeshivah and tucked his long ponytail under the back of his shirt. His dog Chika sat in the open-ended back of the truck, panting patiently for his master to return.

Ben walked into the yeshivah and asked to see Rabbi Freifeld. Ben had called for an appointment just an hour earlier, and was surprised when Rabbi Freifeld said without hesitation, "You can come over right now!" He was led to the office and welcomed inside. Rabbi Freifeld was a tall, imposing figure with a robust personality. When his words were strong, they were thunderous and overpowering. When they were soft, they penetrated the hearts of the cynical and the skeptical. He understood human nature like few in his generation, and when he was with you, you felt he had no other care in the world.

Ben was taken aback by Rabbi Freifeld's queries. He wanted to know how to catch deer, how to determine the freshness of elk tracks. He was interested in the mechanics of hunting. These were the last topics Ben ever thought he would be discussing with a rabbi. Though it lasted less than 20 minutes, the conversation drifted along a wide gamut of topics, from the Hungarian Navy to the harsh winters of South Dakota, from plant life to human life. Before Ben left, Rabbi Freifeld asked, "Why are you hiding your hair in your shirt? Your hair is so beautiful!"

Ben left the office mesmerized. He wanted to come back. He needed to know this man — or maybe more importantly, he needed this man to know him. Ben returned the next morning, but was startled at the large crowd that had assembled in the *beis midrash.* He was told that a *bris* was taking place. He stood sheepishly in the back looking at the swarm of people gathered around Rabbi Freifeld, near the *Aron Kodesh.* Somehow Rabbi Freifeld spotted Ben. He summoned his son-in-law Rabbi Avraham Halpern and told him to bring Ben up to the front. Ben saw his first *bris* up close. He was touched that the rabbi would even recognize him, but he wished he hadn't watched the actual procedure.

During the next few weeks Ben and Rabbi Freifeld spoke for hours on end. They would usually speak in his office, which was bejeweled with thousands of *sefarim* on all aspects of Torah. Each of the bookshelves was filled to capacity, similar to the many bookcases that Rabbi Freifeld had in his home. It was said that he had over 15,000 *sefarim.*

One afternoon as they conversed in the office, someone came in and told Rabbi Freifeld he was needed in the *beis midrash.* Rabbi Freifeld excused himself and told Ben he would be back in a few moments.

Being alone in the office, Ben got up from his chair and began walking around gazing at the overflowing bookcases of *sefarim* that Rabbi Freifeld had. He walked near where Rabbi Freifeld had been sitting and noticed something unusual in the kneehole of the desk. There were a number of books lying on the floor! It didn't make sense. These were all holy books — how could they possibly be on the floor?

He bent down and picked them up. And when he did — that changed his life, for the books were about Indian culture and reservations! "It was then," says Ben, "that I realized how much the *rebbi* really loved me."

Rabbi Freifeld was studying those books so he could understand where Ben was coming from. By taking time to *understand* and not merely to *be* understood, Rabbi Freifeld validated Ben's concerns and quest for meaning in life.

Ben studied at Shor Yoshuv for years, where he developed into a remarkable *talmid chacham,* an incredible human being and became (in his mind) Rabbi Freifeld's most beloved *talmid.*

Goal!

Throughout the thirty-two years that I knew Rabbi Sholom Schwadron (1912-1997), the Maggid of Jerusalem, he was known around the Jewish world as a master orator who moved his audiences with his heartwarming and spellbinding *drashos* (lectures) and as a *talmid chacham* who wrote, annotated and published over fifty *sefarim.*

In his younger years, he was a master *mechanech* (Torah educator), who served as *Mashgiach* in Yeshivas Tiferes Tzvi (the secondary division of Yeshivas Chevron) and later became *Rosh Yeshivah* in Yeshivas Oholei Shem. His *talmidim* knew that he genuinely loved them and that his words of *mussar* (spiritual and ethical teaching) were only meant to build and not break them. In the following story, we witness his imaginative intelligence in dealing with students.

In the late 1940's, after the establishment of the State of Israel, Reb Sholom and a number of friends organized evening Torah classes in Jerusalem for teenaged boys, who would otherwise have been on the streets. The scent of liberation was in the air and children were intoxicated with the pursuit of sport and pleasure. Yeshivos had not yet proliferated in *Eretz Yisrael* and many boys needed direction.

One boy, Chezky Berkowitz,* had been coming to learn every evening — then he missed two nights in a row. Reb Sholom was surprised at his absence, and when Chezky missed the next night as well, Reb Sholom decided to visit him at home. Perhaps he was ill.

At the Berkowitz house, Chezky himself answered the door. He looked like the picture of health. "Are you all right?" asked Reb Sholom.

"Oh yes, I am fine," Chezky answered. "Why do you ask?"

"Well, our learning program is voluntary, so you are not obligated to come, but you have been coming for weeks and you seemed to enjoy it. Now you missed three days in a row; I thought you might be sick so I came to visit you."

"Thank you for coming," replied Chezky. "But I'm not sick at all. Don't worry, I'll be back sometime next week."

"Next week?" Rav Sholom asked incredulously. "What about the rest of this week? Is there anything going on in your family that's troubling you?"

"No, everything is all right," replied Chezky, somewhat embarrassed at his evasive answers.

"So tell me," insisted Reb Sholom, "is anything bothering you at the classes?" Reb Sholom presumed that everything was fine in the study groups, but wished to get Chezky involved in conversation so he would reveal the truth.

Chezky was hesitant to talk, but Reb Sholom said, "Look, don't be embarrassed. You know that I like you. I'm your friend."

---

*Name has been changed.

Chezky relaxed and said slowly, "You see, I live for soccer. I love to play the game and I love to watch the tournaments. The next few nights are when the tournaments are being played and I want to watch them. It's important to me. But I promise when they are over I'll be back in the classes."

Reb Sholom listened intently and said, "Tell me, how do you play soccer? What's the object of the game?"

"There are two separate teams," explained Chezky, who surmised that Reb Sholom had never played soccer because he was always involved in learning. "There are nets on both sides of the field, and each team has to try and kick the ball into the net. When they do, it is absolutely the most exciting thing!"

Chezky's eyes lit up as he visualized a soccer ball flying off the foot of a player who just kicked a perfect line drive into the embrace of the net's webbing.

Reb Sholom looked surprised and said, "What's so special about that? Come with me, I'll show you I can kick twenty balls one after the other into the net."

"I forgot to explain," said Chezky, smiling that he had forgotten such an important fact. "There is a goalie — a man who stands in front of the net trying to block the ball from going in."

"I see," said Reb Sholom, slowly absorbing the scenario. "But listen, does the goalie stand there all day and all night?"

"Of course not," laughed Chezky at the ridiculous question. "He's only there during the game. Afterwards he goes home and he leads his regular life."

"So that's wonderful," exclaimed Rav Sholom in excitement. "Let's you and I play after the goalie goes home and then we can kick as many balls as we please into the net."

"But there's no point to that," Chezky said, exasperated. "The whole objective is to try and score a goal when there is an obstacle there — when the goalie is trying to thwart your efforts. If you're able to do that — then you've done something special."

Reb Sholom waited for a moment to see if Chezky himself understood the practical application of what he just said. "That's exactly what I mean," said Reb Sholom softly. "You just said it yourself! The accomplishment of scoring a goal is noteworthy only because one must overcome the obstacle — the goalie. If the goalie is not there and he's gone home, then even little children can kick goals in the wide-open net. That's no trick!"

"If you come next week, " said Reb Sholom, "that's no trick — because nothing is standing in your way. This week if you come, now that would be special. Overcoming that obstacle in front of you, that's the real goal."

The next night Chezky showed up to class.

Score one for Reb Sholom.

The Shot Heard Around the World

The phone rang in the fashionable office in downtown Tel Aviv. Joe could see from his newly installed Caller ID that it was his wife calling. He was proud that his office telephone system was one of Israel's few state-of-the-art systems. This was the 1980's and many in Israel did not even have touch-tone phones, let alone elaborate communication features.

"Joe," his wife of eleven years said, "I didn't get to cook today, there were meetings and shopping to tend to. Would you mind stopping off on the way home and getting some food for the kids."

"No problem," he answered with his usual casual confidence, "I'll be home at 6:30."

In secular terms, Joe, or Yossi as he was known to his Israeli friends, was a model success story. Born in Israel, he moved abroad with his parents to New York, before his *bar mitzvah*, where he grew up in a rough and tumble neighborhood in the Bronx. Joe learned "street smarts" from the gangs he fought with and against, but he was determined to major in engineering at an American university. He graduated from City College at the top of the class.

He married and returned with his wife to Israel in order to serve in the Israeli army. He rose to the rank of captain, and had nearly completed his obligatory service when the Yom Kippur War broke out in October, 1973. Yossi extended his term of duty until the crisis was over, and then moved back to the United States. There, he used his military experience and engineering skills to create an aircraft parts, helicopter and weapons business that became internationally known and very successful. Once it was established, he moved his base of operations to Israel. To his friends, Joe was a hero; he had overcome the poverty of his parents who were Holocaust survivors, he had shown loyalty to Israel by fighting in one its wars, and he had returned to Israel a successful capitalist.

People could not imagine that at times he felt an emptiness.

Joe left his office at 5:30 and made his way to the *Misadah HaPil* (The Elephant's Restaurant) known for its *basar lavan* (pork) and *pita*. It was a hot steamy day and the line to get into this trendy eatery was out the door. Joe figured out just how many portions he would need for his children, who devoured this kind of treat. It was going to be a humid evening, he thought to himself, as he began feeling impatient, uncomfortable and a little out of place. His mind began wandering and suddenly he recalled a story that had taken place decades earlier. He had heard the story numerous times in the family, but now the story loomed larger than ever before.

The story was about his maternal grandfather, Shraga Feivel Winkler. He came from Feldesh, a small town outside Debreczyn, Hungary, and was known as the most pious man in his town. He was a *melamed* (teacher of children) who was revered and respected by all who knew him.

In 1944, Reb Shraga Feivel was taken from his home by the Nazi S.S. and interned in a slave labor camp outside Hungary. He could not contact his family members, and had no idea of their whereabouts. As the War was coming to an end and the camps were about to be liberated, Nazi soldiers wanted to humiliate as many Jews as they could before they were freed. They decided to make an example of Reb Shraga Feivel, whom they sneeringly called "the rabbi of the camp."

The Nazi soldiers summoned Jews from all the barracks and ordered them to form a wide circle. Reb Shraga Feivel was brought to the middle of the circle. One could already see clouds of smoke rising from the Allied tanks and trucks that were making their way to the camps. "In a few hours you will all be free," a Nazi officer announced. "You will be reunited with your families — or whatever is left of them. But you, rabbi," he said, pointing to Reb Shraga Feivel, "you must first pass this test. I have a piece of pig's meat in my hand. If you want to live and see your family again, you must eat this in front of everyone." The Nazi roared, as he drew his pistol, "Otherwise you will be our last victim."

Reb Shraga Feivel had starved himself throughout his stay in the camps rather than eat anything that was not kosher. He existed on water, dirty fruits and vegetables, and anything else he knew was kosher. He had not eaten meat in years, not even soup that may have had pieces of non-kosher meat in it. Reb Shraga Feivel's fellow prisoners stood by nervously as he was confronted with his life-and-death decision. Some could not bear to watch his ordeal and looked down at the ground.

"I will not eat this meat!" he announced defiantly. The sudden crack of gunfire ruptured the air, as a bullet exploded into Reb Shraga Feivel's head, killing him instantly.

Now, in the hot humid evening outside *Misadah HaPil,* Reb Shraga Feivel's grandson closed his eyes, envisioning that late afternoon, decades ago in the slave labor camp. Joe thought to himself, "I am standing in a long line waiting to buy pork — meat that my grandfather gave up his life for. Had he eaten just one piece of that pork, he would have been reunited with his family that he hadn't seen in over a year. I have my family. I have anything I desire — and I am waiting on line for this? Either *I* am not normal or *he* was not normal." And then he thought, "I cannot believe that my grandfather was not normal. I must find out why he would do something that seems to me to be crazy!"

He left the line and bought supper at another store. He came home a perplexed and troubled man. After supper, Yossi had a long talk with his wife. They talked about their purpose in life, their future — and the emptiness that gnawed at their souls. They wanted a solution, but where could they find it?

A few days later, Yossi heard about a seminar called *Arachim* (Values) that was being given by two scientists, Dr. Sholom Srebrenik and Mr. Tzvi Inbal. The academic credentials of the men giving the seminar were impeccable. Joe, who had a scientific bent, decided to attend.

For four days he listened, questioned, absorbed, discussed, evaluated, deliberated and reflected. At the end of the seminar he was convinced. His previous life was over. Yossi Walis became a new person, determined that others would see what he saw, feel what he felt, and understand what he now understood.

He asked Dr. Srebrenik, "How can you not be getting this message out to thousands of people? What you have said here is literally incredible."

"It's a matter of money," replied Dr. Srebrenik sadly. "If we had the money we could get the message out."

"I will take care of it," Yossi said with firm confidence. And take care of it he did. Overnight he became *Arachim's* General Director, a title he holds until this day.

Today *Arachim* seminars are given throughout the world. Over the last twenty years it has become one of the most effective *kiruv* (outreach) organizations in Israel and the Diaspora. Dedicated *Arachim* lecturers have delivered their talks throughout the world, in such countries as Australia, South Africa, Thailand, India and Hungary, aside from those they have given in countless European and American cities. *Arachim* was the forerunner of the Aish Hatorah Discovery Program and the Gateways seminars. More than 120,000 people have attended *Arachim* seminars and more than 50,000 of them have been brought back to authentic Judaism. Yossi recently estimated that more than 60,000 children have been born to couples who have become *baalei teshuvah* by virtue of graduating *Arachim* seminars.

One man, one life, one goal. This can be said of Reb Shraga Feivel Winkler and it can be said about his grandson Yossi Walis. When each one was confronted with a challenging crisis — he rose to the occasion.

Before his death, Moshe *Rabbeinu* told the Jewish nation, שְׁאַל אָבִיךָ וְיַגֵּדְךָ זְקֵנֶיךָ וְיֹאמְרוּ לָךְ, *Ask your father and he will relate it to you, and your elders and they will tell you (Devarim 32:7).* The word זְקֵנֶיךָ can also be translated as *your grandfathers.* The verse talks of *asking* your father. Most people have that opportunity in life. The verse however talks of *your grandfathers telling you.* Many people don't have the opportunity to *ask* their grandfathers, but somehow, by virtue of their example, such grandfathers are able to *tell* their grandchildren about the *values* of life.

Reb Shraga Feivel Winkler never saw his grandson Yossi, but what he told him affected tens of thousands of people around the world.

Now that's a message!

Outreach

One of the most remarkable men in our generation is Rabbi Nosson Tzvi Finkel, *Rosh Yeshivah* of Yeshivas Mir in Jerusalem. Originally from Chicago, Rav Nosson Tzvi first came to Mir in the 1960's while in high school, visiting the *Rosh Yeshivah* of the time, Rabbi Eliezer Yehuda Finkel (1875-1965), his grandfather's brother. (See *Echoes of the Maggid,* p. 239.)

Today, more than forty years later, Reb Nosson Tzvi has built Mir into one of the largest yeshivos in the world, encompassing a network of buildings in Jerusalem's Beis Yisrael neighborhood and beyond, that house thousands of *bachurim* and *yungerleit* from all corners of the globe. Reb Nosson Tzvi has accomplished all this despite his ill health.

His speech is occasionally difficult to understand, but it is obvious that his words emanate from a heart brimming with love for a fellow Jew. Hence his *shiurim, mussar shmuessen* and *sichas chullin* (ordinary conversation) touch people in an unexpectedly compelling manner. The awe and reverence his *talmidim* have for him is fervent, for they recognize his genuine concern for each of them. (I personally am indebted to him, since my two sons and two of my sons-in-law are or were students of Mir.)

This story about Reb Nosson Tzvi was told in a speech given by Mr. Howard Schultz upon his receiving an honorary degree in Business Ethics from the Columbia Business School.

During a recent summer, a group of secular Jewish-American businessmen were brought to Rav Nosson Tzvi so they could have an audience with a prominent English-speaking rabbi. Among the high-powered executives was Mr. Howard Schultz of Seattle, chairman and chief global strategist for Starbucks, a colossal retail coffee company, with more than 50,000 employees working in 3500 stores throughout the United States. The men were escorted to Rav Nosson Tzvi's modest home and waited for the meeting to begin.

The visitors were seated at the table where Reb Nosson Tzvi had given hundreds of *shmuessen* over the years. They felt like schoolchildren in the principal's office. Rav Nosson Tzvi noticed that their eyes were aimed elsewhere rather than on him. They hadn't known of his ill health. "Gentlemen," he said. "I have only a few minutes for you because I know you're all busy American businessmen."

Mr. Shultz wondered if that was a putdown. Did the rabbi intend to make them feel like spoiled, self-centered stuffed shirts? Anyone who knows Reb Nosson Tzvi knew that nothing could be further from the truth. He eyed his guests and asked, "Who can tell me the lesson of the Holocaust?"

The *Rosh Yeshivah* called on one of the men, who was surprised to be singled out. He began meekly, "We will never, ever forget ..."

Rav Nosson Tzvi indicated that it was not the right answer. No one wanted to be called on next. Mr. Schultz was sweating like a fifth-grader, avoiding eye contact with the teacher so he wouldn't be recognized. One of the men spoke up. " We will never, ever again be a victim or a bystander, " he suggested boldly.

Rav Nosson Tzvi dismissed the answer. "Gentlemen," he said softly but firmly, "let me tell you the essence of the human spirit.

"As you know, during the Holocaust, the people were transported in the worst possible inhumane way, by railcars. They all thought they were going to a work camp. We all know that they were going to a death camp. After hours and hours in this stifling crowded cattle car — with no light, no bathroom, no room to sit — they arrived in the camps freezing cold. The doors of the railcars were swung wide open, and the people inside were blinded by the light. Men were separated from the women, mothers from their daughters and fathers from their sons. They were herded off to bunkers to sleep.

"Only one person out of six was given a blanket. When they went to bed, the person who had the blanket had to decide, 'Am I going to push the blanket to the other five people who did not get one, or am I going to pull it toward myself to stay warm?' "

Rav Nosson Tzvi continued. "It was during this defining moment that we learned the power of the human spirit, because Jews pushed the blanket to five others."

With that, Rav Nosson Tzvi stood up and said, "Take your blanket. Take it back to America and push it to five other people!"

Chazal (Sanhedrin 20a*)* illustrate the greatness and praise the level of Torah study of the generation of Rabbi Yehudah the son of Rabbi Elai by exclaiming, that though his disciples were smitten with abject poverty, to the point where six students had only one blanket for the whole group, still they toiled diligently in their Torah study and were rewarded by reaching high levels of comprehension in Torah *(Sanhedrin* 20a*).*

In a talk regarding preparation for *Shavuos* and *Kabbalas HaTorah* (see *Sichos Mussar, Maamar 7*, 5731), Rav Chaim Shmulevitz, the Mirrer *Rosh Yeshivah*, once said, "Normally it is impossible for one blanket to cover six people, yet it was accomplished because each individual was genuinely concerned for another. Hence all those in need were 'covered.' That is the essence of a yeshivah, thinking of others and assisting them in time of need. If however," warned Rav Chaim, "*talmidim* are self-centered and not focused on the requirements of others, it is not a yeshivah."

From study halls to corporate halls, outreach creates a unified effort.

Submission Accomplished

Change is difficult. It takes a concerted effort to acclimate to a new environment or assume a new position in life. The security and comfort of the familiar is reassuring; uncertainty is unnerving. Yet tens of thousands of Jews throughout the world have become *baalei teshuvah* — changing their unfulfilled way of life to one of satisfaction and attainment.

For this they are so highly regarded that the Sages declare, מָקוֹם שֶׁבַּעֲלֵי תְשׁוּבָה עוֹמְדִים שָׁם צַדִּיקִים אֵינָן עוֹמְדִים שָׁם, *The [exalted] level where penitents stand, the righteous do not stand* (*Sanhedrin* 99a, see *Rashi* ibid.).

What motivates people to make a fundamental change in their lives? The catalyst for change may be an unusually meaningful event. It may be a lecture given by a *kiruv* professional, such as the Aish Hatorah Discovery Program, which presents three hundred seminars to over twenty thousand participants a year.

Rabbi Yaakov Salomon, a Brooklyn, New York psychologist, is one of the noted lecturers for Discovery. He frequently travels throughout the United States, conducting seminars for people who are curious about authentic Judaism, the veracity of Torah, the role of Hashem in our daily lives, and the significance of *mitzvos*. His warmth, sincerity, and intelligence motivate audiences.

The following episode took place at a *Shabbaton* — a weekend seminar in Minneapolis where R' Yaakov was a presenter. Fifty non-observant Jews had gathered in a downtown hotel to hear lectures by the Aish Hatorah speakers. As they sat in a cozy dining room, R' Yaakov had the participants identify themselves. Sitting on R' Yaakov's left was a refined Russian fellow in his 60's, a former scientist from Leningrad. As he rose to introduce himself he announced with conviction, "My name is Michael and I am an atheist."

"Really," said R' Yaakov, undaunted. "If you don't have an open mind, why did you come to the seminar?"

"I came here because a friend of mine insisted that I come," said Michael. "He said I would find it interesting."

"I hope so," R' Yaakov said with a smile and guarded optimism.

Throughout the weekend lectures, the participants were encouraged to ask questions and seek clarifications and indeed many of them did. However, no one asked more pointed questions than Michael. His queries were sharp, his comments intelligent, and his participation exhibited a bright and perceptive mind. Numerous times, R' Yaakov and Michael fenced verbally as the other attendees listened in fascination.

Many topics were presented, as matters of Jewish heritage and Torah perspectives were discussed and analyzed. In an atmosphere of congeniality and spirituality, the participants heard ideas and concepts that they had never associated with Judaism. Most of the attendees had no idea of the Torah's ideas on such topics as marriage, parenting, and business ethics.

After the final lecture on Sunday afternoon, Discovery participants are customarily asked to compress their feelings about their weekend experience in one word.

"What word would you use to describe what you feel now that you have heard these lectures?" asked R' Yaakov.

One participant declared, "Informed," another said, "Exhilarated," a third exclaimed, "Inspired." A fourth confessed that he was "perplexed." Every person had an answer. R' Yaakov noticed, however, that Michael had not responded.

"So, Michael," R' Yaakov said with a little smile, "We have heard from almost everyone. What about you, how do you feel about this weekend?"

All eyes turned to Michael. For the first time throughout the weekend he seemed unsure and hesitant. It wasn't like him to be silent, so everyone waited in quiet and respectful anticipation for his reply. After a few long seconds, Michael got up from his chair. He paused for yet another moment and then said softly, with reverence and appreciation, "G-d bless you."

In 36 hours the atheist had seen reality — *baruch Hashem.*

Heartspeak

The relationship between a *talmid* and his *rebbi* transcends physical boundaries. A true *talmid* is often a reflection of his *rebbi,* in speech, in mannerisms, and certainly in his thought processes.

The Hebrew expression רַבּוֹ מוּבְהָק is usually interpreted as *primary teacher,* but it means more. The *Tosefos Yom Tov* (*Bava Metzia* 2:11) writes that the root of the word מוּבְהָק is בהק, *to shine* or *glow.* Accordingly a *rebbi muvhak* is the teacher who inspired his *talmid* to shine.

A bright star in the world of *chinuch* (Torah education) today is Rabbi Noach Orlowek of Jerusalem. He is a *Mashgiach* in Yeshiva Torah Ore, a lecturer in various seminaries, author of books on *chinuch,* and an adviser to hundreds of young men and women in Israel and America. Rabbi Orlowek says that the *rebbi* who had the greatest influence on him was Rabbi Simcha Wasserman (1899-1992), the son of the world-renowned Rabbi Elchonon Wasserman, (1875-1941), and *Rosh Yeshivah* of *Ohr Elchanan* in Jerusalem.

Rabbi Orlowek is a New Yorker who went to study in Reb Simcha's yeshivah in Los Angeles when he was 13 years old, and maintained a very close relationship with his *rebbi* for the next thirty-two years, in America and in Jerusalem.

In this moving episode told by Dr. Chona Chaim (Howie) Lebowitz (see p. 44), now living in Lakewood, New Jersey, we get a glimpse of a profound *rebbi-talmid* bond.

Near the end of his life Reb Simcha was seriously ill and was cared for by his only surviving relatives, who lived in Boston, where he was admitted to the coronary care unit of Brigham and Women's Hospital. Reb Simcha was so frail that every movement he made, even to sit up in bed, caused the heart monitor to leap wildly, as if he were suffering from a series of small heart attacks.

One day, Dr. Lebowitz, a staff doctor at Brigham and Women's, was told that a rabbi from Jerusalem was in the Coronary Intensive Care Unit (CICU). Curious, he went there and was surprised to see that it was Reb Simcha. The doctor had heard much about Reb Simcha when he was studying in Aish Hatorah in Israel, from one of his teachers, Rabbi Noach Orlowek.

Dr. Lebowitz visited Reb Simcha every day and sometimes helped him put on his *tefillin.* Reb Simcha could not speak; he would only hold Dr. Lebowitz's hand in gratitude. Dr. Lebowitz would talk softly to Rav Simcha, assuring him that he was getting the best care. Dr. Lebowitz promised that he would always be available when needed. He couldn't help but notice the monitor, which showed the constant unsteadiness of Reb Simcha's heartbeat.

One morning Dr. Lebowitz mentioned that Rabbi Orlowek had been his teacher in Aish Hatorah. When he mentioned Rabbi Orlowek's name he noticed a sudden change on the heart monitor. The heartbeat slowed down and became stable. Reb Simcha's heart and respiratory condition had come closer to normal; the monitor reflected an inner serenity. Dr. Lebowitz was astounded!

That afternoon he visited Reb Simcha again, and once more, when he mentioned Rabbi Orlowek's name, the monitor indicated that Reb Simcha's heart was relaxed. Obviously the thought of his beloved *talmid* calmed him.

Dr. Lebowitz decided to use this as therapy, so every day he visited Reb Simcha and spoke about Rabbi Orlowek and something he had taught at Aish Hatorah. The response was always the same. The lines on the monitors no longer danced in frenzy; they progressed at a steady, even keel. Whenever Dr. Lebowitz passed the nurses' station and noticed that the monitors indicated an unstable condition, he would rush to Reb Simcha's room and begin chatting about Rabbi Orlowek.

A while afterwards Reb Simcha was transferred to a hospital in New York, and it was there that he passed away.

A few months later when Dr. Lebowitz returned to Israel, he met Rabbi Orlowek. "I understand that you were with my *rebbi* when he was in the Boston hospital," said Rabbi Orlowek. "Can you tell me anything he said?"

"Not really," replied Dr. Lebowitz sadly, realizing how much a thought from Reb Simcha would have meant to Rabbi Orlowek. "When I saw him he was no longer able to speak."

"Did he say anything at any time? You don't remember him saying some thought or some words?" Rabbi Orlowek pleaded almost desperately.

Once again Dr. Lebowitz told Rabbi Orlowek that Reb Simcha was no longer able to converse during his hospital stay. Rabbi Orlowek shook his head in despair, "I can't get over the pain of his having passed away," he said.

Then Dr. Lebowitz recalled the phenomenon. "I can tell you this," Dr. Lebowitz said. "When I came into his room and mentioned your name there was a noticeable change in his condition. Before that the monitor would indicate that his heart was in distress, but when I spoke about you, suddenly his heart became calm. You couldn't tell anything from the outside but the monitor definitely reflected a change. And to tell you the truth, once I realized that, I used it as therapy. The mention of your name had a subconscious soothing effect."

Tears welled in Rabbi Orlowek's eyes. He turned away.

A few days later he told Dr. Lebowitz, "Many people have tried to comfort me since my *rebbi* passed away, to no avail. But your words gave me comfort. I know how close I felt to my *rebbi.* To know now that he felt that way about me is my greatest consolation."

When Yehudah described the loving bond that Yaakov *Avinu* had with his youngest son Binyamin, he said: וְנַפְשׁוֹ קְשׁוּרָה בְנַפְשׁוֹ, *his soul is bound up with his soul (Bereishis* 44:30*).* One can justifiably use that phrase for Reb Simcha and his beloved *talmid.*

The Mouth, the Message and the Medium

The *Midrash* teaches that during the Hellenistic era, the Syrian-Greeks ordered Jews, under threat of death, כִּתְבוּ עַל קֶרֶן הַשּׁוֹר שֶׁאֵין לָכֶם חֵלֶק בֵּאלֹקֵי יִשְׂרָאֵל, *Inscribe on the horn of an ox, "We have no share in the G-d of Israel" (Bereishis Rabbah* 2:4, *Vayikra Rabbah* 15:9; see also *Midrash Tanchuma, Tazria* 11).

Commentaries explain that because Jews had many oxen, this blasphemous declaration of heresy, carved on the oxen's horns, would become widely known. Another interpretation for this strange decree was that the horn of the ox was a stinging reminder of the Jews' sin of the Golden Calf, just weeks after they had received the Torah at Mount Sinai. The Syrian-Greeks wished to insure that Jews would be shamed by recalling that dark moment in our history.

When I discussed this Midrash with Rabbi Avraham Gurwicz, the *Rosh Yeshivah* of Gateshead, England, he told me an interesting insight he had heard from his late father, Reb Leib. Reb Leib had a colleague in London's Yeshiva Eitz Chaim, Rabbi Hirsch Meir Bendas (1877-1958), who once visited the British Museum to view ancient utensils used in Talmudic times, so he could better understand the *Mishnayos* in *Mesechta Keilim* that discuss the spiritual purity and impurity of various vessels and utensils. As Rabbi Bendas surveyed the artifacts he noticed an ancient "baby bottle." It was a horn of an ox that was hollowed out so that it could contain milk or water. There was a tiny opening at the tip of the horn, which would be inserted in the baby's mouth, so that the liquid would drip out, drop by drop.

Rabbi Bendas remembered the aforementioned *Midrash* and suggested that perhaps the Hellenists insisted that Jews place the sacrilegious message in a place where even infants would see it. The symbolic message was that people should be taught from earliest infancy that their religion is false. (Inculcate the youth and they will be yours when they grow up, as we see today in the hate-filled textbooks of the Palestinians and other purveyors of hate.)

Conversely, we must recognize that the Torah's positive messages must be transmitted at the earliest stages of life. *Chinuch* begins from the day a child is born. It is never too early to start educating children on their level.

Indeed there is a correlation between the word חִנּוּךְ (education) and the word חֲנֻכָּה (*Chanukah*). A significant part of the *Chanukah* celebration was that the *Chashmonaim* reinaugurated the use of the *Beis HaMikdash*. Jews were free to worship Hashem and Torah could be learned without disruption. Authentic *chinuch* could be taught. No longer would Jews have to inscribe public heretical messages on oxen. Hence, חֲנֻכָּה meant the availability of חִנּוּךְ. And just as a חֲנֻכַּת הַבַּיִת (the inauguration of a new home) is done with excitement and enthusiasm so too the חִנּוּךְ of children should be practiced with excitement and enthusiasm.

Role Call

Rabbi Shimon Schwab (1908-1995), the beloved rav of Khal Adath Jeshurun in Washington Heights, New York for close to five decades, was known for the penetrating insights he mined from verses in *Tanach* and from words of *Chazal*. The following critical lesson in *chinuch*, from his *Maayan Beis HaShoeivah, Haftarah Parashas Naso*, p. 310, is imperative in parenting and crucial in education.

Manoach and his wife Tzelelponis, the eventual parents of Shimshon (see *Shoftim* 13 and *Bava Basra* 91a), were childless for many years. One day an angel appeared to Manoach's wife and informed her that she was pregnant and would give birth to a son who by Hashem's decree would be a *Nazir*. The angel told her she should not drink wine or eat anything that was *tamei* (spiritually contaminated).

When she came home and related her startling encounter with the angel to her husband, he said to Hashem, "אִישׁ הָאֱלֹקִים אֲשֶׁר שָׁלַחְתָּ יָבוֹא נָא עוֹד אֵלֵינוּ וְיוֹרֵנוּ מַה נַּעֲשֶׂה לַנַּעַר הַיּוּלָּד, *May the man of Hashem come now again and teach us what we should do with the lad who is to be born*" (*Shoftim* 13:8).

One must wonder: Would Manoach not trust his righteous and virtuous wife with the accuracy of the events and the description of the angel's instructions? "What is remarkable," says Rabbi Schwab, "is that the angel did come back and his reply to Manoach seems puzzling: מִכֹּל אֲשֶׁר אָמַרְתִּי אֶל הָאִשָּׁה תִּשָּׁמֵר, *Everything that I told your wife you must do!* (ibid. 13:13). The angel did not add anything to what he said to Manoach's wife earlier. If so, what was the purpose of his returning?"

Rav Schwab suggests a creative approach to this scenario. Undoubtedly Manoach believed his wife's description of the meeting with the angel. However Manoach was concerned about a *chinuch* (educational) issue. How could a father be instructed to raise his child in a manner in which he himself did not behave? How could he be expected to raise a child to refrain from drinking wine and abide by the additional prohibitions of a *Nazir* when he himself did not abide by them? It was to ask these specific questions that Manoach sought the angel's return and counsel.

In this light, the angel's answer is telling: "מִכֹּל אֲשֶׁר אָמַרְתִּי אֶל הָאִשָּׁה תִּשָּׁמֵר, *Everything that I told your wife you must do.*" This meant that Manoach was indeed to become a *Nazir* himself! For it is impossible to raise a child in a manner in which the parents don't conduct themselves. Rav Schwab then adds emphatically, "If a person will tell his child to follow a fine code of behavior that he does not maintain — even if he demands it a hundred and one times — he will not be successful." Thus in order for Shimshon to be raised as a *Nazir,* Manoach also had to become a *Nazir.* (See also *Meshech Chochmah's* commentary to *Shoftim* 13:14, cited in *Haftarah* of *Parashas Naso.*)

> Children learn what they see, not what they are told. This applies to coming on time to *davening,* talking in *shul,* speaking *lashon hara,* making time to learn Torah, maintaining standards of *kashrus* and being honest in business.
>
> This point was brought home to me by a delightful story I heard from Reb Pinchus Kornfeld of Belgium.

In a kindergarten in Antwerp, the *morah* (teacher) wished to teach the little boys and girls in her class about Shabbos and its observance in the home. She told each of the children to bring various items that would be needed for their Shabbos table. "Chaim, you bring wine; Sarah, you bring *challah;* Meir, you bring in some silverware, and Leah, you bring a tablecloth."

By Wednesday morning all the children had brought in what they were asked to and the class Shabbos table was set beautifully. The *morah* said, "Chaim, you will be the *tatty* (father)."

Chaim sat himself proudly at the head of the table with all the authority he could muster. "Fine," said the *morah.* "You may now begin."

Chaim looked around at everyone, plopped his head back on his chair and said with a sigh, *"Oy! Hub ich ge'hat a shvereh vuch!"* ("Oh! Did I have a difficult week!").

> As the angel taught Manoach, children imitate and emulate. Only unthinking parents and educators would deny it.

Parental Prayer and Presence

During a recent trip to Bnei Brak, Israel, my son and daughter-in-law and I visited the venerable *Rosh Yeshivah,* Rabbi Michel Feinstein. Reb Michel is the son-in-law of the Brisker Rav, Rabbi Yitzchok Zev (Velvel) Soloveitchik (1887-1959), and a nephew of Rabbi Moshe Feinstein (1895-1986).

During the visit I asked Reb Michel's wife, Rebetzin Lifsha, if she would share with us a thought on *chinuch* that she heard from her great father, Reb Velvel. She thought for a moment and told us, "I will tell you an incident that I can never forget.

"Back in Brisk, there were some horrible people. There were communists, socialists, and people with distorted *hashkafos* (philosophical perspectives). One day, two brothers with opposing political views about Zionism got into a very nasty public confrontation. The manner in which they conducted themselves was appalling and disgraceful. It was all anyone talked about in the community. It was a terrible *chillul Hashem,* and a humiliation for their family. That evening someone came to our home and asked my father, 'How is it that your children are all so fine and upstanding and so respectful of each other? They would never behave as those two brothers did.'

"My father didn't answer, but after the questioner left, my father said to me and to my siblings, *"Vus kainer vaist nisht is vifil treren, Tehillim, tanneisim, und umshlofedigeh necht ich hub gegeben az meineh kinder zullen zain vee zai zennen."* ("What no one knows is how many tears, [recitation of] *Tehillim,* days of fasting, and sleepless nights I endured so that my children would be as they are today.")

Rav Velvel understood that even in the finest families there can be children who veer from the paths of their parents. Hence, parents must constantly beseech Hashem that they merit that their children follow the ways of Torah and *yiras Shamayim.*

In his *sefer, Z'riah U'binyan B'chinuch* (p. 35), Rabbi Shlomo Wolbe, the world-renowned *Mashgiach* now living in Jerusalem, writes that if he has achieved anything in Torah it is due to his mother's prayers on his behalf. He would see her praying for him, sometimes even ten times a day! He notes that we can never pray enough for our children and cites a special prayer for parents written by the *Chazon Ish,* Rabbi Avraham Yeshayah Karelitz (1878-1953, *Igros* I:74).*

Rav Wolbe notes that many people include this prayer in their *Shemoneh Esrei* and / or recite it after candle lighting on Shabbos or *Yom Tov.* (See English edition, *Planting and Building: Raising a Jewish Child,* p. 33, and ArtScroll's *The Chazon Ish,* p. 159.)

---

*The text of the prayer is: יְהִי רָצוֹן מִלְּפָנֶיךָ ד׳ אֱלֹקַי וֵאלֹקֵי אֲבוֹתַי שֶׁתְּרַחֵם עַל בְּנִי (שֵׁם הַבֵּן) בֶּן (שֵׁם הָאֵם) וְתַהֲפֹךְ אֶת לְבָבוֹ לְאַהֲבָה וּלְיִרְאָה שְׁמֶךָ וְלִשְׁקֹד בְּתוֹרָתְךָ הַקְּדוֹשָׁה וְתָסִיר מִלְּפָנָיו כָּל הַסִּבּוֹת הַמּוֹנְעוֹת אוֹתוֹ מִשְׁקִידַת תּוֹרָתְךָ הַקְּדוֹשָׁה וְתָכִין אֶת כָּל הַסִּבּוֹת הַמְּבִיאוֹת לְתוֹרָתְךָ הַקְּדוֹשָׁה., *May it be Your Will, Hashem my G-d, and G-d of my forefathers, that You have mercy on my son (son's Hebrew name) son of (mother's Hebrew name), and direct his heart to love and fear Your Name, and to be diligent in the study of Your Holy Torah. May You remove from before him all circumstances that can deter him from diligent studying of Your Holy Torah and may You establish all the conditions that will bring him (closer) to Your Holy Torah.*

See also a beautiful prayer for parents (beginning רִבּוֹן כָּל הָעוֹלָמִים, *Master of All Worlds)* cited at the end of the weekday morning *Shemoneh Esrei* in the *Siddur Otzar HaTefillos.*

Interestingly, Rabbi Velvel Soloveitchik was once asked, "If, as people say, the apple does not fall far from the tree, how is it that there are children that don't follow in the paths of their parents?"

Reb Velvel's pithy answer was classic. "It depends how strong the winds are!"

Indeed when the winds of materialism, immorality and secularism are so virulent, there are no guarantees that children won't be influenced by these frightful forces. *Tefillah* and Hashem's help are imperative.

Another *gadol* (great Torah sage) in Jerusalem, who tragically had a son who veered from the path of his family and became irreligious, was also asked the same question about the apple not falling far from the tree. His answer was also perceptive, "It depends," he said with sadness, "how high the tree is."

If parents are so busy, even with good things, that they are removed from their children in the sense that they have no time for them, they could be the most prominent people in the community, but their children may falter. Children need time, love and attention to help assure that they blossom in the image of their parents.

Rav Wolbe once told me, "There are two things that parents must give children — love and time." When he was asked, "How much time?" His answer was short and sharp: "As much as they need."

The Right to Rebuke

Rabbi Avraham Kleinkaufman, a *maggid shiur* in Yeshiva Derech Ayson in Far Rockaway, New York, was a *talmid* of Rabbi Yitzchak Hutner (1904-1980) in Yeshivas Rabbeinu Chaim Berlin for twelve years. The brilliance and vigorous personality of Rabbi Hutner influenced his *talmidim* for decades after they left Chaim Berlin. A seemingly insignificant event that once occurred with Rabbi Kleinkaufman and his *rebbi* illuminated Rabbi Hutner's creative understanding of the words of *Chazal.*

Chazal teach that when a *rebbi* and *talmid* walk together, the *rebbi* should always be on the right to symbolize the *rebbi's* prominence (see *Yoma* 37a). (This is why the chair for the *sandak,* the person holding the infant during the *bris,* is set up on the left side of the *Kisei Shel Eliyahu,* the chair set up for Elijah the Prophet, as Elijah is the distinguished teacher and thus is on the right side (*Derech Pikudecha*; see ArtScroll's *Bris Milah,* pp. 77 and 97).

One day Rabbi Kleinkaufman was walking on Rabbi Hutner's left, when he noticed that the sidewalk ahead narrowed, as part of a building jutted outward. For a moment, Rabbi Kleinkaufman moved behind the *Rosh Yeshivah.* When space allowed, Rabbi Kleinkaufman resumed his position on the *Rosh Yeshivah's* left.

"What indeed is the meaning of a *talmid's* walking on the *rebbi's* left side?" asked Rabbi Kleinkaufman.

Rabbi Hutner thought for a moment and responded, "*Chazal* teach: לְעוֹלָם תְּהֵא שְׂמֹאל דוֹחָה וִימִין מְקָרֶבֶת, *Always let the left [the weaker hand] push away [a student, with gentle rebuke] but the right [the stronger hand] should draw [the student] close [with encouragement and friendship]* (*Sotah* 47a)."

"Any *talmid* can accept the יְמִין מְקָרֶבֶת, *strong encouragement,*" said Rabbi Hutner with a smile, "but only a true *talmid* can accept the שְׂמֹאל דוֹחָה, *gentle rubuke.*"

Another incident with a *talmid* illustrates Rav Hutner's genius and wit. When Rabbi Nota Schiller was about to leave America and move to Israel to create the now legendary Yeshiva Ohr Someyach, he went to his *Rosh Yeshivah,* Rav Yitzchak Hutner, to receive his blessing and good wishes.

Rabbi Schiller brought some liquor to the *Rosh Yeshivah's* home to make a *l'chaim.* As Rav Hutner lifted his glass, he said, "Usually when *chassidim* make a *l'chaim* [on a *yarhzeit*], it is so that the *neshamah* (soul) *[of the departed one]* will have an *aliyah* (a [spiritual] ascension). My blessing to you is that your *aliyah (ascension [to Israel])* should have a *neshamah*!"

A Seed Grows in the Midwest

The 12- and 13- year-old boys from Flint, Michigan* had been to *bar mitzvahs* before, but never one like this. Their friend Jonathan Waxman* had left Flint a year ago in October 1955, the day the Brooklyn Dodgers won the World Series (that was their frame of reference), to study in Yeshiva Beis Yehudah in Detroit. Now, in May 1956, Jonathan had come home to celebrate his *bar mitzvah.* Few Jewish boys in Flint had ever heard of Beis Yehudah, but when Jonathan told them that his rabbis in the yeshivah had actually studied in that famous city where the Dodgers played, they became instant celebrities. Maybe they had even seen the Dodgers play! The two rabbis, Rabbi Sholom Goldstein and Rabbi Avraham Abba Freedman, were *talmidim* of Rabbi Shraga Feivel Mendelowitz (1886-1948) at Mesivta Torah Vodaath, and had come to Detroit at his request to build Torah in the Midwest.

The rabbis had made the three-hour trip to Flint to celebrate with the Waxman family, and it was they, more than anyone else, who made the *bar mitzvah* special. They spoke beautifully about the importance of Torah study, a topic that was seldom heard at *bar mitzvahs* in Flint. They led the singing and dancing and praised Jonathan as the boys had never heard him praised before. These enthusiastic rabbis were sure that Jonathan had a great future. Jonathan's friends couldn't help but be a bit envious. "He must feel like a million dollars," thought the impressionable Michael Lerman.*

Michael thought fleetingly and longingly about what it must be like at Beis Yehudah, but he was an only child and he knew his parents would never let him leave home, certainly not to go to a yeshivah. The *bar mitzvah* was over and within days most people forgot about it — that is, most people except Michael. There was something majestic about those rabbis, he thought. His friend Jonathan was a lucky boy.

Throughout the summer, Michael kept talking about the *bar mitzvah* and the rabbis from Detroit, so when Rabbi Yechiel London and Rabbi Reuvain Mann of Yeshiva Haichal Hatorah in New York

* The name has been changed.

came to Flint that summer on a fundraising trip for the yeshivah — and possibly to recruit new *talmidim* — the local Orthodox rabbi told Rabbis London and Mann that there were a few possible candidates, especially Michael, who had started to come to the Orthodox *shul* on his own.

Rabbi London met with Michael and was impressed. He invited him to attend a summer camp in upstate New York that was directed by himself and his older brother Rabbi Yaakov. Camp Machneh Torah in Mountaindale wasn't the best-equipped camp in the Catskills, but Rabbi London assured Michael's parents that he would have a fun-filled, educational, and inspiring summer there.

Reluctantly and with lumps in their throats, the Lermans sent their child off to Machneh Torah for the second half of the summer. The head counselor was R' Schneur Aisenstark (today the dean of the Bais Yaakov of Montreal) and Michael's counselor was R' Chaim Bressler (today the *Rosh Yeshivah* in Yeshiva Beth Moshe of Scranton, Pennsylvania).

R' Schneur and R' Chaim picked up where Rabbis Goldstein and Freedman left off. They spoke glowingly of the significance of *mitzvos* and Torah study and they made Michael feel that he was indeed part of a special nation. They also encouraged him to come to Haichal Hatorah, where they studied. At the end of the summer, R' Dov Wolowitz (today a noted community leader in Lawrence, New York) spoke convincingly to the campers about making the full-time commitment and going to a yeshivah. Michael was convinced.

Once back in Flint, Michael was able to persuade his parents to let him go to Haichal Hatorah. In 1956, not many American parents were willing to make the sacrifice of sending a child to an out-of-town yeshivah, but the Lermans saw how much it meant to their beloved son, so Michael started in Haichal Hatorah that autumn. Showing exceptional diligence and seriousness, he moved up the ranks in the yeshivah and within a few years he was accepted in Beth Medrash Govoha in Lakewood. There he became the *chavrusa* (study partner) of Rabbi Chaim Bressler, his former camp counselor, who was by then married and a member of the Lakewood *kollel.*

Michael became an outstanding *ben Torah* and today is a noted *talmid chacham* and supporter of Torah in Lakewood. He attributes the whole chain of events to the inspiration that Rabbis Goldstein and Freedman provided at the *bar mitzvah* of Jonathan Waxman. Sadly, Jonathan didn't go back to Beis Yehudah the next year. He attended public school and dropped all connection to *Yiddishkeit*. Rabbis Goldstein and Freedman made an extra effort to travel over eighty miles to celebrate the *bar mitzvah* of one of their *talmidim.* They did it for Jonathan, and perhaps they felt heartbroken that they had failed. Perhaps they never knew about Michael Lerman whose success is to their credit. Their efforts were not for naught.

In her book, *Facing Adversity with Faith,* Rebbetzin Chavi Wagshal of Manchester, England cites a perceptive expression, "Any fool can count the seeds in one apple, but only the Highest Power (Hashem) can count the apples in one seed."

Years ago in Flint, a seed was planted. Who could have imagined that it would produce an apple from another grove.

Driving Lesson

When Rabbi Jay Marcus, the former rabbi of the Young Israel of Staten Island, was a young man he would drive Rabbi Moshe Feinstein (1895-1986) from Mesivta Tifereth Jerusalem on the Lower East Side of Manhattan to the Yeshiva of Staten Island, where Rav Moshe's son, Reb Reuven, is the *Rosh Yeshivah,* to deliver a *shiur.*

As they were driving on the Staten Island Expressway, Rabbi Marcus was speeding. A policeman pulled him over and gave him a summons.

Rabbi Marcus was somewhat embarrassed at having been ticketed in the presence of Reb Moshe. Sheepishly, he said, "I thought שְׁלוּחֵי מִצְוָה אֵין נִזוֹקִין, *Those sent to [perform] a mitzvah are not harmed" (Kiddushin* 39b*).*

"You are right," said Reb Moshe, "that's exactly why the policeman stopped you, so that you would not get hurt!"

A Judgment Call

The Sages teach: כָּל הָאוֹמֵר תְּהִלָּה לְדָוִד בְּכָל יוֹם שָׁלֹשׁ פְּעָמִים מוּבְטָח לוֹ שֶׁהוּא בֶּן הָעוֹלָם הַבָּא, *Anyone who recites* [Psalm 145 which begins] *"A praise by David" three times every day is assured that he is [worthy of] the World to Come" (Berachos* 4b*).* This psalm is commonly referred to as *Ashrei,* because in our *siddurim* it is introduced by two verses which begin with that word: אַשְׁרֵי יוֹשְׁבֵי בֵיתֶךָ, *Fortunate are those who sit in Your House (Tehillim* 84:5*),* and אַשְׁרֵי הָעָם, *Fortunate is the people* (ibid. 144:15).

One of the reasons *Ashrei* is so distinctive is that it contains the verse: פּוֹתֵחַ אֶת יָדֶךָ וּמַשְׂבִּיעַ לְכָל חַי רָצוֹן, *You open Your hand and satisfy the desire of every living thing* (ibid. 145:16*).* That verse is followed by צַדִּיק ה׳ בְּכָל דְּרָכָיו וְחָסִיד בְּכָל מַעֲשָׂיו, *Righteous is Hashem in all His ways, and magnanimous in all His deeds.* Rabbi Shimon Schwab (1908-1995) writes that he once heard a beautiful explanation from Rabbi Joseph Breuer (1882-1980), the founder of Khal Adath Jeshurun in Washington Heights, regarding the juxtaposition of these two verses.

Sometimes a person struggles to earn an adequate livelihood and comes to feel that Hashem is not treating him the way he wishes. Sometimes it is health, children or happiness that a person desires, and it hasn't come yet. If so, the present tense of the verse *You open Your hand* seems to be inaccurate. Cases where the participants do not see their livelihood materializing are the subject of the next verse, the intent of which is akin to צדוק הַדִּין (a prayer said for the acceptance of Hashem's strict judgment). When man does not understand the ways of Hashem he expresses his faith by saying that He (Hashem) is just in all His ways. (See *Maayan Beis HaShoeivah, Shemos* 5:22 and *Rav Schwab on Prayer,* p. 179.*)*

These thoughts brought to mind a remarkable episode I heard from Rabbi Zev Smith, of Brooklyn, concerning a visit he paid to Rabbi Mordechai Schwab (1911-1994) of Monsey, New York, a younger brother of Reb Shimon, who was revered as a man of unusual piety.

When Rabbi Smith studied in Yeshiva Bais Shraga in Monsey, he became very close to Rabbi Mordechai Schwab, who was the *Mashgiach,* a bond they maintained for many years. After he was married and with a family, Rabbi Smith would travel to Monsey every *Chol HaMoed* to visit his *rebbi.*

During the last year of his life, Rabbi Schwab was extremely weak and frail. He was confined to bed and his appearance deteriorated dramatically. Before *Succos* 1994, the Schwab family feared that Rabbi Smith would become frightened at the sight of his *rebbi* after not having seen him since *Chol HaMoed Pesach,* six months earlier. The Schwab family called to tell him that he should brace himself for how his *rebbi* would look.

Rabbi Smith thanked the Schwabs for the courtesy of their call, and he readied himself for the visit that *Chol HaMoed.* However, when he arrived and saw his revered *rebbi,* he was aghast! The change was so severe, the seriousness of his illness so blatant, that Rabbi Smith's face could not hide his shock and fright. Rav Schwab realized it at once and said immediately to Rabbi Smith, *"Ich leb b'simcha, ich leb b'simchah."* ("I live with happiness, I live with happiness.")

Rabbi Schwab continued, "I wasn't able to go to *shul* this *Yom Kippur*. I wasn't able to *daven* nor am I able to learn anymore. I can't concentrate. But I am living חַיִּים בִּרְצוֹנוֹ" *(Tehillim* 30:6*).*

> These words written by David *HaMelech* mean *life results from His pleasure. Rashi* explains that by pleasing Hashem and gaining His good will, one assures long life. Rabbi Schwab, however, used these two words from *Tehillim* to express the idea that he happily accepted his condition because that is how Hashem wants him to live at this moment. He understood the words חַיִּים בִּרְצוֹנוֹ to mean: *My [present condition in] life is in accordance with His will.*
>
> Undoubtedly this great *tzaddik* would have wanted to be in *shul* on *Yom Kippur.* Unquestionably he missed being able to study and delve into Hashem's Torah.
>
> But if it was Hashem's will that he not be able to do these things anymore, then he was satisfied and accepted it, and

expressed his personal צִדּוּק הַדִּין (acceptance of the harsh judgment) on his difficult condition.

He lived in practice what his brother taught in theory.

אַשְׁרֵי יוֹלַדְתָּם, *Fortunate are those who bore them.*

Heights of Humility

Rabbi Sholom Schwadron, the Maggid of Jerusalem, and Rabbi Yehudah Zev Segal, the Manchester *Rosh Yeshivah,* shared a great mutual esteem and affection. Whenever they met, each spoke to the other like a *talmid* to a *rebbi.* They would ask one another how to handle character flaws they each perceived they had (and probably didn't), and they sought guidance from one another in attaining higher levels of *yiras Shamayim* and punctiliousness in *mitzvos.* My brothers, R' Kolman and R' Arye, who were close to both of these saintly men, had the opportunity to witness many of these meetings, and they always came away astonished at the modesty and submissiveness that Reb Sholom and Rav Segal showed one another.

The following exchange between them is a case in point. It is recorded in the introduction of *Kol Dodi Dofek,* a compilation of Reb Sholom's thoughts on the awesome days of *Elul* and repentance.

Shortly after he became 70 years old, Reb Sholom met Rav Segal and said, "I feel bad because I have lost the opportunity to perform the *mitzvah* of מִפְּנֵי שֵׂיבָה תָּקוּם, *In the presence of an old person you shall rise (Vayikra* 19:32*),* for the law is *(Yoreh Deah* 244:8*)* that one elderly person (i.e. 70 years old, see ibid. :1) is exempt from standing up for another elderly person."

"Nu, Nu," replied Rav Segal, "so from today you'll perform the *mitzvah* like someone who is an אֵינוֹ מְצֻוֶּה וְעוֹשֶׂה, *not commanded to perform the mitzvah but does so anyway."* This is a lower level of *mitzvah* fulfillment than that of one who is obligated to perform the *mitzvah,* but it is still a meritorious deed (see *Kiddushin* 31a).

"However," added the venerable sage, "there is an added benefit to your having become 70. When someone stands up for a *talmid chacham* (a Torah scholar), the *talmid chacham* must be careful that he does not feel a trace of haughtiness because of the respect and reverence being shown him. However when you are 70, you need not worry about that, because the *yetzer tov* will counter, 'They are standing up for you because of your advanced age, not because of your wisdom.' "

Afterwards Reb Sholom would often cite Rav Segal's counsel and add, "The antidote for a *talmid chacham* not to feel haughty when people stand up for him is for him to imagine that he was walking into a *beis midrash* holding a *Sefer Torah.* Everyone would stand up immediately, but it would be foolish for the *talmid chacham* to think they are standing for him. They stand for the *Sefer Torah.* The same applies to the Torah knowledge that the *talmid chacham* possesses. He should consider that when people stand in his presence it is for the Torah knowledge that he carries in his mind — equivalent to carrying a *Sefer Torah* — for which they stand, not for him."

An Age-old Syndrome

When Rabbi Aaron Soloveitchik (1917-2001) *Rosh Yeshivah* of Yeshivas Brisk in Chicago, was 6 years old, he was standing and *davening* on a fast day next to his illustrious grandfather, Reb Elya (Feinstein) Pruzhener (1842-1928).

The congregation was reciting *Selichos* (prayers of supplication), and they were up to the moving supplication שְׁמַע קוֹלֵנוּ, *Hear Our Voice.* The Ark was opened and the *baal tefillah* led everyone in the verses that are recited responsively.

As Reb Elya cried out each verse with emotion, little 6-year-old Aaron recited them with as much fervor as a 6-year-old can muster. The recitation of each verse built on the crescendo of the previous verse.

When they came to the verse, אַל תַּשְׁלִיכֵנוּ לְעֵת זִקְנָה, *Do not cast us away in old age,* Reb Elya exclaimed it with the same passion as the other verses. The little boy, however, lowered his voice and recited the verse almost in an undertone.

After the *davening* Reb Elya said to his grandson, "I noticed that there was one *pasuk* that you didn't say with the same enthusiasm that you said the others."

Little Aaron was surprised at his grandfather's attentiveness. "*Zaide,*" he replied, "those words are not for me. I'm only 6 years old!"

Reb Elya smiled at his grandson's perception and said, "Let me tell you what intent lies in these words besides their literal meaning. At times when an elderly person is confronted with a challenge he says, 'I am too old and tired to deal with this problem. Let others take charge. I don't have the strength or the willingness to get involved.'

"With older people," said Reb Elya, "it is understandable. But sometimes even young people give up when they have a problem. They say, 'I can't deal with it. I'm too tired and it's too hard. Let others do it.' They have been smitten with the mind-set of the elderly. We therefore ask Hashem, 'Do not let us develop the attitude of those elderly people who have lost their enthusiasm to accomplish.' "

This concept brought to mind a stirring talk delivered at an Agudath Yisroel convention by Dayan Chanoch Ehrentreu, the *Av Beis Din* (head of rabbinical court) in London.

Rabbi Ehrentrau posed the following question: When Rachel gave birth to her first son Yosef, Yaakov Avinu said to his father-in-law, Lavan, שַׁלְּחֵנִי וְאֵלְכָה אֶל מְקוֹמִי וּלְאַרְצִי, *Grant me leave that I may go to my place and to my land* (*Bereishis* 30:25). *Rashi* notes that Yaakov felt a surge of confidence that Hashem would protect him in the merit of this newborn child. Therefore he wished to return to the land of Canaan.

"But why now?" asked Dayan Ehrentreu. "Yaakov already had prominent sons such as Yehudah, the ancestor of royalty, Levi the ancestor of priesthood, and Yissachar who represented Torah learning. What was it about his new son that assured Yaakov of his future?"

Citing the *Shem M'Shmuel* (*Vayeitzei* 5681) by the Sochatchover Rebbe, Rabbi Shmuel Borenstein (1855-1926), Dayan Ehrentreu said that the answer lies in the name — Yosef. The meaning of Yosef is "to add." Knowing that a man's name defines him (see *Berachos* 7b), Yaakov knew that this child more than any other would never be satisfied with the status quo. He would always strive higher, achieve more, and constantly add to his accomplishments. For this reason, Yaakov Avinu was confident that he would have Hashem's protection in Yosef's merit.

Thus our prayer that we not be "cast away" to the mind-set of the elderly, who have no expectation of growth, is in consonance with Yaakov Avinu's confidence due to Yosef's overwhelming virtue of always striving for advancement.

Part F:

Perceptions and Perspectives

Travel Plans

Rav Elya Baruch Finkel, a grandson of the late Mirrer *Rosh Yeshivah*, Rav Lazer Yudel Finkel (1875-1965), is today a *maggid shiur* at the Mirrer Yeshiva in Jerusalem. As a young man, R' Elya Baruch studied in the Mirrer Yeshiva and befriended many of the American *bachurim* who went to Israel to study. The following episode took place in the spring of 1974, with a friend of his, Ezra Weingast,* of Kansas City.

Ezra had studied in Mir for more than two years and was planning to return home for Pesach and remain in the States, where he would continue his studies. A few weeks before his trip, R' Elya Baruch suggested to Ezra that he go to Bnei Brak to get a *berachah* (blessing) from the revered *Mashgiach* (spiritual dean) of the Ponevezher Yeshiva, Rav Chatzkel Levenstein (1885-1974). Ezra liked the idea but asked R' Elya Baruch if he would come along. "My *Yiddish* is not that great and you could be my interpreter," he said apologetically. R' Elya Baruch agreed to accompany him.

A week later, as Bnei Brak celebrated Purim with merriment and festivity, R' Elya Baruch and Ezra made their way through the town's crowded streets, dodging children in colorful costumes, romping happily alongside their parents, delivering *shalach mannos.* The two of them came to the home of the saintly *Mashgiach,* whose constant cognizance of Hashem's presence always kept him stern and serious.

After introducing himself, R' Elya Baruch said to Rav Chatzkel in Yiddish, *"Der bachur hut ge'lernt in Mir fahr tzvei yohr, und er gait tzurik tzu America. Er bet der Mashgiach fahr ah berachah."* ("The boy

*The name has been changed.

has studied in Mir for two years and is going back to America. He is asking the *Mashgiach* for a blessing.")

Rav Chatzkel turned to Ezra and said, *"Nu, mit vus gaist du?"* ("Well, with what are you going?")

"Mit El Al" ("With El Al"), Ezra answered enthusiastically, as he failed to grasp Rav Chatzkel's intent.

Realizing that Ezra misunderstood the question, Rav Chatzkel tried again, *"Nain, ich main, vus nemst du mit?"* ("No, I mean, what are you taking with you?")

"Tzvei peklach" ("Two suitcases"), came the inappropriate reply.

Once again, Ezra had misunderstood the question. Embarrassed for his friend, R' Elya Baruch explained to him the meaning of Rav Chatzkel's words. Ezra then explained that indeed he was "taking along" hundreds of *blatt* (folios) of *Gemara* he had studied.

Ezra's futility at understanding the *Mashgiach's* intent brought to mind a penetrating thought from the *Meiri* in his introduction to *Shas.* The *Meiri* states that one must "take along" a lesson from every one of life's experiences, be it joyous or — Heaven forbid — tragic, as there is always something to be learned from an event. Otherwise it is a lost opportunity.

Additionally, says the *Meiri,* every holiday affords each of us an occasion for spiritual growth. One should not come away from *Pesach* merely with the knowledge that he ate *matzos,* nor come away from *Succos* with the mere memory of his having sat in a *succah.* "Without a fresh insight from the holiday," says the *Meiri,* "one is like a donkey who carries grapes in the grape season and wheat in the wheat season. There may be a physical change because of the season but there is no spiritual change or intellectual growth. Hence the simple donkey remains the same donkey."

The intelligent person derives a lesson from every event and every experience. Thus, in our voyage through life, the baggage we carry from destination to destination must be spiritually first class.

Living Life

Rabbi Shlomo Freifeld (1926-1990), founder and *Rosh Yeshivah* of Yeshiva Shor Yoshuv in Far Rockaway, New York, was a charismatic, effervescent, inspirational man, who understood human nature like few in his generation. From his towering frame flowed a rushing brook of confidence, a hearty laugh, an infectious joy and love of life and Torah. His friends, acquaintances and *talmidim* craved to be in his presence, hoping that his vibrancy would electrify their lives as it did his.

He motivated people in unique ways. Rabbi Moshe Greene relates that Rabbi Freifeld once gave a plaque prepared in beautiful calligraphy to a young man with a learning disability. He had just completed learning his first page of *Gemara*, after months of struggle to comprehend it. The plaque read, "If you know this *amud* of *Gemara*, then you can know all of *Shas*. The next *amud* is not harder, it is just different."

I once attended a *siyum* where two of Rabbi Freifeld's former students, who were already in the work force, were celebrating their completion of Tractate *Kiddushin*. Rabbi Freifeld told them, "Don't be discouraged if you have forgotten some of what you learned because even if the Torah you studied went in through one ear and out the other, at least it went through your head!"

Rabbi Freifeld taught that being "brainwashed" by Torah concepts meant that one cleansed his thinking process.

The following story, told by the Braunstein family of Brooklyn, typifies Rabbi Freifeld.

Rabbi Shlomo Braunstein and his wife Rebbetzin Zahava had just married off their son and were making *Sheva Berachos* (lit. Seven Blessings; a festive meal tendered during the first week of marriage, at which seven blessings are recited in honor of the newlyweds). The Braunsteins and Freifelds had been friends for decades, and it was natural for the Freifelds to be in attendance.

Unfortunately Rabbi Freifeld was already quite ill and confined to a wheelchair. The Braunsteins arranged the *Sheva Berachos* in

Rabbi Freifeld's home, so that he could participate. When he spoke, Rabbi Freifeld told the following story:

The Kotzker Rebbe, Rabbi Menachem Mendel Morgenstern (1787-1859), once came to a *cheder* (school for young boys) to test the children. The boys had just finished the first *sedrah* in the Torah — *Bereishis* — and one little boy was asked to recite some verses near the end of the *sedrah,* which detail the genealogy of the generations from Adam to Noah. The syntax of the respective verses (*Bereishis* 5:3-32*),* is identical. ... וַיְחִי אָדָם ... וַיָּמֹת ... וַיְחִי שֵׁת ... וַיָּמֹת וַיְחִי אֱנוֹשׁ ... וַיָּמֹת, *Adam lived... and he died, Sheis lived ... and he died, Enosh lived ... and he died,* and so on. The little boy was translating the verses fluently and confidently: וַיְחִי, *Un er hut gelebt* (and he lived); וַיָּמֹת, *Un er is geshturben* (and he died). Then again by the next descendant, וַיְחִי, *Un er hut gelebt* (and he lived); וַיָּמֹת, *Un er is geshturben* (and he died).

The Kotzker Rebbe stopped the boy and said, "That's not how you say those verses. Recite them again."

The boy was surprised; he was repeating them exactly as he had heard them from his *rebbi,* but he obeyed. Once again he said, וַיְחִי, *Un er hut gelebt;* וַיָּמֹת, *Un er is geshturben.* The little boy was sure that he had said it right this time.

However the Kotzker said: No, that's not how these *pesukim* are said. This is how you say them: He called out in a bellowing voice, וַיְחִי — *UN ER HUT GELEBT*! (AND HE LIVED!). And then in a barely audible voice he whispered in a hush, וַיָּמֹת, *Un er is geshturben* (and he died). The Kotzker exclaimed again, וַיְחִי, *UN ER HUT GELEBT* (AND HE LIVED), and in a soft, low voice, וַיָּמֹת, *un er is geshturben* (and he died).

Rabbi Freifeld smiled as he continued. The Kotzker's lesson was obvious. One must live with verve and vibrancy. A hushed and sedate demeanor is reserved for dying. Vim and vigor are essential ingredients of life.

And then with clever innovative insight, Rabbi Freifeld added, "And that is what I believe is the *p'shat* (meaning) of David *HaMelech's* words: לֹא אָמוּת כִּי אֶחְיֶה וַאֲסַפֵּר מַעֲשֵׂי יָ-הּ, *I shall not die! I shall live and recount the deeds of Hashem (Tehillim* 118:17*).*

"The words are usually understood as David's exclamation that he will survive his enemies' attempts to kill him, and live to recount the deeds of Hashem Who saved him from his foes. I feel there is another meaning as well," said Rabbi Freifeld. "לֹא אָמוּת כִּי אֶחְיֶה, *I shall not die **while** I am alive!* As long as I am blessed with life, I will live with intensity and enthusiasm, not indifference and half-heartedness."

Rabbi Freifeld was echoing the thoughts of the Kotzker, because that was exactly how he lived.

Dipping Into the Past

Rabbi Isaac Bernstein (1939-1994), rabbi of the Finchley Synagogue in North London, was a dynamic, spellbinding orator who delivered weekly *parashah shiurim* to capacity audiences at the Ner Yisroel Community Center in Hendon. Born in Dublin, Ireland, he had a lyrical British-Irish accent that blended well with his exuberance and enthusiasm. His first rabbinical position was at the largest *shul* in Ireland, the Terenure Hebrew Congregation, where his father had previously served as rabbi.

Though I never had the opportunity to meet him, his delight in a fresh Torah insight or clever perception of a *pasuk* or *Chazal* is readily apparent on any of his many tapes. In a lecture about *Pesach* he presented the following incredible insight about the *Seder.* The lesson is applicable in our daily lives.

Chazal teach that as people were walking home from the *Beis HaMikdash* (the Holy Temple) with their *Pesach* offerings, they carried them slung over their backs like Arab merchants *(Pesachim* 65b*)*.

"Why did Jews have to recall Arab merchants at the moment they were carrying their *Pesach* offering?" asked Rabbi Bernstein.

He suggested the following. *Rabbeinu Manoach,* one of the classic commentators on the *Rambam,* writes that we use *karpas* as the vegetable to be dipped at the *Seder* for it recalls for us the *kesones pasim,* the fine woolen tunic that Yaakov *Avinu* made for his son Yosef *(Rambam, Hilchos Chametz U'Matzah* 8:2; *see Bereishis* 37:3*)*. "Just as the brothers dipped the *kesones pasim* in blood (to make their father think that Yosef was dead), so, too, we dip the *karpas* in saltwater," explained Rabbi Bernstein.

"Rabbeinu Manoach's comparison of the *karpas* to the *kesones pasim* begs explanation," exclaimed Rabbi Bernstein. "What is the connection between the two?"

Rabbi Bernstein directed his listeners to *Rashi's* comments on the words כְּתֹנֶת פַּסִּים *(Bereishis* 37:3*)*. Rashi uses the word כַּרְפַּס in describing the garment. He writes that כַּר means colored wool and פַּס means a fine woolen tunic. Hence כַּרְפַּס is a synonym for כְּתֹנֶת פַּסִּים, a fine woolen colored tunic.

On the night of *Pesach*, Jews the world over celebrate the freedom from Egyptian bondage. "However, one must ask," Rabbi Bernstein cried out, "what led to the bondage? How did the Jews wind up in Egypt in the first place? The answer is because brothers could not get along. There was jealousy and strife that led the older sons of Yaakov to sell their younger brother Yosef."

Perhaps that is why the *karpas* ritual is one of the first rituals at the *Seder* — because before we can celebrate how we were freed from bondage we must understand what got us into bondage. Hence we dip the *karpas* to remind us of another dipping years before, which symbolized the strife that led to the enslavement in Egypt.

And that may be, suggested Rabbi Bernstein, why the Jews carried the *Pesach* offering in the manner of Arab merchants. The Torah (*Bereishis* 37:25*)*, tells us that after Yosef was cast into the pit, וַיֵּשְׁבוּ לֶאֱכָל לֶחֶם וַיִּשְׂאוּ עֵינֵיהֶם וַיִּרְאוּ וְהִנֵּה אֹרְחַת יִשְׁמְעֵאלִים בָּאָה, *They [the brothers] sat to eat food; they raised their eyes and they saw, behold! A caravan of Ishmaelites [Arabs] was coming ...* to whom Yosef was eventually sold.

Again, the same message. Indeed, we celebrate our redemption by offering the *Pesach* lamb, but we must also be aware of how we lost our freedom in the first place. It started with episodes that led to betrayal within a family, leading to the sorrowful sale of a brother to Arab merchants.

The *Midrash Tanchuma (Nitzavim 1)* teaches: אֵין יִשְׂרָאֵל נִגְאָלִין עַד שֶׁיִּהְיוּ כּוּלָּן אֲגוּדָה אַחַת, *The Jewish nation will not be redeemed until they are one unit.* One's family is a microcosm of the family of Jews. If we can achieve unity in our families, we can hope to extend that unity to all Jews. At Mount Sinai the Jewish nation was united, like one person with one desire (*see Shemos* 19:2 *and Rashi*), thus they merited to receive the Torah. May we as a nation once again achieve that oneness, so that we merit Mashiach and redemption in our time.

A Clean Slate

Rabbi Binyamin Finkel, *Mashgiach* of Yeshiva Mishkan Yisrael in Jerusalem, is known lovingly as "Reb Binyamin HaTzaddik," the appellation given to the righteous charity collector mentioned in *Bava Basra* 11a. The humble, soft-spoken Rabbi Finkel is the son of the revered *Mashgiach* of the Mirrer Yeshiva, Rabbi Aryeh Finkel. He lectures throughout Israel on ethical behavior, and is one of the *baalei tefillah* in Mir during the *Yamim Noraim*. He is cherished by all who know him.

One year on *Chol HaMoed Succos* (the Intermediate Days of *Succos*) my family and I visited Rav Binyamin in his *succah* in Givat Shaul. He spoke endearingly of his late mother, Rebbetzin Esther Gitel, who he said had a powerful effect on the sanctity of her home and the behavior of her children. Her brother was the noted *Maggid*, Rabbi Shabsi Binyamin Yudelevitz (1924-1996) of Jerusalem. Reb Binyamin gave the following example of her perspective on life, but prefaced it with an insight found in the *Daas Zekeinim MiBaalei HaTosafos* on *Vayikra* 2:13.

The Torah instructs us: וְלֹא תַשְׁבִּית מֶלַח בְּרִית אֱלֹקֶיךָ מֵעַל מִנְחָתֶךָ עַל כָּל קָרְבָּנְךָ תַּקְרִיב מֶלַח, *You may not discontinue the salt of your G-d's covenant from upon your meal-offering — on your every offering shall you offer salt (Vayikra,* ibid.*).* The *Daas Zekeinim* explains that since salt never spoils, this long-lasting quality of salt signifies the atonement achieved by bringing a *korban*.

The *Shulchan Aruch (Orach Chaim* 167:5*)* writes that this verse is the reason it is proper to have salt on the table before one makes *Hamotzi,* since one's table is likened to the Altar in the *Beis HaMikdash.* Additionally, having salt on the table serves as a protection from punishment (see *Mishnah Berurah* ibid. notes 30-32*).*

When one brings a *korban* his forgiveness is permanent just like salt. Hence he is careful not to sin again for he does not wish to "soil" his "clean slate." It is similar to a person wearing new clothing. He is careful that it not become dirty or damaged in the slightest way. Similarly people with new cars drive and park cautiously so the car does not get even the smallest scratch. However once the barrier is broken and man has repeated his sin (or has soiled his clothing or scratched his car), he is more apt to repeat it yet again. (See *Moed Katan* 27b.)

The *Daas Zekeinim* offers a novel interpretation on the verse: בְּכָל עֵת יִהְיוּ בְגָדֶיךָ לְבָנִים, *Let your garments always be white (Koheles* 9:8*).* By always wearing "pure white clothes," i.e. having a spiritually "clean slate," one will hesitate to sin for he will not want to defile himself.

"It was with this concept in mind," said Rabbi Binyamin Finkel, "that our mother would gather us together every *erev Pesach.* She would point to the walls of the house that had just been thoroughly washed down with a lime solution so that they were glisteningly white. '*Taiyereh kinderlach* (dearest children), these fresh white walls have never heard *lashon hara,'* she would say. 'Let's see if we can keep them in that pure state by our not speaking any *lashon hara* in their presence.'"

Rabbi Finkel smiled warmly as he recalled the sanctity of his mother's words. He added, "Our home suddenly felt holy. We all felt elevated. We all made silent commitments to a fresh observance of *shemiras halashon* (proper speech)."

Location, Location, Location

Rabbi Chaim Shmulevitz (1902-1978) offered a poignant parable to explain a statement in *Mesechta* (Tractate) *Shabbos* regarding one of the thirty-nine categories of prohibited labor on the Sabbath.

The thirty-fifth *melachah* is סוֹתֵר, *dismantling*. The *Gemara (Shabbos* 31b*)* explains: סוֹתֵר עַל מְנָת לִבְנוֹת בִּמְקוֹמוֹ הָוֵי סוֹתֵר, עַל מְנָת לִבְנוֹת שֶׁלֹּא בִּמְקוֹמוֹ לֹא הָוֵי סוֹתֵר, *Dismantling for the purpose of building [something else] in the same place is deemed [the biblical labor of] "dismantling." [Conversely, dismantling] for the purpose of building in* another *place is not deemed "dismantling."*

Rabbah challenges this premise: We derive all prohibited labors on the Sabbath from the labors performed in connection with the Tabernacle (see *Shabbos* 49b*)*. Yet in the Tabernacle the act of dismantling was performed with the purpose of erecting again in *another* place. [In the Wilderness the Jews would dismantle the Tabernacle when they broke camp, and would re-assemble it when they pitched camp in their next location. Thus the very source for the forbidden labor of dismantling is for the purpose of building in a different place — not the same place!]

Ulla replied to Rabbah, "Since it is written in the Torah עַל פִּי ה׳ יַחֲנוּ [וְעַל פִּי ה׳ יִסָּעוּ], *By the word of Hashem they would encamp [and by the word of Hashem they would journey] (Bamidbar* 9:23*)*, it is tantamount to dismantling for the purpose of building in the very same place."

Why? How does *"the word of Hashem"* transform another place into the same place?

Rabbi Chaim Shmulevitz *(Sichos Mussar, Maamar* 22, 5733*)* likened it to a mother carrying her infant on a long trip. Rav Chaim says, "Were you to ask the baby, at the beginning of the trip, 'Where are you?' if the baby could speak it would say, 'I am in my mother's arms.' If you were to ask the baby an hour into the trip, 'Where are you?' it would give the same answer, 'I am in my mother's arms.' They could be traveling for thousands of miles, but to the child, the location is always the same — it is with its mother. The geographical location is irrelevant, the child and its mother are inextricably bound together. He is with her and she is with her baby."

Similarly, the Jews who traveled in the Wilderness were anchored to Hashem. As long as their every move was at His command, wherever they encamped they were "with Hashem." עַל פִּי ה׳ יַחֲנוּ [וְעַל פִּי ה׳ יִסָּעוּ], *By the word of Hashem they would encamp [and by the word of Hashem they would journey].* The locale on the map was insignificant; their connection to Hashem was primary. Since the Tabernacle was always "with Hashem," it could be considered halachically בִּמְקוֹמוֹ, *in the same place.*

Interestingly, Rabbi Yaakov Yisrael Bifus of Rechasim, Israel, author of *Lekach Tov,* writes (ibid.) that after World War II, when the *rebbeim* and *talmidim* of the Mirrer Yeshiva were crossing the Pacific Ocean from Shanghai to America, Rabbi Shmulevitz was writing his *Kuntres Toras Hasefinah* on the *Shev Shmaatsa.* The long trip took weeks, and seemed endless. One day one of the *talmidim* was on deck peering out over the ocean wondering when the trip would finally end. He turned to Reb Chaim and asked, *"Ahvu zehnen mir?"* ("Where are we?")

Reb Chaim answered spontaneously, *"Mir haltehn by Shmaatsa Gimel."* ("We are up to the third [essay of the] *Shmaatsa.*") Reb Chaim's location was determined by the Torah he was learning, not where his ship might be traveling. He was like the Tabernacle in the Wilderness.

Roaring Rejoinder

At his *drashah* following *Kol Nidrei* on *Yom Kippur* eve, our rav, Rabbi Shlomo Teitelbaum, of Khal Adas Yeraim in Kew Gardens, New York, made an interesting observation to set the tone for the observance of this most hallowed day of the Jewish year.

He cited the verse: אַרְיֵה שָׁאָג מִי לֹא יִירָא, *A lion has roared; who will not fear?* (*Amos* 3:8). Commentators note homiletically that the word אַרְיֵה is an acronym for the awesome days of reflection and repentance: אֱלוּל (the month of *Elul*), רֹאשׁ הַשָּׁנָה (*Rosh Hashanah*), יוֹם כִּפּוּר (*Yom Kippur*) and הוֹשַׁעְנָא רַבָּה (*Hoshana Rabbah,* the day G-d completes the task of sealing the results of the Days of Judgment). These are days of reflection and repentance and, indeed, as they approach wouldn't any thinking Jew be anxious and fearful as he faces judgment for his conduct throughout the past year?

Rabbi Teitelbaum recalled that he had once gone to the Bronx Zoo and as he walked along the flowered promenade from area to area, he suddenly heard a ferocious roar from a nearby lion. And he wasn't frightened! Fascinated perhaps, but not afraid. Why? "Because the lion was in a cage and there was no way he could harm me," he explained.

"I deduced from that," he said, "that if the *Ribono Shel Olam's* days of *Elul, Rosh Hashanah, Yom Kippur* and *Hoshana Rabbah* 'roar' at us and we are not frightened, then perhaps it is because there is a barrier between us and the *Ribono Shel Olam*."

He concluded, "It is our mission to remove that barrier and sensitize ourselves to the seriousness of the moment."

Indeed, in the concluding prayer of the *Hoshana Rabbah* service we ask: יְהִי רָצוֹן מִלְּפָנֶיךָ ... וְתָסִיר מְחִצַּת הַבַּרְזֶל הַמַּפְסֶקֶת בֵּינֵינוּ וּבֵינֶיךָ, *May it be Your will ... and remove the iron partition separating us from You.*

Interestingly, the gentile prophet Balaam said of the Jews, הֶן עָם כְּלָבִיא יָקוּם וְכַאֲרִי יִתְנַשָּׂא, *The people will arise like a lion cub and raise itself like a lion* (*Bamidbar* 23:24).

Rashi comments, "When they get up from their sleep in the morning, they exert themselves like a lion cub and like a lion to grab commandments: to wear a *tallis*, to read the *Shema* and to put on *tefillin*." Hence we have it within us to respond to the "roar" of *Elul* and the subsequent Days of Awe.

Fear? Yes. Apprehension? Certainly.

But along with it should come confidence that we can respond. We can meet the roar head on, with remorse, regret, reflection, reaction and repentance.

Who Owns What?

Each of the Patriarchs tithed from their wealth. Of Avraham the Torah writes: וַיִּתֶּן לוֹ מַעֲשֵׂר מִכֹּל, *And he gave [to Shem son of Noach] a tenth from everything (Bereishis* 14:20*)*; of Yitzchak the Torah states: וַיִּמְצָא בַּשָּׁנָה הַהִוא מֵאָה שְׁעָרִים, *in that year he reaped a hundredfold* (ibid.

26:12*)*, to which *Rashi* notes, אוֹמֶד זֶה לְמַעְשְׂרוֹת הָיָה, *this estimation was done for tithes.* Yaakov pledged to Hashem, וְכֹל אֲשֶׁר תִּתֶּן לִי עַשֵּׂר אֲעַשְּׂרֶנּוּ לָךְ, *whatever You will give me, I shall surely tithe (*ibid. 28:22*).*

Giving *maaser* is not only a benefit for the recipient; it benefits the giver as well. *Chazal* (*Taanis* 8b-9a) expound that the message in the Torah's commandment, עַשֵּׂר תְּעַשֵּׂר, *then you shall surely tithe* (*Devarim* 14:22), has the additional meaning of "Tithe so that you shall become wealthy." (This homiletic interpretation relates the words תְּעַשֵּׂר, *you shall tithe,* to the word עֹשֶׁר, *wealth*).

Rabbi Moshe Feinstein often stated that the commandment to tithe obligates one to contribute not only a tenth of one's income, but also a tenth of one's time and energy.

When I first became a professional *mohel* in 1966, Rabbi Sholom Schwadron (1912-1997), the Maggid of Jerusalem, who stayed in my parents' home when he was in America, stressed the importance of my keeping a ledger in which I would enter all earnings, so that at a designated time (either every week, every other week or every month) I would deduct a tenth of my income (after expenses) for charity.

Rabbi Shimon Schwab (1908-1995) had such a book in which he dutifully kept an exact account of the money he earned and the money he dispensed to charity. Every year on his birthday he would begin a new book with a new account regardless of how much more than the required tithe he had given the year before. His son R' Moshe explained to me that his father's gratitude to Hashem for giving him another year of life inspired him to express his thanks in this manner.

Rabbi Schwab's approach to his finances brought to mind an incident told by the noted lecturer and *kiruv* activist, Rabbi Jonathan Rietti of Monsey, N.Y.

For the last ten years of his life, Rabbi Schwab was confined to a wheelchair because his legs were ailing. His grandson, Nosson Schwab, once asked him, "It has been years since you have been able to walk. Yet, *Oma* (grandmother) tells me that you have never complained about it. How can you maintain a serene smile on your face when you are so restricted?"

Rabbi Schwab smiled and replied, "Imagine that a wealthy man lent you a million dollars and let you keep it to use as you wished for seventy years! After the seventy years he told you that he wanted a hundred or a thousand dollars back. Would you be angry with him? *Could* you be angry with him? He gave you the opportunity to use a special gift for so long, he is entitled to take any part of it back whenever he wants. My feet were a gift from Hashem and He has the right to take them back. I am not my feet. They are not *my* assets. Their loss is nothing more than an inconvenience."

Rabbi Schwab realized that *everything* he possessed — his money, his home and even his body — was a gift from Hashem. Nothing was his own; he was merely a guardian for all that Hashem had permitted him to use as long as he was in this world.

Is then *maaser* — one tenth — too much to give in return for all that Hashem has given us?

Then Rabbi Schwab added to his grandson, "And besides, I have a wife, a family, over fifty children, grandchildren, and great-grandchildren who are all following in the ways of my fathers and forefathers; I have had the privilege of leading the Kehillah in Washington Heights for over fifty years. And I should complain? I should be without a smile?"

What values! What priorities! What perspectives!

Prescriptions for Longevity

The Talmud (*Megillah* 27b-28a) records that numerous elderly *amoraim* (rabbis of the Talmud) were asked: בַּמֶּה הֶאֱרַכְתָּ יָמִים, *On account of which [meritorious practice] have you attained longevity?* Each of them mentioned a trait they had practiced for years, which they felt was responsible for their long life. For example, Rav Preida said: מִיָּמַי לֹא קְדָמַנִי אָדָם לְבֵית הַמִּדְרָשׁ, *In all my days, no one ever came to the study hall before me.* Rav Elazar ben Shamua said: מִיָּמַי לֹא עָשִׂיתִי קַפֶּנְדַּרְיָא לְבֵית הַכְּנֶסֶת, *In all my days, I never used a synagogue as a shortcut [to get from one street to another].* Rav Zeira said:

מִיָּמַי לֹא הִקְפַּדְתִּי בְּתוֹךְ בֵּיתִי, *In all my days, I never showed anger in my house.* Rav Nechunya ben Hakanah said: מִיָּמַי לֹא נִתְכַּבַּדְתִּי בִּקְלוֹן חֲבֵרִי, *In all my days, I never derived honor from the shame of another person.* Twenty other *amoraim* gave reasons for their longevity.

We all want to live long — but how do we choose a trait, or even a number of them, to assure our longevity?

Rabbi Yechezkel Munk, *Rosh Yeshivah* at Yeshivas Telshe in Cleveland, told me that the commentators find a common denominator in the replies of all the *amoraim.* Each one of them prefaced his words by saying: מִיָּמַי, *In all my days ...,* indicating that they were consistent in their behavior. The primary virtue was this constancy in never deviating from a practice they undertook. Their long lives resulted more from their never having deviated from their noble traits than from the traits themselves.

The *Netziv,* R' Naftali Tzvi Yehudah Berlin (1817-1893), writes in *Haamek Davar (Bamidbar* 15:41*)*: "All people do not serve Hashem in the same manner. Some study Torah all day, some are totally involved in prayer, while others occupy themselves with *gemillus chassadim* (benevolence and kindness). And each group sincerely intends to connect with Hashem in its chosen way of life."

Even in the study of Torah, continues the *Netziv,* there are different methods of learning (בְּקִיאוּת vs. עִיּוּן — erudition and familiarity with a broad range of topics vs. profound analysis of the subject matter under discussion). So, too, with the performance of *mitzvos.* Although all Jews are required to observe them all, different people give particular emphasis to different *mitzvos.* Some pay scrupulous attention to the observance of Shabbos, while others are meticulous in *tzitzis,* and so on. (See *Peirush HaMishnayos L'Rambam, Makkos* 3:16.)

The *Netziv* cites the *Yerushalmi (Kiddushin* 1:9*)* which states: "*Anyone who performs one mitzvah will be blessed with goodness and longevity ... provided that he never violates the mitzvah he singled out [for scrupulous performance].* Consistency is imperative.

Interestingly, R' Yehudah HaChassid (1150-1217) writes (*Sefer Chassidim,* note 210): "If you see a *talmid chacham* who enjoys longevity, know that he has accepted upon himself [seemingly] trivial and minor [meritorious] deeds that others don't do. As we see in *Mesechta Megillah* (ibid.), [when a*moraim* were asked]: 'On account of which [meritorious practice] have you attained longevity?' they each spoke of deeds they performed that were not [even] *d'oraisa* (ordained by the Torah). They attached significance to practices that some people might consider to be trivial."

In light of the above, the following story adapted by Rabbi Avrohom Chaim Feuer in *Tehillim Treasury* (p. 149) from *P'ninei Rabbeinu Yechezkel* (part II p. 43) is illuminating.

Rabbi Yechezkel Abramsky (1886-1976) was the head of the London *Beis Din* (rabbinical court) during World War II. One day while the *Beis Din* was in session regarding a divorce procedure, the city was bombed by the German Luftwaffe. A bomb struck the *Beis Din* building and the husband was killed instantly, leaving his wife a widow instead of a divorcee.

The impact of the explosion threw Rabbi Abramsky out of his chair and he lay sprawled on the floor on the other side of the room. A moment later a huge chunk of the roof caved in and crashed on the spot where he had been sitting. He said afterwards, "Had I still been in that seat I would have been crushed to death."

A few weeks later Rabbi Abramsky told friends, "I have often asked myself: In what merit did Hashem save me from death? Why did I merit Divine salvation? I thought about this carefully and concluded that I always take special pains to don my *tallis* with concentration." Rabbi Abramsky was known to devote special attention to the *mitzvah* of *tzitzis.* Often he could be seen lovingly caressing the *tzitzis* on his *tallis,* which was always immaculately clean.

Rabbi Abramsky continued, "Every morning I wrap myself in the *tallis* and recite the verses from *Tehillim* (36:8-11) printed in the *siddur.* As I say the first verse, מַה יָּקָר חַסְדְּךָ אֱלֹקִים וּבְנֵי אָדָם בְּצֵל כְּנָפֶיךָ יֶחֱסָיוּן, *How precious is Your kindness, O G-d! The sons of man take refuge in the shadow of Your wings,* I feel enveloped by G-d's embrace, protected by His invincible might. Perhaps this was the merit that saved my life!"

When recounting the story, Rabbi Abramsky would add, "The building that housed the London *Beis Din* was very large, but I assure you that the total of all the chapters of *Tehillim* that I recited in that building far outnumbered its bricks. I have no doubt that those chapters of *Tehillim* also protected me in the explosion."

Perhaps it behooves us to undertake a trait or two to enhance our chances for longevity.

Should it be a commitment to say all *berachos* (blessings) out loud? Rabbi Chaim Volozhiner (1749-1821) always recited them aloud so that someone present could answer *Amen.* He based this practice on the *Zohar,* which compares a blessing made without someone answering *Amen* to אִיגַּרְתָּא דְלָא פְּתִיחָא, *an unopened letter.* It would be wise to consult with Torah scholars as to which *mitzvah* or trait one should lavish additional concentration on. The *amoraim* in *Mesechta Megillah* chose from a wide gamut of behavior patterns reflecting both בֵּין אָדָם לַמָּקוֹם, *Man to G-d,* and בֵּין אָדָם לַחֲבֵרוֹ, *person to person* relationships.

In reality it doesn't matter which *mitzvah* or trait is chosen. But once it has been selected be sure that you perform it with consistency. And may you then merit a long and good life.

Under Lock and Key

Rabbi Aryeh Levin (1885-1969) was known for his compassion and concern for every Jew. His kind words and easy smile encouraged all who came in contact with him. In the 1940's when Jews were imprisoned by the British authorities who ruled Palestine, Reb Aryeh was one of the rare individuals who had permission to visit them. The prisoners loved and revered him.

One *Chol HaMoed Pesach,* Reb Aryeh visited the prisoners. "How was your *Seder?"* he asked, genuinely interested in their welfare.

One of the prisoners smiled and quipped, "Everything was fine, we were able to fulfill all the *halachic* requirements of the *Seder* except one. When we came to: שְׁפֹךְ חֲמָתְךָ אֶל הַגּוֹיִם אֲשֶׁר לֹא יְדָעוּךָ, *Pour Your anger on the nations that do not want to know You,* they wouldn't let us open the door!" {Customarily Jews open the front door of the home prior to reciting this part of the *Haggadah* as an affirmation of trust in Hashem's protection on לֵיל שִׁמֻּרִים, *the night for protection* — the first night of Pesach (see *Shemos* 12:42).}

Reb Aryeh returned the inmate's smile and said, "You are mistaken. You do have the key to freedom — the key to your heart, which can give you spiritual freedom." He continued, "We are prisoners in our own bodies, but we can be freed of the bondage to our materialistic desires. By opening our hearts and allowing ourselves to gain control, we become truly free."

> And the effort is not that exhaustive, as the *Midrash* teaches: Hashem exhorts us: פִּתְחוּ לִי פֶּתַח שֶׁל תְּשׁוּבָה כְּחוּדָּהּ שֶׁל מַחַט וַאֲנִי פּוֹתֵחַ לָכֶם פְּתָחִים שֶׁיִּהְיוּ עֲגָלוֹת וּקְרָנִיּוֹת נִכְנָסוֹת בּוֹ, *Open for Me an aperture of repentance no bigger than the eye of a needle and I will make openings for you through which wagons and carriages can pass (Shir HaShirim Rabbah* 5:2:2). As the Talmud teaches, בָּא לְטַהֵר מְסַיְּיעִים אוֹתוֹ, *One who comes to purify himself will indeed be helped (Shabbos* 104a*).* A little effort goes a long way.

The concept of one being a prisoner in one's own body brought to mind a puzzling reference *Chazal* make regarding marriage. In a discussion on how matches are made, the Sages *(Sotah* 2a*)* cite a verse in *Tehillim:* אֱלֹקִים מוֹשִׁיב יְחִידִים בַּיְתָה מוֹצִיא אֲסִירִים בַּכּוֹשָׁרוֹת, *Hashem gathers individuals into a home, He releases the prisoners at suitable moments (Tehillim* 68:7*).*

The first part of the verse is an obvious reference to marriage, as it speaks of Hashem bringing two individuals together to build a home and family. However, the second part of the verse seems irrelevant to marriage. It describes the season of the year in which Hashem chose to take the Jews out of Egypt. The winter would have been too cold for the Jews to walk through the desert and the summer too hot so Hashem selected springtime as the ideal time for redemption. But what do prisoners leaving bondage have to do with marriage? How do the two halves of the verse relate to each other?

Perhaps the idea is that before people marry, they are prisoners within their own bodies in the sense that there is much latent potential within them that lies dormant until an opportune moment or environment stimulates the potential to blossom. Marriage can provide such opportunities; when individuals are blessed with an עֵזֶר כְּנֶגְדּוֹ, *a helpmate alongside themselves* (*Bereishis* 2:18), their potential for achievement is unlimited.

Thus the intent of the verse is that Hashem brings individuals together in marriage so that they can liberate from each other the dormant potential they each possess.

> For inmates or soul-mates, fulfillment and freedom can flourish. The key element is to bring out the best within ourselves and our partners.

The Strength of Softness

> The piercing sounds of the long even blasts and the short staccato blasts of the *shofar* on *Rosh Hashanah* are meant to awaken us to repentance. According to Rav Saadiah Gaon they remind us, as well, of the great and awesome Judgment Day of the future (see ArtScroll's *Rosh Hashanah*, p. 60).
>
> As is often the case, it is not merely the message but the messenger that adds urgency to the task at hand. Hence the *baal tokei'a* (one who blows the *shofar*) who delivers this message of repentance and judgment is often a humble, saintly individual, who personifies allegiance to Torah and *mitzvos* at the highest levels.
>
> The following story is about one such *baal tokei'a*.

Rabbi Moshe Betzalel Alter (1869-1942), the third son of the *Sfas Emes* — Rabbi Yehuda Leib Alter (1847- 1905) (the second Rebbe of Ger) — was a pious, humble man. When he was born, his father, sensing his holiness, decided not to name him after a deceased relative, but after holy people mentioned in the Torah. Since he was born during the week of *Parashas Vayakhel,* he was named after two people appearing in that *sedrah,* Moshe and Betzalel, who was in charge of building the *Mishkan* (Tabernacle).

When the *Sfas Emes* died, his eldest son, Rabbi Avraham Mordechai Alter (1866-1948), the *Imrei Emes,* became Rebbe. During his tenure, the *Imrei Emes* appointed his younger brother, Reb Moshe Betzalel, to blow *shofar* on *Rosh Hashanah.* Reb Moshe Betzalel spent much time every *Elul* reviewing the *halachos* involved. The *kehillah* was moved every year, not only by his *tekios,* but also by the intensity of the *berachos* he recited before the *tekios.*

One year the *tekios* lacked the power and strength of previous years; they were soft and barely audible. At their conclusion, Rav Moshe Betzalel was visibly disappointed and walked away from the *bimah* dejected.

Noticing his brother's discontentment, the *Imrei Emes* sought to comfort him. After *davening* he told him a homiletical insight offered by the P'shis'cha Rebbe, Reb Simchah Bunim (1767-1826).

"It says in the *U'nesaneh Tokef* prayer: וּבַשּׁוֹפָר גָּדוֹל יִתָּקַע, *When the shofar is blown by a great person,** then even if וְקוֹל דְּמָמָה דַקָּה יִשָּׁמַע, *a still, thin sound is heard,* still וּמַלְאָכִים יֵחָפֵזוּן וְחִיל וּרְעָדָה יֹאחֵזוּן, *the angels will hasten, a trembling and terror will seize them,* וְיֹאמְרוּ הִנֵּה יוֹם הַדִּין, *and they will say, 'Behold, it is the Day of Judgment.'"*

A Share of Wealth

We often hear the well-known teaching of the *Mishnah* (*Avos* 4:1), אֵיזֶהוּ עָשִׁיר? הַשָּׂמֵחַ בְּחֶלְקוֹ, *Who is rich? He who is happy with his lot.* The conventional understanding of this statement is that in order for us to be content, we should be satisfied with whatever Hashem has blessed us. Those who are always focused on what they don't have are doomed to unhappiness and disappointment.

*The conventional sense of the phrase is that at the time of Judgment, וּבְשׁוֹפָר גָּדוֹל יִתָּקַע, *the great shofar will be sounded,* וְקוֹל דְּמָמָה דַקָּה יִשָּׁמַע, *and a still, thin sound will be heard,* signifying Hashem's appearance (see *I Melachim* 19:12 and *Yeshayah* 27:13).

The *Chasam Sofer*, Rabbi Moshe Schreiber (1763-1839), understands the phrase שָׂמֵח בְּחֶלְקוֹ in a unique manner. Coupled with a concept of the *Or HaChaim*, his insight offers tranquility and inspiration.

The *Chasam Sofer* notes that the word בְּחֶלְקוֹ can be translated as *his fraction*. In His infinite wisdom and foresight, Hashem does not allot an individual the full measure of compensation for the Torah he has learned or for the *mitzvos* he has performed. He dispenses only part of the reward — the amount that is appropriate for the person's needs. Hashem withholds the full reward for one of numerous reasons. First, so that the individual may receive his compensation in the World to Come. Second, so that the person will not squander his reward foolishly, or, third, so that the newly acquired compensation will not adversely effect the person's personality and character. (See *Visions of the Fathers* by Rabbi Abraham Twersky M.D. *Avos* ibid.)

The *Or HaChaim (Shemos* 20:6*)* offers another reason, based on the phrase in the *Aseres HaDibros* (Ten Commandments), וְעֹשֶׂה חֶסֶד לַאֲלָפִים *[Hashem] Who shows kindness for thousands [of generations].* This teaches that when Hashem withholds part of someone's due reward, it is to benefit the person. The balance of the reward may be conferred on the person's descendants generations later, as protection or assistance.

If someone feels that he has not received just reward for his Torah observance, he may be right. Hashem may be giving him only a *portion* of what he deserves — so that the rest of it can be meted out later in his lifetime or to his descendants in the future generations. Someone who understands this is indeed שָׂמֵחַ בְּחֶלְקוֹ, *happy with his "fraction."*

These thoughts brought to mind a story that Rabbi Avraham Pam (1913-2001), *Rosh Yeshivah* of Mesivta Torah Vodaath, wrote in his *sefer, Atarah LaMelech* (p. 120).

In 1976 he and his wife Sarah, were vacationing in Bethlehem, New Hampshire. One summer day, he was suddenly stricken with a very high fever and felt faint. He called out to his wife that he was afraid he would fall. She ran to get a citrus fruit and the only one available was a lemon. "Bite into this, bite into this," she exclaimed, "it will help you."

Rabbi Pam writes that he devoured the lemon, squeezing and slurping every drop of liquid he could draw from it despite its bitter taste. Within moments he felt revived.

A number of days later, as Rabbi Pam related this incident to his son, he expressed surprise at the uncouth way he had devoured the lemon. He couldn't recall ever seeing anyone eating food with such ravishing zeal. He was embarrassed at his own behavior, though he readily understood it. Suddenly he remembered an incident that had occurred twenty years earlier.

Rabbi Pam had gone to a convalescent home to visit a friend who had terminal cancer. He took along some fresh oranges to give as a gift, but his friend thanked him for the gesture and explained that he didn't want them.

In the same room lay an elderly rabbi who was paralyzed from the waist down. Rabbi Pam offered him an orange. The rabbi was so hungry that he devoured the orange, sucking its juice like a lion devouring its prey. The man was so weak that he could no longer speak, but his sparkling eyes conveyed the message of gratitude in a manner that moved Rabbi Pam whenever he thought about it.

Now, talking to his son, Rabbi Pam realized that Hashem had paid him מִדָּה כְּנֶגֶד מִדָּה, *measure for measure.* He had stored Rabbi Pam's recompense for twenty years and delivered it (the juicy lemon in exchange for the luscious orange) just when he needed it most, when he was ill and about to faint. It was then that the *Rosh Yeshivah* understood a new meaning to the verse in *Yeshayah* (40:31), וְקוֹיֵ ה' יַחֲלִיפוּ כֹחַ, *Those whose hope is in Hashem will have renewed strength.* The word יַחֲלִיפוּ comes from the word חֲלִיפִין, *exchange,* writes Rabbi Pam. Thus the expression can be understood in this context to mean that Hashem makes an exchange with man by rewarding him מִדָּה כְּנֶגֶד מִדָּה, *measure for measure.*

With these thoughts in mind, no one need be envious of what others have. Hashem gives everyone the portion he needs now. As for the rest, whatever he deserves will come later.

Flood Protection

The *mispalelim* (congregants) in the Emunas Yisroel *Shul* in Boro Park under the leadership of Rabbi Moshe Wolfson, the *Mashgiach* in Mesifta Torah Vodaath, are known for their extraordinary fervor and conscientiousness in *davening*. Each *mispallel* is encouraged to pray slowly and concentrate on every word. Even the daily *Shacharis* takes an hour and a half.

In a *drashah* regarding *tefillah,* Rabbi Wolfson told his *mispallelim* a beautiful thought he heard from his *rebbi,* Reb Shraga Feivel Mendlowitz. It typifies the attitude of the Emunas Yisroel community.

Rav Mendlowitz cited an interesting homiletical interpretation of the *Baal Shem Tov.* When Hashem told Noach to build the Ark, he instructed him, צֹהַר תַּעֲשֶׂה לַתֵּבָה, *[A source of] brightness shall you make for the Ark* (*Bereishis* 6:16). Some say it was a skylight, others say it was a precious stone that glittered luminously (see *Rashi* ibid.).

"The word תֵּבָה can also mean *word,*" said the *Baal Shem Tov.* "Hence, the expression can also imply, *You shall make an illumination for the word,*" i.e. every word of *tefillah.* Each word should sparkle with the proper intent, pronunciation and knowledge of its meaning."

Rabbi Mendlowitz added, "The תֵּבָה (Ark) rescued Noach and his family from the flood. Similarly, the תֵּבוֹת (words) of *tefillah* can save each of us from the flood of immorality, dishonesty and secularism that threatens to overrun our society. By concentrating on every word of the *davening,* we come to appreciate our total dependence on Hashem's beneficence, and we become cognizant of His *Hashgachah Pratis (*Divine Providence*) (*see *Mishnas Rav Aharon* Vol. 1, *Essays on Tefillah,* pp. 84,92). This in turn leads us to be more observant and attendant to the words and ordinances of Hashem."

This is a message that should inundate our daily lives.

At a *Sholom Zachar* for my grandson, in the Sanhedria Murchevet section of Jerusalem, Rabbi Chaim Dvir, one of the *askanim* (community activists) of the neighborhood, told the following story. He became a *talmid* of Yeshivas Chevron at the age of 17, while it was still in the Geulah section of Jerusalem. The *Rosh Yeshivah*, Rabbi Yecheskel Sarna (1895-1969), was already elderly and in poor health due to his advanced case of diabetes.

Customarily on *Yom Kippur*, Reb Chatzkel was called to the Torah for *Maftir Yonah*. The third person called to the Torah at *Minchah* has the honor or reading (or having read for him) the entire Book of *Yonah*, which is the textbook of repentance and mercy. Its concepts of atonement and forgiveness are indelibly identified with *Yom Kippur*.

On Rabbi Dvir's first *Yom Kippur* in the yeshivah, Reb Chatzkel was still strong enough to be there for most of the day, and was honored with *Maftir Yonah*. By the next *Yom Kippur*, 5730/1969, he was confined to bed and had to remain in his apartment, which was adjacent to the yeshivah, all day.

Reb Chatzkel's grandson, R' Daniel Farbstein, wanted the *Rosh Yeshivah* to receive his customary *Maftir Yonah*, since it would raise his spirits and show him that he was not forgotten.

R' Daniel organized a number of *bachurim* from the *beis midrash* to make a *minyan* for *Minchah* in the *Rosh Yeshivah's* apartment. Chaim Dvir was one of them.

A makeshift *bimah* on which the Torah would be read was set up and Reb Chatzkel's bed was placed next to the *baal korei* (the reader of the Torah). They used the Torah that Reb Chatzkel always kept in his home. He was given his *aliyah* and he recited the blessings while lying in bed and *Maftir Yonah* was read. Under such circumstances, with the *Rosh Yeshivah* so incapacitated, a fear and trepidation of the Day of Awe enveloped everyone in the room.

When *Minchah* was completed, the *bachurim* took their *machzorim* and began leaving the apartment, to return to the huge *beis midrash* of the yeshivah. Rav Chatzkel suddenly called out to them,

"*Bachurim,* please stay here. Let's make a *minyan* for *Ne'ilah.*" The *Ne'ilah* service is the climax of the *Yom Kippur* prayers. It is the last opportunity to entreat Hashem for forgiveness on the holiest of days. The *bachurim* wanted to be back in the yeshivah together with their colleagues and *Roshei Yeshivah,* who would be praying with great intensity and thus would inspire them as well.

Rav Chatzkel understood why they preferred to go back to the *beis midrash.* He said, "*Rabosai,* if you stay here and *daven* with me, then you will be rewarded every minute for the mitzvah of *bikkur cholim* (visiting the sick) which is part of וְאָהַבְתָּ לְרֵעֲךָ כָּמוֹךָ (*love your fellow as yourself, Vayikra* 19:18), and you will be fulfilling a *d'oraisa* (Torah commandment). If you go back and *daven* with the *chevrah* in the yeshivah, then the most you would be fulfilling is a *d'rabbanan* (a rabbinically ordained ordinance) of *davening* with a *minyan.*"

The boys acquiesced to the *Rosh Yeshivah's* request, as he had taught them a priority they had not thought of.

The morning after I heard this story from Rabbi Dvir, I *davened* with Rabbi Don Segal's *minyan* in the Gush Shemonim section of Jerusalem. Rav Don is a well-known *Mashgiach,* a renowned *talmid* of the Ponevezher *Mashgiach,* Rabbi Chatzkel Levenstein (1885-1974). After his intense and melodious prayers, I approached him and told him the story of Rav Sarna's last *Yom Kippur.*

He thought for a moment and said, "It is so important to tell such a story because it has such a significant lesson of priorities. Rav Shlomo Zalman (Auerbach) often told me that one must learn to always weigh one's actions, especially when they deal with *bein adam lachaveiro* (person to person relationships)."

Ultimate Refinement

In Manchester, England, there are two women, Rebbetzin Chava Wagshal and Mrs. Miriam Younger, who write, collect, and publish inspirational material for the benefit of their community. They co-authored the book (under a pen name) *Facing Adversity With Faith,* which has inspired thousands of people throughout the Jewish world. I thank them for sending me their material, which included this remarkable story.

A group of women had a study group in *Nach* (the Prophets). They were studying *Malachi* and came to the verse: וְיָשַׁב מְצָרֵף וּמְטַהֵר כֶּסֶף, *He will sit smelting and purifying silver* (3:3). The women were puzzled by the verse. Why is Hashem described as a smelter of silver?

After some discussion, one of the women volunteered to speak to a local silversmith and seek permission to observe him at work. She hoped that by watching him at his craft she might get an insight into the verse. She made an appointment for the following week, saying that she wanted to learn about the refining process.

On the appointed day, the woman watched as the silversmith held a piece of silver over the scalding fire. He explained that it was important to hold the piece over the hottest part of the fire to burn away the impurities. As she observed the process, she thought about the verse and remembered that at times Hashem too, puts His people through "fire" — difficult situations — in order for them to shed their impurities.

She thought about the wording of the verse and reflected on the word וְיָשַׁב *He will sit.* She asked the silversmith, "Must you sit here throughout the entire process while the silver is being refined?"

"Yes, of course," came the reply. "If I wasn't sitting and watching closely, there could be catastrophe. If the silver were in the heat even a moment too long, the whole piece would be destroyed!" For her that was an allusion to Hashem's constant vigilance over His people.

The woman thought for a moment and asked, "How then can you tell when it's perfect and completely refined?"

The silversmith smiled softly and said, "I know its perfect when I see my image in it!"

The message in the verse was now clear. When Hashem will see His image in our thoughts and deeds — that will herald that we, His precious people, have become perfectly refined.

What indeed is the most defining image of Hashem? Perhaps it is His Oneness, His singular Holiness and unmatched, incomparable capacities. The prophet Balaam stated: הֶן עָם לְבָדָד יִשְׁכֹּן וּבַגּוֹיִם לֹא יִתְחַשָּׁב, *Behold, it is a nation that will dwell in solitude, and not be reckoned among the nations* (*Bamidbar* 23:9). The time will come when Jews will be so uniquely outstanding and so exceptionally elevated that they will not be reckoned as a nation like all the other nations. Their greatness will render them outstanding, separate and unique. That uniqueness will be Hashem's image within us. It is then that we will merit the coming of Mashiach.

Indeed the *Baal HaTurim* (ibid.) notes that the *gematria* (numerical value) of the words לְבָדָד יִשְׁכֹּן, *will dwell in solitude,* are בִּימֵי מָשִׁיחַ, *in the days of Mashiach.* May we merit to witness it in our day.

Indices

Index of Personalities

Note: Included in this index are those historical personalities who played a role (or made a comment about) the stories which appear in this book. Excluded are most fictionalized names, minor characters, and narrators of the commentaries cited in the text. Page numbers indicate the first page of the story in which the person appears.

All titles have been omitted from this index to facilitate finding names.

Index of Topics

Note: Included in this index are topics from all five Maggid books. **MS** indicates *The Maggid Speaks;* **AMT** indicates *Around the Maggid's Table;* **FM** indicates *In the Footsteps of the Maggid;* **MJ** indicates *Along the Maggid's Journey;* **EM** indicates *Echoes of the Maggid;* and **RM** indicates *Reflections of the Maggid.*

Index of Sources

Scriptural and Talmudic Index for all five Maggid books.

Note: **MS** indicates *The Maggid Speaks;* **AMT** indicates *Around the Maggid's Table;* **FM** indicates *In the Footsteps of the Maggid;* **MJ** indicates *Along the Maggid's Journey;* **EM** indicates *Echoes of the Maggid* and **RM** indicates *Reflections of the Maggid.*
Page numbers reflect the page on which stories begin.

Rambam

Shulchan Aruch

Other Sources

Glossary

Aggadah – the homiletical, non-halachic teachings of the Sages
aliyah – call to the Torah at the public reading
amkus – depth
Amoraim – rabbis of the Talmud
amud – page
Aron Kodesh – Holy Ark
Aseres HaDibros – Ten Commandments
askanim – community activists
avinu – our father
avreichim – students in an advanced yeshivah
ayin raah – detrimental eye
ayin tovah – benevolent eye

baal korei – the reader of the Torah
baal tefillah – leader of the prayer service
baal teshuvah – one who returns to Jewish life, observance and study
bachur – unmarried young man
badekken – the placement of the veil on the bride before the wedding ceremony
balabatim – laymen; householders
baruch Hashem – thank G-d
basar lavan – (lit. white meat) pork
Beis HaMikdash – the Holy Temple
beis midrash – study hall
bentsched – blessed
berachah – blessing
bikkur cholim – visiting the sick
bitul Torah – waste of time from Torah study
blatt – folio pages
bris – circumcision

chadarim – religious elementary schools
challos – braided Sabbath loaves
chassan – bridegroom
chassid – a pious individual; follower of a chassidic Rebbe
chatzos – midday
chavrusa – study partner
chazzan – leader of the prayer service
chessed – benevolence; kindness
chessed shel emes – kindness without expectation of reward
Chevrah Kaddisha – Burial Society
chiddush – innovative Torah thought
chillul Hashem – desecration of G-d's Name
chillul Shabbos – desecration of the Sabbath
chinuch – education
Chumash – the Five Books of Moses
Chupah – wedding ceremony

d'oraisa – a Torah commandment
d'rabbanan – a rabbinically ordained ordinance
Daf Yomi – worldwide Talmud study project in which all Jews study the same folio – page of the Talmud every day
daven – to pray
dayan – rabbinical judge
divrei Torah – Torah thoughts
drashash – sermon or discourse on Torah

ehrlicher Yid – a religious Jew
Eretz Yisrael – the Land of Israel

Frau – Mrs.

gadol hador – leading Torah sage of a generation
Galus – Diaspora
Gemara – Talmud
gemillus chassadim – benevolence and kindness
geneivah – stealing

hachnasas kallah – the mitzvah of aiding someone to get married
hakaras hatov – gratitude
halachah – Jewish law
hamelech – the king
hanavi – the prophet
hashavas aveidah – returning a lost item
Hashgachah Pratis – Divine Providence
hashkafah – Jewish perspective
hasmadah – diligence in Torah study
hatzlachah – success
havanah – understanding
hesped – eulogy

kabbalas panim – reception before the wedding ceremony
Kabbalas Shabbos – the Friday evening service
Kaddish – prayer sanctifying G-d's Name
kallah – bride
kapota – long jacket
kappel – yarmulke
karpas – vegetable eaten at the Passover Seder
kashrus – laws of keeping kosher
kesones passim – a fine woolen tunic
kesubah – the marriage contract
Kever Rachel – Rachel's tomb
Kiddush – sanctification of the Sabbath and festivals, usually recited over wine
kiddush Hashem – sanctification of G-d's Name
kittlach – shroud-like garments worn on certain solemn occasions
Klal Yisrael – the entire Jewish community
kochos hanefesh – inner strengths
Kol Nidrei – prayer recited at the beginning of Yom Kippur
kollel – post-graduate yeshivah, usually for married students
korban – offering
kos – (*Kiddush*) cup

l'chaim – traditional toast, "To life!"
leichter – candelabra
levayah – funeral
limudei kodesh – sacred learning

Maariv – the evening prayer service
maasim tovim – good deeds
maggid shiur – Talmudic lecturer
mantel – cover for a Torah scroll
mara d'asra – the leader of the community
mashgiach – spiritual guide
Mashiach – the Messiah
masmid – diligent student
mechanchim – Torah educators
mechitzah – divider between men's and women's sections in a synagogue
melamed – teacher of children